A Jet Power

inspiration for a lifelong career in aviation. I was fortunate to interview Glenn. He passed away at the age of 93 in June 2016.

Kathy O'Sako, Paulson's longtime secretary at Gulfstream Aerospace, shared a wealth of experiences about her former boss. Crystal Christensen, Paulson's granddaughter, recalled the personal side of his life. Her insights into the dynamics existing within the family, before and after the industrialist's death, proved invaluable. A special find was a collection of eight typewritten pages consisting of remembrances dictated by Paulson about his youth and career. I thank Crystal for sharing it. Cheryl Nicholson, daughter of the industrialist's brother, Art, offered information about the family's early history. Murray Smith, founder and publisher of *Professional Pilot* magazine, offered other fascinating insights. Still another contributor was Alex Kvassay, a close friend of Paulson who sold airplanes to world leaders, business moguls, and celebrities.

I wish to thank a number of people who contributed photos: Clay Lacy, Crystal Christensen, Kathy O'Sako, Neil Aird, Heidi Fedak at Gulfstream Aerospace, Jan Southern at Georgia Southern University, and contributors of images donated for the American Aviation Historical Society archives.

In addition to the interviews, my research involved delving into the archives of media sources. In no particular order, the principal ones include *Cable News Network (CNN)*, *Aviation International News*, the *New York Times*, *Business & Commercial Aviation*, *Flying*, *Business Week*, the *Chicago Tribune*, *Professional Pilot*, *Blood-Horse*, *Savannah Morning News*, *Airport Journal*, the *Los Angeles Times*, the *Wall Street Journal*, and perhaps fifty other newspapers, magazines, books, and websites too numerous to acknowledge here. I'm particularly indebted to *Aviation Week & Space Technology* and *Flight International* for providing digital access to the archives of all their magazines. Locating detailed accounts about Paulson and his airplanes helped me piece together the seasons of his life and craft a manuscript that portrays the man as accurately as possible.

In common with my *Howard's Whirlybirds* book, profiling Howard Hughes and his helicopter empire, I'm inspired to continue my writing by keeping in mind the eternal guidance of my late mother, Elsie, also a published writer. I credit my wife Rita for her solid support over a four-year period as I toiled writing and rewriting before finally saying, "It is done."

Table of Contents

Preface

Browsing through books listed on Amazon, it appears to me that most movers and shakers who've built Fortune 500 companies have at least one book written about their exploits. Someone who didn't make the lists is Allen Eugene Paulson—perhaps because his name isn't a household word like many others. But his story *is* an engrossing one, climbing from a penniless childhood to the top tier of the aviation business, a modern day Horatio Alger. But that's not all. In the spirit of today's luminaries such as Elon Musk of SpaceX fame, or airplane designer Burt Rutan, builder of the first civilian craft to enter space, Paulson was relentless in conceiving and *doing* when it came to furthering progress in aviation. Outside of that industry, where he made his mark, and even within it for that matter, there's little written about the man. Shunning publicity, he didn't write an autobiography or talk much in public. The airplanes he conceived and developed, together with the famous racehorses he owned, shined in the spotlight, but not he. Although his name may be unrecognized by most of the public, a list of his friends reads like a who's who of America's mid-century culture.

I had the occasion to meet Paulson in 1973. It was to talk about the possibilities of forming a business venture together. From the moment we met I took note of his unpretentious manner and inquisitiveness, observing that he did need a few minutes to warm up and look at ease. We conversed in the nerve center of his American Jet Industries operation, crowded into two huge hangars situated along the western edge of the Hollywood-Burbank Airport. From his unpretentious office on the mezzanine level of one of the hangars, the panoramic view looked down on a four-engine Lockheed Electra parked inside, surrounded by an army of fast-moving workers. His mechanics were "cutting it in half," the slow-talking industrialist told me, to convert the airliner from carrying passengers to transporting freight. The modifications seemed incredibly laborious to me. Something else caught my eyes. Resting on the carpet around the edges of his sparsely furnished office sat a dozen or so travel agency–size airplane models. They represented the hundreds of airliners he had owned at various times. I came to the conclusion that the man loved anything to do with aviation.

Although Paulson didn't share much about himself that morning, I did walk away with the feeling that he had far more expansive plans in store than what I witnessed in the hangars. Five years later, when I read in a newspaper that he bought Grumman American Aviation, it didn't surprise me one bit. The prized Gulfstream business jet program came with the deal. Within a few years he made history by transforming the company from a loser into a Fortune 500 goliath.

Our meeting ended cordially, my proposed venture with him didn't materialize, and each of us went our own way to never cross paths again. He died in 2000.

Allen Paulson didn't miss much of what life has to offer. From impoverished farm boy to aviation mogul meant that his story was too captivating for me to *not* write this book.

Introduction

Tom Brokaw's best-selling *The Greatest Generation* says it best: "These were children of the Depression with fresh memories of deprivation, and the postwar years were abundant with opportunities to make real money. They didn't want to miss out."

Those words describe Allen Paulson.

It is little wonder he received the Horatio Alger Award. According to the association presenting that honor, awardees are "dedicated community leaders who demonstrate individual initiative and a commitment to excellence as exemplified by remarkable achievements accomplished through honesty, hard work, self-reliance, and perseverance over adversity."

The first quarter of the twentieth century witnessed the advent of commercial flight. Pioneers Douglas, Boeing, and Lockheed are acknowledged as the principal figures bringing about that achievement.

The meteoric rise of Lockheed, in particular, curiously paralleled the course that Paulson would travel a half-century later. Lockheed posted annual sales of more than $1 million by 1928. The prosperity didn't last, however, when the Depression drove the manufacturer into bankruptcy. In 1932, an investor group led by Robert Gross bought the company's assets for $40,000. Throughout the decades to come, Lockheed grew into Lockheed-Martin, today's largest aerospace corporation. Gross remained at the helm for much of that growth. In 1978, Paulson replicated what Gross accomplished, albeit on a smaller scale. He acquired the builder of Gulfstream business jets from Grumman for what was termed a bargain, the manufacturer nearly bankrupt. He's credited with popularizing the airplane, the undisputed Rolls-Royce of business jets. Through his vision, Gulfstream Aerospace morphed into a Fortune 500 corporation. Gross and Paulson saw value where others missed it.

Aside from aviation, Paulson bred equine equivalents of his $25 million jets, hundreds of the horses boarded on farms he owned in Kentucky, Florida, and California. During the 1990s, his racehorse named Cigar racked up an amazing sixteen straight wins to delight hundreds of thousands of fans; the horse is a legend to this day.

Left to fend for himself at the age of thirteen, Paulson scrubbed the floors of a hotel in Clinton, Iowa, while his mother languished in a sanitarium as a long-term tuberculosis patient. His father, reeling from the effects of bankruptcy upon losing the family farm, sought a divorce and trekked to California in search of work. Young Paulson found room and board at the hotel in exchange for the janitorial duties. Restless by fifteen, he bought a one-way bus ticket to California and landed a job on a dairy farm in Marin County. It was there that he assisted with rescue efforts following the fatal crash of an airliner—the event profoundly influencing the future course of his life. Two years after graduating from high school he joined Trans World Airlines as an apprentice mechanic, followed by enlisting in the Army Air Force. World War II ending, he rejoined TWA and soon promoted to flight engineer. Along the way, he came to know Howard Hughes, the airline's owner.

In 1953, Paulson began selling aircraft parts to the airlines. Stripped from war-surplus Wright R-3350 engines, they formed the basis for his early success as an entrepreneur. In less than ten years, his California Airmotive Corporation evolved into the nation's largest buyer and seller of airliners. Upon merging it with Gulfstream, his net worth grew to nearly $500 million by 1984.

A quietly competitive, self-made man who abhorred collaboration, Paulson called all the shots and wanted nothing to do with naysayers chortling, "It can't be done." His pioneering research for developing the world's first supersonic business jet is a vivid example.

Unusual for a CEO, Paulson could be seen in an airport hangar, attired in a white, short-sleeve dress shirt, hands stained with oil, and wielding a wrench to tighten a bolt. He wouldn't refrain from showing his mechanics a shortcut or two. It was a simpler era, before hordes of nattily attired MBAs arrived on the corporate scene. His thousands of employees always knew where they stood with him.

Nothing came effortlessly for the self-effacing entrepreneur. He stumbled three times in attempting to manufacture the Super Pinto, Hustler, and Peregrine airplanes—before striking gold with the Gulfstream. Forging ahead and not agonizing over unsuccessful projects, he sprang back from such failures and achieved success.

During his years in the White House, President Dwight Eisenhower was a houseguest and companion of Paulson on the golf course in Palm Springs. Presidents Gerald Ford and Jimmy Carter enjoyed his friendship. Other notables included Frank Sinatra, Bob Hope, Danny Kaye, Kirk Kerkorian, Lee Iacocca, Bill Lear, Jack Conroy, Teddy Forstmann, Cliff Robertson and Donna

Douglas. Entertainer Kaye and aviator Clay Lacy helped him sell more Lear Jets than anyone else. Following two divorces, Paulson met Madeleine, his third wife. Five years after his death in 2000, she went on to marry billionaire Texas oilman T. Boone Pickens.

Paulson was mechanic, pilot, engineer, entrepreneur, gambler, investor, sportsman, philanthropist, and inveterate tinkerer. Despite a string of achievements, he wasn't popular on Wall Street, considered a crapshooter who made investments that a CEO answerable to an outside board wouldn't dare pursue. Multiple world speed records flying Gulfstream jets brought him aviation's most prestigious awards. Over the years, he was presented six honorary doctorates. In spite of the accolades, he was not recognized as one of the twentieth century's major innovators and industrialists. Upon acquiring the Gulfstream program, *Aviation International News* announced the event by posting the headline "Allen Who?"

He was positive and opinionated, but welcomed a good argument. A flexible thinker, he could be persuaded to shift from what appeared to be an adamant stand. The man possessed the ego of a natural leader, but was blessed with a virtue that many leaders don't have—knowledge of his weaknesses.

Paulson was more comfortable posing with a racehorse in the winner's circle than standing in front of a microphone addressing thousands of people thanking him for his philanthropic generosity. He donated millions to universities, even though his own education ended with high school. On the outside, he appeared tanned, relaxed, and confident. But inside, he faced conflict throughout his life. He became sensitive, even touchy, when discussing his lack of a college education.

Paulson's commitment to aviation was so strong that he continued developing aeronautical technology while fighting cancer during the final year of his life. Six months before his passing, a patent was issued to him for an airship stationed at high altitudes to replace communications satellites. His lifelong love of aviation had never dimmed.

Both dreamer and doer, Paulson toiled for a quarter-century developing airplanes and setting flight records that intrigue people to this day. It was a long journey from a small farm in Iowa to the front office for this member of the greatest generation.

1

Turning Point

It started out as any other winter day for sixteen-year-old Allen Paulson. After waking at four in the morning, he would have gulped down a quick breakfast of buttered toast, grabbed a lantern to light the path to the barn, milked the cows, and flagged down a bus for the bumpy, 10-mile trip to classes at Tomales High School. Living on a farmhand's monthly income of twenty dollars, Paulson paid for a shared room and consumed three meals a day—*if* there was enough food in the cupboards to go around. The setting was a dairy farm in Northern California's pastoral Marin County, where lush meadows and rolling hills extend to the Pacific Ocean.

On that drizzly, overcast Tuesday morning of November 29, 1938, Paulson became caught up in a tragedy that would influence the direction of his life. A United Air Lines DC-3A ditched in the ocean a half-hour before dawn, 30 miles from the farm where he worked. Four passengers, two pilots, and a stewardess were aboard. The captain of ill-fated United Trip 6, forty-two-year-old Charles Stead, had learned to fly in the U.S. Army Air Corps during World War I and accumulated a respectable 8,649 hours with the airline. Thirty-year-old Lloyd Jones occupied the right seat as copilot, having accrued 3,284 hours in the air. Stewardess Frona "Bobbie" Clay, age twenty-four, a registered nurse who'd flown with United for almost three years, tended to the needs of their passengers.

United placed the first Douglas DC-3A in service during June 1937. The airplane was a technological marvel, capable of a cruising speed reaching 207 miles per hour and a maximum altitude of 24,300 feet.[1]

The DC-3's rudimentary cockpit instrumentation included a low-frequency radio receiver required to navigate along what was called the "range." By the mid–1930s, the U.S. government had established a network of tower-mounted radio transmitters across the country for aerial navigation purposes. They were built along well-traveled routes known as airways. A radio receiver in the cockpit enabled pilots to follow a narrow radio beam to their destinations. The transmitters projected four radio beams, each with a constant tone audible to the pilot when on course. When the airplane strayed "off the beam," to one side or the other, different sounds were heard. The system, however, wasn't always reliable. It was affected by lightning, the reflection of signals bouncing off the sides of mountains, and even interference from distant stations, especially at night.

Pilots of the 1930s communicated with a dispatcher who worked for their airline and not directly with an air traffic controller employed by the government. The pilot would file an instrument flight plan with the dispatcher who forwarded the information by phone or telegraph to a controller at the flight's departure airport. Assuming there was adequate physical separation from other aircraft on a chosen airway, the controller would issue a clearance to the dispatcher who passed it on to the pilot. As the airplane flew through authorized airspace, the pilot radioed his position to the dispatcher, which was relayed to the controller who updated the aircraft's approximate position on a chalkboard. Decades before radar tracking of all flights became routine, this cumbersome air traffic control system had to suffice.

In 1937, the nation's fledgling airline fleet totaled fewer than 400 airplanes serving 200 cities. Of the airports in those cities, only ninety-six had night lighting. The Bureau of Air Commerce employed a mere sixty inspectors to check on the safety performance of 14,000 licensed pilots and all kinds of aircraft. With commercial pilots flying up to 100 hours a month, fatigue was considered a contributory factor in an increasing number of accidents. Regulation was a hit-and-miss proposition during this primitive era of commercial air transportation. For Captain Stead, fatigue was only one of the challenges he would face.

United Trip 6 began its journey in Seattle with a flight plan calling for a routine "milk run" to Portland and Medford in Oregon, followed by stops at several airports along the California coast before terminating in San Diego.

Thomas Van Sceiver, a dispatcher in Oakland employed by United, was responsible for authorizing the flight's departure from Medford. After conferring with a U.S. Weather Service meteorologist at the Oakland airport, the men agreed the flight should stay on the ground. On Monday at 11:34 p.m., Van Sceiver sent a radiogram to Medford: "With frontal system off coast and strong south wind and heavy rain reported at Farallon Islands and Oakland conditions decreasing, suggest holding trip 6–28 for weather improvement at Oakland, probable daylight."[2]

At 11:41 p.m., following an abbreviated three-way phone call between Van Sceiver, Stead, and United's station manager at Medford, the decision was reversed based on an updated forecast. Trip 6 was cleared for departure to Sacramento, California, one of the interim stops on the way to San Diego. Stead's insistence on departing Medford was considered questionable by fellow captains, who thought it prudent to sit out the deteriorating weather and delay their own flights. At midnight, Van Sceiver's shift ended and Philip Showalter in Oakland assumed his tasks.

Departing to the south from the Medford runway at 12:03 a.m., United Trip 6 climbed to a cruising altitude of 12,000 feet, flying above cloud-shrouded hills in light rain. Stead continued in a southerly direction along the 330-mile leg to Oakland, the first airport where he would land, located 6 miles east of San Francisco. The flight plan called for covering the distance in 2 hours and 10 minutes. At 1:10 a.m., he received approval to climb to 14,000 feet in order to fly above a solid layer of clouds. In addition to fighting a stiff headwind, a layer of rime ice began to form on the leading edges of the wings, which further slowed his progress. At 1:34 a.m., Stead climbed to 15,000 feet as he and the copilot donned oxygen masks in the unpressurized cabin.

The airliner worked its way south of the Oregon-California border, west of Mount Shasta. Starting at 2:09 a.m., contact stopped between Showalter and the other dispatchers at United who were monitoring the company's radio frequency. The silence raised concern that something was amiss. In the cockpit, atmospheric conditions were causing heavy static on the low-frequency radio, resulting in questionable heading information and spotty communication.

At 3:08 a.m., Stead finally got through to Showalter: "We are at ten thousand five hundred in the clear between layers with a big break ahead. Believe we will drop down through it. What is the Oakland weather?" Showalter replied a minute later: "Oakland weather nineteen hundred, overcast, lower broken, visibility four miles, light rain."[3]

Another 11 minutes elapsed before Showalter cleared the flight to proceed to the radio range at Oakland. Stead reported he was "definitely" tracking the northeast leg of the Oakland range after descending to 6,000 feet. After flying the leg for 15 minutes, he began to realize there was a serious problem. "If it had been correct, I should be over Oakland," Stead radioed Showalter. "Am dropping down to see what is below. There is something wrong with this course."[4]

At 4:05 a.m., experiencing only sporadic radio contact with the pilot, Showalter reported the airliner as overdue in Oakland. Coast Guard and Navy operations in San Francisco were notified that an aircraft was flying somewhere over the ocean west of Oakland—or may have crashed. A government investigation later determined that these rudimentary rescue measures were "inadequate to meet the requirements of such an emergency."[5]

At 4:10 a.m., Showalter got through to the captain: "At 3:17 a.m., you reported definitely on northeast leg of Oakland range."

Stead radioed back: "I have been over fifty minutes from there ... am thirty degrees off in my computations. I have sixty gallons of gas. Don't know exactly where I am. I am going to come down slowly."[6]

At 4:14 a.m., Showalter tried reaching Stead again: "What is your altitude now?" Under extreme stress in the cockpit, the captain replied, "Can't tell, I am descending now." At 4:58 a.m., he reported, "Visibility excellent; few scattered clouds."

Two more minutes elapsed before he told Showalter, "At sixty-five degrees [heading], can see a beacon light. Will you get the wind at Farallon Islands? That is the first light I have seen." Concerned over how much fuel remained, the dispatcher asked: "Will you give us another gas check?" Stead replied, "about twenty gallons."[7] He again queried the dispatcher about the wind strength in the Farallons—a strange request, as the islands, located 33 miles west of the Golden Gate Bridge, were nowhere near where the airliner was supposed to be. There was no doubt that Stead didn't know how far off course he'd taken the airplane. He was lost over the ocean, far from the Oakland airport. Unsure of his position, he made a 180-degree turn while descending to 300 feet. Switching on the landing lights, he was shocked to see he was flying closely over ocean waves.

The DC-3 continued to drone on about a mile from the shoreline, 20 miles north of San Francisco, while burning off 20 gallons of fuel remaining from the 450 gallons they had taken on at Medford. With Stead running a lean mixture to save what was left, the engines began to belch and backfire. Climbing to 1,800 feet in an easterly direction, he sighted the Point Reyes Lighthouse at 5:03 a.m.

Showalter made contact with him again at 5:06 a.m.: "If a light, ten miles south of [your] course, it is Farallons and, if it is Point Reyes, it will be on the north side of range." Stead immediately replied: "How far from shore am I?" At 5:13 a.m., Showalter told him: "Do not land on the beach. Land on the beach on shore side of light. It is level, and it is rough along the shore." Five minutes later the nervous dispatcher said, "If you get to Point Reyes and have enough fuel after you pass the light, you will find a sandy beach on the east side of Drake's Inlet. Follow the shore, and there is a big, wide beach there."[8]

Time was not on Stead's side. At 5:19 a.m., he radioed, "Ready to land now; we turned at the lights. And there are two lights. One looks like a ship. We are still over the water. We are right now turning south to a point [with] some lights. We are practically out of gas. We are over water, right on the shore." Showalter replied with no hesitation: "Follow the shore line, and if it is Point Reyes light you will find a sandy beach on south side."

At 5:22 a.m., the final transmission from Trip 6 came in over the dispatcher's loudspeaker: "The shore is too rough for landing."[9]

As the DC-3 approached the shore, Stead circled the lighthouse twice, dropping a flare each time. After completing the second orbit, the pointer on the fuel quantity gauge snapped to read zero. Consuming the last gallons of

onlookers, he saw a newspaper photographer scouting an angle to photograph the wreck. Spotting young Paulson, the photographer asked him to pose for a couple of shots. Dripping wet, short of breath, and suffering from rope burns, he forced a smile for the camera—at the same time remembering that his shirt and pants had been swept out to sea. As he reached the road paralleling the cliff, the crowd followed him to hear what he'd seen inside the airplane. He responded that no one was inside but refrained from talking about the shocking condition of Stead and Edelstein. Another news photographer snapped a picture. "And there I was in my skivvies. In the San Francisco newspaper, they had pictures of me pulling mail sacks from the plane. The headline read, 'United Pilot Saves the Mail.' Well, the United pilot was I."[21]

The accident investigation report prepared by the Civil Aeronautics Authority blamed the crash on Stead making a navigational error. It concluded that the probable cause was "failure of the pilot to definitely establish the position of the aircraft through standard orientation procedures within a reasonable time after intersecting a leg of the Oakland radio range at 3:17 a.m., and of company flight dispatchers, charged with the responsibilities of directing the operation of the trip, to properly safeguard the flight, resulting in forced landing of the aircraft at sea due to exhausted fuel supply."[22] The CAA recommended revoking the licenses of Stead, Van Sceiver, and Showalter. As for Edelstein, following hospitalization, he didn't get to leave the United States as planned. The publicity that arose from the accident caused detectives in other parts of the country to identify him as a suspect in a variety of crimes. He went on trial and endured more years of imprisonment.

The bodies of the copilot and one passenger were recovered. Those of the stewardess and two other passengers were never found.

In an ironic coincidence, on September 30, 1951, following a weekend visit with his family in Seattle, Clint Eastwood, the future actor-director, hitched a ride on a Navy AD-1 Skyraider destined for Mather Air Force Base south of Sacramento. A U.S. Army enlisted man, twenty-one-year-old Eastwood had been on leave from Fort Ord in Monterey. When the torpedo bomber ran out of fuel, the pilot ditched it in the ocean two miles off Point Reyes—within sight of where Stead had ditched the DC-3 in 1938. He and the pilot climbed out of the cockpit of the sinking airplane and swam to shore, escaping serious injury. Eastwood separated from the Army in 1952 and moved back to Seattle to work as a lifeguard.

It's not unusual for a teenager to pursue a career prompted by adolescent experiences. When it came to Paulson, the adventure of examining the innards of a big airliner combined with the notoriety of being hailed as a "rescuer" may have been the motivation that led him to pursue a career in aviation. Or perhaps, the impetus was less conscious and more primal. After starting out in business as a seller of used airplane parts and reconditioning aircraft, he would struggle with the conflict inherent in attempting to fix the fractured and reassemble the broken in both his personal and professional lives.

In California for less than a year at the time of the airliner's ditching, the young man's life had begun in a broken family 2,000 miles to the east. The locale was a bustling farming town called Clinton, situated along the Mississippi River in Iowa. The lessons learned from growing up in the Depression would prepare him to tackle seemingly insurmountable challenges as an adult.

Perched near the middle of a forty-acre corn farm in eastern Iowa, just outside the town of Clinton, sat a compact clapboard house owned by Harry and Lillian Paulson. Married on February 4, 1913, the couple and their children were about to welcome a new addition. Allen Eugene came into the world on April 22, 1922. He joined four brothers, Marvin, Carl, Art, and Vern.

Before planting time arrived, work around the Paulson farm centered on fixing fences and adjusting the plow to prepare for what Harry hoped would be a bountiful harvest. The snowy winter months made life miserable for farming families in the Great Plains states. The arrival of spring saw the frozen land thaw—a signal to get busy with the plow. The days were filled with adults and kids weeding, tilling the earth, and moving corn plants into place, acre after acre. The backbreaking tasks stretched from dawn to dusk during the month that Allen was born.

It wasn't the best time for twenty-six-year-old Lillian to bear another child, the farm surviving on a hand-to-mouth financial basis. Allen became the family's seventh mouth to feed.

A devastating recession in the early 1920s almost landed the farm in bankruptcy, in common with the owners of neighboring farms. But at the age of twenty-nine, Harry, a tall, energetic man with a slim frame was blessed with an unshakeable work ethic and struggled through each day unscathed. He kept debt collectors at bay and pulled in enough cash from crop sales to put food on the table.

Twenty-eight miles north of Moline, Illinois, Clinton is Iowa's easternmost city. Located on the western shore of the Mississippi, it has the most expansive riverfront of any city along the nation's longest waterway. In 1922, the fields surrounding the town were covered with feedlots, granaries, and railroad yards. Corn, soybeans, and hay were the crops most in demand. By the late 1920s and early 1930s, farmers harvested and shipped incalculable truckloads of corn.

At the age of four Allen was kicked by a cow, which broke his leg. It was his earliest memory of life on the farm. Long before graduating eighth grade he helped build fences, cleaned the barn, milked cows, and endured a daily regimen of backbreaking work in the fields. Attending class and completing homework assignments were sandwiched between the chores. On the farm, chores always came first. Rising at four in the morning to milk the cows wasn't enough; he needed to milk them again at eight-thirty in the evening. The dawn-to-dusk routine spanned seven days a week without a break. "We had just a little forty-acre farm, with corn, a few pigs, a few cows, and I remember pulling a lot of weeds," he recalled of his early years.[23]

Farm boys of the 1930s were an inventive bunch, especially good with their hands. They had no choice. Their hard-driving fathers expected them to maintain simple farming equipment and tools in tip-top condition. If something broke it meant losing a day's crop yield. Allen spent long hours in the barn. On his own, he figured out how to bring ailing farm machinery back to health. At an age when boys living in major cities played with toy cars, he worked on man-size machines.

Away from the monotonous chores, life at home was anything but pleasant. His parent's anger, fueled by the farm's precarious financial condition, resulted in a remoteness that took a toll on the kids. During the evening meal in a dimly lit dining room, mom sat at one end of a long wooden table with dad at the other end. Not much of interest to the children was discussed. Marvin sat closest to Allen, accessible to his kid brother to offer emotional support whenever a negative remark was directed his way. "He and Marv stayed close for their entire lives," recalled Mary Lou Paulson, Allen's second wife.[24] Kathy O'Sako, his future secretary, agreed: "Allen was the baby but he always felt that Marvin was the special child. He never explained why he thought that, but he always loved Marvin."[25]

Allen's oldest brother, Art, attended high school through the ninth grade, then quit to work full time to help support the family. "He'd do anything available, find someone to show him what was needed, and do it," daughter Cheryl Nicholson recalled. "He was a hunter, which helped put meat on the table, especially during the Depression."[26]

After class, scant time remained for Allen to get involved in teenage escapades in sleepy Clinton. The town typified rural America. On Saturdays, he and his buddies didn't have much to do other than bet nickels playing cards or occasionally catch a movie. Adventure films, such as *Devil Dogs of the Air*, starring Jimmy Cagney, filled the time vacuum and expanded Allen's interest in the exploits of daredevil pilots, not unusual with boys his age.

He wasn't considering a future in aviation or any other career at the time, although he did enjoy hiking across town to Clinton Municipal Airport to watch biplanes land on the dirt strip and refuel. Away from the rigors of farm and school life he cherished the few hours that remained to read engineering books at the Clinton Public Library on Eighth Avenue. And was intrigued learning about the adventures of aviator Charles Lindbergh as reported in *The Clinton Herald*.

Harry had purchased the farm with the hope it might become a major player in corn production within the county. In years past it threw off sufficient income to pay the mortgage and provide household necessities. He expected to keep the property in the family upon retiring, turning over its reins to his sons. It was a noble dream but one fast fading. The Depression had cut the volume of business that he and nearby farmers were capturing. The future looked anything but certain.

Allen hoped to enter his teenage years with the promise of long-term prosperity at home. It was not to be. In the Midwest, farmers were shipping only sixteen bushels of corn per acre. The proceeds earned for those efforts were so insignificant that it became wiser to feed the corn to hogs on the farm rather than trying to sell it. "Corn was so cheap that it was selling for two or three cents a pound," Paulson recalled. "It was a rough time for my family."[27]

On the home front, the situation worsened. Lillian stopped buying coal to heat the house. Instead, she burned piles of unsold corn stacked up in the barn. There weren't enough customers in sight to buy the only commodity they had. It was a traumatic time for Allen's proud, fiercely independent parents.

The Depression dragged on longer than any economic calamity in American history. One of the most intense droughts on record followed, exacerbating the pain. In 1934, extraordinarily dry conditions brought havoc to 80 percent of the nation's land. On May 13, a dust storm swept across the prairies of several states, including Iowa. Some farmers called the string of bad luck a "double whammy"—economic collapse accompanied by drought. Bone-dry weather prolonged the economic ills, especially for farmers in the Great Plains states who were desperate to try anything legal to earn a living.

Without rain, farmers could grow few if any crops. A non-existent harvest meant that howling afternoon winds blew powdery topsoil from the unplowed fields into dust storms. As the storms intensified, crop yields continued to decline—corn prices plummeting to a new low. Families in metropolitan areas couldn't afford to buy corn or other produce. In communities near the farms, schools canceled classes, not for tornados, but due to the choking dust. Life got tougher by the day.

Harry tapped whatever cash remained in Lillian's cookie jar to pay at least something on the unpaid bills piling up. The jar was almost empty. No longer able to keep pace with paying the mortgage, he threw in the towel, declaring bankruptcy and losing the homestead to his lender. Overnight, the family's income went from little to nothing.

It was inevitable that dissention would erupt between Harry and Lillian about how to survive the deepening chaos. Neither had a satisfactory answer, communication broke down, and the couple became emotionally distant. There were rumors circulating that before Harry filed for bankruptcy, he and Lillian were seeing people outside of marriage. By 1935, it became clear that divorce would be the outcome for the splintered relationship. The family's dynamics remained seared in Paulson's memory a half-century later when he abruptly recalled: "I was thirteen years old when my father divorced my mother."[28]

Unemployed and homeless men drifted from town to town across America seeking work of any kind. More than thirty million Americans had no income. Thousands of farmers were making the long trek from the Dust Bowl to a promised land called California. When an acquaintance of Harry told him that jobs were plentiful on the West Coast, he wasted no time to pack a suitcase and make his way across the country. His goal was to seek work on a farm north of San Francisco, the region known as dairy country. California was named the Golden State and considered the land of opportunity. He intended to determine if the slogan was really true. The promise of making money in California was his last-ditch hope. Three of his older sons, all able-bodied young adults, weren't far behind him moving west. Carl decided to stay behind in Clinton and take up residence at a downtown hotel. Still attending junior high, Allen was too young to make the westward jaunt, so Carl, four years older, took the youngest brother under his wing.

Adding to the tribulations, their once strong mother contracted tuberculosis and was admitted to a local sanitarium for a prolonged stay. The relocation of Allen's father and three of his brothers left him stuck in Clinton to navigate life with eighteen-year-old Carl, who wasn't always the best role model. Like it or not, Allen was on his own as Carl's paltry income was a hit and miss proposition and their parents had no money to contribute toward the boys' support.

Coming of age in the Depression, when economic despair hovered over the land like the plague, Allen had watched his father lose the farm, his wife, and his hopes. It became obvious that for Allen to survive, he would need to live one day at a time and not repeat his parent's mistakes or even relive them in his mind.

Harry, resettled in California while Lillian remained ailing in the sanitarium, caused Allen to take action and bolster his independence. He began selling newspapers. But by day's end, the pennies and nickels he'd collected were barely enough to pay for a fifteen-cent ham sandwich and nickel soda at the corner cafe. He set his sights a notch higher.

A shy, quiet boy who didn't converse about nonsensical things, he did master the art of making a positive impression when introducing himself to strangers. He went to talk with the manager of the Lafayette Hotel on 629

South Second Street, where Carl had rented a room. He convinced the man that he'd be the best employee working there. Impressed with what he heard, the manager's only concern was the boy's age. Remarkably, he nailed the job. It called for scrubbing the hotel's floors and cleaning its toilets. Fortunately, he'd grown muscular enough to endure constant bending and lifting. Carl was happy hearing the news as Allen agreed to split the room rent with him. They would bunk together.

During earlier years, the Lafayette served as a venue for vaudevillians appearing in Clinton. Opening in 1906, it grew into the finest hotel in Iowa. By the time Allen and Carl shared a room, the type of clientele the hotel had once attracted changed dramatically. Many of its guests were farmers who had fallen on hard times or retirees needing nothing more than shelter and meals. The hotel's glory days were past.

Sharing the room with Carl, Allen did his best in attempting to sleep on a stiff, single mattress, it needing to accommodate his brother as well. When Carl invited a girlfriend to the room, Allen spent time in the lobby or wandered around the docks bordering the Mississippi.

"While I was there I went to junior high," he said. "I didn't get any salary, only room and board, but did all kinds of things besides school. I remember going down the alley, finding a little wagon, and picking up scrap steel, copper, or whatever I could find and selling it to the local junkyard. I also peddled papers in the morning before I went to school and did everything possible to make anything I could because things were rough at that time."[29] He had no safety net.

"I was on my own when I was thirteen," he continued. "When I look back, it's probably the greatest thing that ever happened to me. I was an entrepreneur early in life. I had to make it on my own."[30] He remembered the edict often voiced by his stern father—don't complain and just get the job done. Much like his father, Allen came to exemplify what's sometimes termed the Depression-era work ethic.

When not studying or scrubbing floors, he polished his ability with a deck of cards, ready for any game he could hustle up. The hotel's residents were mostly older men with plenty of time on their hands. They looked forward to card games to wile away those hours. It was here that Paulson mastered the nuances of dealing a deck and outsmarting the moves of other players. "I learned how to keep score [when I was] pretty young, playing pinochle with those old guys at the hotel," he recalled.[31] Keeping a pair of dice in his pocket, he was also prepared for a game of street craps with anyone willing to put money on the line. More often than not, he walked away from those games a dollar or two ahead.

2

New Beginning

Blessed with unshakeable ambition and boundless energy, young Paulson balanced the duties of his menial jobs with schoolwork. Turning fifteen in 1937, he felt stuck in a rut. Graduating from junior high and well into high school, he began to think it might make sense to quit school as brother Art had done. He thought of traveling to California to join his father and land a full-time job but wasn't sure how to make it happen.

"I was ready to go, but I couldn't afford the bus fare," he said. "My dad was working at a ranch out there, somewhere north of San Francisco. He wrote and said if I could find a way out there he could help me find a job. I wasn't too close to my dad, but it sounded pretty good to me."[1] These were difficult times for the teen, coping with disturbing thoughts concerning his parent's broken marriage. He loved both of them, despite not being close emotionally, and remained upset by having witnessed the marital and economic disillusionment they endured. His mother's continuing ill health brought on further anxiety.

Saturday afternoon at a downtown movie theater found him playing keno with a couple of high school buddies. He enjoyed their camaraderie during weekends, hanging out at the theater or going for a swim at the YMCA on Third Street. Anything that was free or cheap. During this particular weekend, the theater owner sponsored a keno contest as a promotion. The boys won—and split a $100 jackpot, big money in the 1930s.

"We each got thirty-three dollars and thirty-three cents," he recalled. Walking back to the hotel room with cash in his pocket, the newfound wealth solidified his plan to head west. On Monday, he quit the janitorial job and didn't bother going to school. Later that day, "I went to the Greyhound bus depot and bought a ticket," he said.[2] The price was twenty-five dollars. The remaining eight dollars would stay in his pocket to buy snacks along the way.

It took three sleepless days and nights sitting in the noisy Greyhound to traverse the 2,000 bumpy miles to Northern California. It was either too hot or too cold. "It was quite a tiresome trip," he recalled. However, the journey did provide plenty of time for the boy wanderer to ponder what his future might hold. Disembarking in the San Francisco area, he caught a glimpse of steel workers stationed high above the bay completing the Golden Gate Bridge. Down to the last of the eight dollars, he hitchhiked out of the city to join up with his father. Harry was working and living in a rural settlement in Marin County just off State Route One near Tomales Bay. Situated 60 miles north of the Golden Gate, the region was home to dairy farmers. Frequent downpours, fanned by gentle offshore breezes, irrigated grazing lands that spread across the rolling hills. The farms were populated with herds of cows, supplying milk for dairy products destined for consumption by urbanites in San Francisco.

His only possessions consisting of the clothes he wore and the contents of a makeshift suitcase, Allen greeted his father at the farm. Within a week, Harry lined up a job for him on another farm about six miles away in Marshall, a tiny community hugging the northeast shore of the bay. Free of the burden he faced in Clinton, Allen dove into this new life with enthusiasm. Strolling around the neighborhood, he could sense renewed optimism among the residents. The Depression was showing signs of ending and people were beginning to find work.

"I made twenty dollars a month on the farm with room and board," he recalled. "But the guy who had the farm was a bachelor, so most of my meals [involved] eating chicken noodle soup and toast ... breakfast, noon, and evening. But I survived."[3]

If he had stayed in Clinton it's likely he would have ended up working for the Clinton Corn Processing Co. or the Climax Engine Manufacturing Co., the largest employers in town. Many of his classmates would do so. Instead, he sought more engaging work than packing cartons or assembling widgets on an assembly line. His brothers would remain satisfied during their lifetimes as members of the status quo, but not he. He dreamed of something more, but couldn't put his finger on exactly what it might be.

Most of the farm chores in Tomales were no different than those he handled in Clinton. The room and board provided by the job enabled him to complete his senior year at Tomales Joint Union High School, down along Highway 1. Each weekday, the routine involved finishing the farm chores before heading off to classes. "I used to have to get up in the morning to milk the cows around six a.m.," he recalled. "Then I'd go to school by bus, about ten or fifteen miles to Tomales High. After school, I'd come back to milk cows again. It would be nine or ten o'clock before I'd get to bed. I did that seven days a week, all the way through high school."[4] At school, he discovered that math and science classes intrigued him the most. Literature and history were another matter. Strong and agile, he did make the football team. After school was dismissed for the day, he looked forward to riding a farm horse across the meadows, sometimes with a friend. The older farmhands working with him gradually matured and toughened him. They convinced him that farm work would always be a life offering little more than a small paycheck.

Ensconced in the neighborhood library, he came across an article in the *San Francisco Chronicle* about Howard Hughes setting airplane speed records. On January 19, 1937, Hughes flew from Los Angeles to Newark in a remarkable 7 hours, 28 minutes, 25 seconds. But the triumphant flight faded into history by July of that year when Amelia Earhart's Lockheed 10 Electra, after departing Oakland Municipal Airport in California, went missing over the Pacific during her attempt to complete an around-the-world flight. Paulson was learning there were successes and failures associated with most any endeavor in life, including aviation. But when problems arose in flight, the outcome could be fatal. His later exploration of the crashed DC-3 at Point Reyes would bring a greater appreciation of such risks.

Finishing the tasks in the barn, he retreated to his room, sat on the edge of a cot and toiled late into the night piecing together model planes of his own design. He used whatever bamboo, wood, and scraps of cloth he could find. "I'd carve them out of balsa wood," he recalled. "I made a lot of model airplanes. At that time you had to design your own airplanes and make the parts all fit."[5] It was an era before the advent of plastic snap-together model airplane kits, a consuming hobby for later generations of teenage boys.

During the weekend of May 28, 1938, Oakland airport was set to play host to the Pacific International Air Races. The event was expected to attract a full roster of well-known race pilots, their aerial adventures to be viewed by tens of thousands of fans. Spotting a newspaper advertisement promoting the race, Paulson finished his chores by daybreak on Saturday and prepared to drive to Oakland. Firing up a well-used and sometimes cantankerous Ford he'd bought from a fellow worker on the farm, he headed east along a narrow, pothole-filled road to meet up with the highway. Ahead was a 60-mile drive to the airport. It would be a tiring day but well worth the effort for a sixteen-year-old interested in anything to do with aviation.

At Oakland in the afternoon, after watching countless aerobatic stunts and death-defying maneuvers around the pylons, he strolled around the ramp to get a closer look at the airplanes. By chance, he met a pilot by the name of Tex Rankin. When he mentioned that he had never flown, the aviator took him up for his first ride. Returning the favor, he washed dirt and oil stains from the pilot's airplane. He didn't know it then, but forty-four-year-old Rankin was a famous figure in aviation circles. Moving to Hollywood in 1936, he flew airplanes in movies and gave flying lessons to a limited number of students, including actors Jimmy Stewart and Errol Flynn. In 1937, he won the international aerobatic competition in St. Louis. Coincidentally, Rankin had taught Lloyd Jones, the copilot of ill-fated United Air Line's Trip 6, how to fly.[6]

Rankin believed that if teenagers were curious enough to watch airplanes arrive and depart, they might decide to learn to fly. Paulson's brief flight around the traffic pattern with him was enough to hook the teen. Hanging around other pilots during future visits to Oakland, he continued to bum rides. "I guess it got into my blood," he recalled.[7] It became clear to him that he would eventually nail down a job flying airplanes. Flying would be his ticket to leave the farm, a life he saw no reason to pursue. He considered enrolling in the Boeing School of Aeronautics after high school, a major tenant on the Oakland airport, offering both flight and mechanic training programs. The aviation school had grown from 100 students in 1929 to nearly 500 by 1937.

Flames of war were popping up in 1938. Air raids over London and the seemingly unstoppable Nazi war machine were everyday news. Hitler seized Austria and Jews were targeted for elimination. Japan continued a genocidal war against the Chinese. In Russia, Stalin deported rivals in the Communist party to Siberia for execution. A world apart in tranquil Marin County, soothing sounds from the radio came from Benny Goodman and Glenn Miller. Small-town America seemed well insulated from the horrific happenings overseas. Immersed in the drudgery of farm work, Paulson didn't pay much attention to events unfolding on the other side of the world. Milking cows, fixing farm equipment, and keeping his automobile running left little free time.

It was a memorable day on June 6, 1941, when he graduated from high school, his father proudly watching the ceremony. From an academic standpoint, his last year had been a mixed bag. His report card revealed mostly A's and B's for the fall semester, but the spring semester reported C's, and even a couple of D's. Distracted by dreaming about future endeavors, he was ready to leave behind teachers and tests to tackle life's challenges as a young adult.

Nineteen-year-old Allen Paulson dressed for his graduation from Tomales High School in June 1941 (Paulson family archives/Crystal Christensen).

Finding aviation engrossing, as well as fun times with a girlfriend, he began to spend more time at the Oakland airport. Because Rankin was seldom there, he'd wash airplanes for other pilots. Rather than accepting a dollar or two for the work, he'd trade his sweat for a ride. Back in Tomales, he earned extra money by adjusting balky carburetors and replacing screeching water pumps of cars belonging to neighbors. He perfected those skills by fixing his own car, hoping the knowledge would help him land a full-time job. Along that line, an unexpected long distance call came in from brother Carl. It would provide the break he was hoping for. While in Clinton, Carl felt an obligation to watch over his kid brother while their mother was in the sanitarium. The commitment would now continue. Leaving Iowa, Carl worked his way eastward, landing a job in West Virginia. During their lengthy conversation he told Allen that a job was waiting for him, too. Of course, it would require a move from one coast to the other.

"I saved enough money to drive to West Virginia where my brother was working for DuPont on a construction job," he recalled.[8] Carl had found work at the site of the chemical manufacturer where a plant was being plant to produce pure ammonia for the military, the chemical used to manufacture torpedoes. The construction contractor needed hundreds of workers.[9]

The exhausting drive across country was uneventful. Heading into West Virginia, the region's mountains and rolling hills reminded him of California. A day after arriving in the town of Belle, he endured a brief interview and started work as an entry-level construction laborer. On most workdays, he found himself gripping on to tall scaffolding to erect rigging. "I was working there during the day," he said, "then I went to Wheeling and took a night course in electrical engineering." Enrolled as a student at the University of West Virginia, he decided to study engineering, as his superior math skills made it a no-brainer and a prerequisite to enroll. Outside of the classroom, he met someone who would take his life in another direction.

"I ran into Irene," he said of the couple's casual meeting.[10]

Lola Irene Eddy grew up in the rural coal-mining region of McCurdysville. Her father, Esta Ray Eddy, served as sole means of support for wife Blanche and their six children. In 1931, Esta passed away unexpectedly due to his work in the mines. It is unknown whether he died in an accident or as the result of black lung disease. The state was a top coal-producer, second only to Wyoming. Most of the town's men worked in the mines or held jobs that supported mining operations. Regardless of how their father died, nine-year-old Irene and her siblings were forced to mature beyond their years to cope with life's challenges. Upon graduating from Clay-Battelle District High School, the time was right for her to spread her wings. Dating Paulson, a bright and ambitious fellow with big ideas, she foresaw a better life than what the immature young men in her town could offer.

"We went together for just a short time and got married," he said. Both nineteen-years-old, they tied the knot on January 7, 1942, at St. Paul's Methodist Church, not far across the state line in the quaint, Victorian-themed town of Oakland, Maryland. Thirteen months had elapsed since the Japanese attack on Pearl Harbor. During the time that they dated, the U.S. military publicized the fact that it needed all able-bodied young men for wartime service. The newlyweds expected that he'd be drafted at any time but a "greetings" letter from the war department didn't arrive.

The regular paychecks from working on the DuPont project put cash in his wallet but he hadn't forgotten about airplanes. The early inspiration from Tex Rankin kept him thinking about a future in aeronautics. In August 1942, finding no acceptable reason to remain in West Virginia, with Irene equally eager to relocate, they piled their few belongings into his car, headed out of the mountains to join up with U.S. Route 66 in the Chicago area, and began the long journey to California.

Paulson and wife Irene celebrate her twenty-first birthday in September 1943 (Paulson family archives/Crystal Christensen).

After a brief visit in Marin to introduce Irene to his father, Paulson dropped by Transcontinental & Western Air's employment office at the Oakland airport to inquire about a mechanic's position. Something clicked with the interviewer because the newlywed snapped up a job, even though the airline wanted applicants to have a year of aviation experience. All that Paulson had to offer was a high school diploma and a letter of recommendation from DuPont. But he stressed his ability in fixing cars and washing plenty of airplanes. He was hired as an apprentice mechanic and told that he'd be assigned to the airline's maintenance base in Southern California. "When I got to California again, I got a job at TWA as an apprentice mechanic for thirty cents an hour," he recalled.

Reaching Los Angeles, that city celebrated as the nucleus of the nation's fledgling aviation industry, the couple rented an apartment in the San Fernando Valley. He reported for work at TWA's hangar along Hollywood Way on the Lockheed Air Terminal airport in Burbank. Other than odd jobs as a teenager, TWA would become his only employer for more than a decade of his career.

Sandwiched between rolling mountain ranges in the eastern San Fernando Valley, the runways at Burbank came into existence during 1930 to accommodate air traffic for the entire Los Angeles area. Once the country's involvement in World War II appeared inevitable, Lockheed Aircraft Corp. expanded its manufacturing facilities on the field, building hangars on much of the undeveloped acreage. Lockheed bought the airfield in 1940, changing its name to Lockheed Air Terminal, and continued to operate it as a commercial airport.[11]

Not long after Paulson's brief probationary period in Burbank, "They sent me back to Kansas City and I went to school there for about three months," he recalled, spending the remainder of 1942 learning about shop practices to maintain TWA's aircraft. While the couple occupied another temporary home in Kansas City, Irene gave birth to Richard Allen on October 25 of that year, the couple's first child. "Then I went to Washington, D.C.," he said, "and worked on a contract with the government for the intercontinental division of TWA."[12] As a newly assigned mechanic, he took up residence with Irene at an apartment bordering National Airport. The demands of war had created a job with a future for him.

TWA's Intercontinental Division (ICD) was formed when the airline signed a contract with the Army to provide emergency courier flights wherever and whenever they were requested. Flying top government officials, its fleet of four-engine Douglas DC-4s and Boeing Stratoliners also saw duty transporting machine guns, aircraft parts, mail, and medical supplies. Among the unexpected tear-jerking loads were wounded soldiers headed for hospitals or coming home for discharge.

For twenty-year-old Paulson, working at the airport was akin to spending time in paradise. The allure of aviation had become part of his DNA. When an airliner acted up during his shift, he'd rush to help more senior mechanics find a solution to whatever ailed it. Never a complainer, but disliking co-workers who moved in slow motion, he made sure that any job he handled was performed correctly the first time. The can-do style being observed by supervisors, he earned fast promotions from apprentice to mechanic and then lead mechanic. "I went up the ladder pretty quick from lead mechanic to foreman," he recalled about still another promotion. The military draft resulted in a severe shortage of civilian mechanics, creating openings at the airline. He was in the right place at the right time. Before his promotion to foreman, he handled routine tasks such as draining hot, sticky oil from Wright Cyclone R-1820 engines and replacing seals in the leak-prone hydraulic systems of Stratoliners. He learned what made the big ships tick, all the way from their tires to the tips of their vertical stabilizers.

Some of the mechanics Paulson worked with were as colorful and resourceful as the pilots. One of them happened to be a cigar-smoking maintenance supervisor by the name of Roy Davis, later thought as the most famous mechanic in airline history. After the war, he would gain notoriety by rescuing airliners that became stuck in mud or snow alongside runways. Davis was interviewed as a character for a novel—Arthur Hailey's fictitious Joe Patroni, who then made film history as a TWA mechanic in *Airport*.

After the stint with ICD, Paulson was transferred back to Burbank. He was excited to be a player in the company's success, and especially in awe of the airline's owner, Howard Hughes.

Later dubbed the "bashful billionaire," Hughes became the airline's controlling shareholder in April 1939. Other than focusing on strictly technological advances, a consuming interest of Hughes involved expanding TWA's routes, both domestic and international. TWA's corporate culture combined cosmopolitan trendiness and Midwest work ethic. As the airline grew into a global giant, it didn't forget that its roots were tied to America's heartland—Kansas City, Missouri. It became the nation's trendsetting airline. During Paulson's tenure as a foreman, one of his assignments was to make sure that an airplane was always ready for Hughes' personal use. "He was an impressive man to me," Paulson recalled. "I used to get his airplane ready in the morning. For some reason they picked me to go out and run the engines up before he got in the airplane. I was quite proud of that."[13] Paulson made an effort to chat with the elusive industrialist whenever they crossed paths. Although the opportunities were sporadic, they did spark a longer-term association between the men. "He told Mr. Hughes that he hoped to run his company one day," granddaughter Christensen said.[14] "I always had my eye on running

TWA," Paulson continued, even as a young adult. "I thought I could do a better job than what was being done."[15]

Checking the mail each day, Irene expected to find a letter from the government ordering her husband into the military. It never arrived. Instead, Paulson decided to volunteer, in common with some of his friends. "Getting back to work for TWA [in Burbank] after going to Washington, I decided to join the Army Air Corps," he said. "I went to take the test and was accepted." He wasn't required to join because his employment at TWA gave him an exemption. "They had a government contract and I could have stayed out; we were exempt from going in the service, but I wanted to go."[16] He wasn't alone in the desire to serve. Young men were enlisting by the hundreds of thousands. Brothers followed brothers into the military. A sense of devotion and commitment to winning the war were their foremost thoughts as the conflict dragged on. It was how that generation was raised, never questioning a sense of duty to the country. Paulson was expecting that the Army would train him to fly fighter planes. His love of flying stemming from hitching rides at the Oakland airport hadn't diminished the obsession. He had no desire to carry a machine gun slogging through the jungle as an infantryman.

By early 1941, as the threat of global war heated up, the U.S. Army Air Corps was reorganized as the U.S. Army Air Forces (USAAF). To meet a demand for pilots following the attack on Pearl Harbor, the Army relaxed its recruitment prerequisites from previous years. Air cadets needed to have only passed their eighteenth birthday and earned a high school diploma. Most of the recruits were nineteen or twenty years old.

Taking a leave of absence from TWA, Paulson joined the Army toward the end of 1943. He looked forward to earning a pilot's wings and flying combat missions. Unfortunately, the wish was not granted as the military's shifting priorities scuttled the prospect. "Al tried to get in as a cadet but they had reduced pilot training," best friend Clay Lacy said. "He went into a pool they used to pick people." A winning number didn't come up for him. "Instead, he became an aircraft mechanic."[17] Unbeknownst to anyone in 1943, it wouldn't be much longer until world peace arrived.

Disappointed by the turndown, he made the best of the situation. Already sworn in, he had no choice. "They had more pilots than they needed," he recalled. The service sent him to school to learn aircraft maintenance, something he'd already mastered as a civilian. "I was assigned to training fields from Texas to California."[18] Noting his experience as an airline mechanic, the Army assigned him to work on aircraft sitting on the ground rather than flying them. His only time in the air came when he accompanied pilots making test flights of repaired airplanes.

As the end of the war approached, Irene remained at home in the San

Fernando Valley. Her hands were full during the long stretches her husband was in uniform. Richard was now a toddler and she was pregnant with the couple's second child. Exchanging letters with mother-in-law Lillian in Clinton, she living alone after a lengthy stay in the sanitarium, Irene invited her to live with the family in California. "She came to live with Irene for a couple of years while Allen was in the service," Mary Lou Paulson recalled.[19] Irene needed the assistance. On June 26, 1946, Robert Steven Paulson was born.

Paulson was never deployed overseas, spending most of his enlistment at an airfield in Yuma, Arizona, a windswept, sagebrush-covered place he called "Yuma-Jima," with a bit of sarcasm. Discharged at war's end as a sergeant, none of his time in uniform saw him on the front lines. But he and his fellow GIs shared a common mindset. Work well done and honorable military service were enough recognition.

The majority of veterans sought jobs or went on to college after discharge. They intended to make up for the years spent away from family members and from starting a career. Unlike GIs who escaped death during combat, but acquired no job skills transferable to a peacetime economy, Paulson's service equipped him with additional expertise to continue building his career in aviation. He'd matured beyond his chronological years, shaped by the experience of serving and the discipline drilled into him by military regimen.

"Al went right back to TWA after the war, getting his airframe and engine mechanic license," Lacy said.[20] It was a simple matter to get reinstated on the TWA payroll. "If you were

Paulson at home from the Army Air Force in 1946, shown handling babysitting chores with sons Richard and Robert (Paulson family archives/Crystal Christensen).

working for someone, and went into the service, they had to give your job back when you got out of the service," Paulson said. The maintenance department snapped him up immediately. "I went back to work for TWA as a mechanic, and [then] up the ladder to lead foreman—but I wanted to get into flying."[21] The flying part would have to wait.

A day filled with earsplitting racket and clouds of oily smoke shooting from the exhaust stacks of huge piston engines described the work of mechanics that twenty-five-year-old Paulson supervised. Unlike the reliable operation and antiseptic working conditions associated with today's jetliners, the heavy piston-powered airliners kept mechanics on their toes. It was tiring, dirty work.

In December 1946, when TWA moved its west coast operations from Burbank 20 miles south to Avion Drive on Los Angeles Airport, Paulson accompanied the airline. His coworkers knew him as someone who went the extra mile in tackling the most difficult tasks. He became a repeat winner of the "Win a Place in the Sun" contest, TWA encouraging non-reservations employees to entice travelers to buy tickets.[22] He passed muster with subordinates and superiors as a dedicated company man. During off-duty hours, he availed himself of the education benefits offered by the G.I. Bill. He completed flight training in a 40-horsepower Piper J-3 Cub to earn a private pilot's license at Metropolitan Airport in the valley, today known as the Van Nuys Airport.[23]

Restless, he wasn't content working a single job at a time. On the side, he bought, reconditioned, and sold used cars to bring in extra money. "I started a garage on the side fixing automobiles and also bought and repaired airplanes,"[24] he said, the planes mostly the small, single-engine variety. He brought home a steady salary from the airline, plus the cash earned by fixing the cars and planes. It kept the household budget balanced. Fifteen months after Robert came into the world, James Douglas, born on October 12, 1947, joined the family.

In the postwar years, most of TWA's twin-engine DC-3s were relegated to short routes. For longer flights, four-engine Lockheed L-049 Constellations replaced them. The first batch of "Connies" the airline received from Lockheed consisted of converted C-69 troop transports—military versions of the plane that never got a chance to fly for the military before the war ended. The airplanes remained parked outside the Lockheed factory in Burbank, waiting for the government to release them to TWA and other airlines that ordered them before the war. The military olive-drab paint camouflaging their fuselages was stripped, airline-type seats replaced utilitarian troop seats, and aesthetic touches readied the planes for airline service.

As a foreman, Paulson's mechanical skills came in handy supervising the men who maintained this earliest generation of Connies. Integrated into TWA's fleet in 1946, the airline suffered a series of teething problems during the airliner's introductory period. Some of them were downright terrifying. Their intricate eighteen-cylinder, supercharged R-3350 Duplex-Cyclone engines found their way to the top of the problem list. Developed by Curtiss-Wright Corp. in 1937, the same 3,350-cublic-inch engines powered the Boeing B-29 Superfortress heavy bomber—the airplanes that dropped atomic bombs on Hiroshima and Nagasaki. For B-29 aircrews, the engine failures became so frequent that they shrugged them off. For airline passengers and pilots, the expectations were different, of course. "They weren't dependable," Paulson said of the engines. "They had a lot of failures. In fact, you were lucky when you took off that you wouldn't have an engine failure."[25]

It wasn't unusual for Connies to leave the airport behind schedule due to engines that wouldn't start, or if they did, catch fire. The stranded passengers were luckier than the folks who boarded, got in the air, and started praying when an engine caught fire. They could only hope for a survivable emergency landing. Flight crews nicknamed the four-engine airliner the "best tri-motor in the world." The problems became so widespread that fix-it projects for the big Wrights became somewhat like swatting flies—kill one and another soon appears. Although the incidents had different causes, enough evidence existed for the Civil Aeronautics Board to ground all Connies in service until Lockheed and Wright remedied the defects. The L-049 Connies turned into hangar queens while mechanics kept older airliners in service to take their place. The problems were mitigated, but not cured, as the government was under pressure from the airline industry to authorize a return to service for the airplanes. It did so in August 1946.

"Wright 3350 C18 BA-3 engine operations were especially troublesome," wrote Bob Rummel, a longtime engineering vice president at TWA. "False engine fire warnings were rampant."[26] Another problem involved losing oil pressure, causing inflight shutdowns. If two engines quit, it meant that the airliner would lose half its power. Over New York City, the scenario wouldn't raise a captain's ire because the concrete runways of Idlewild Airport were nearby. But over the middle of the Atlantic, multiple engine failures were more problematic, becoming major emergencies and possible ditching at sea. In common with the B-29 engines, one of the problems centered about assuring that sufficient oil reached the valve mechanisms of all eighteen cylinders. Oil lubricated and cooled those critical parts. Without adequate lubrication the valves snapped apart, beating the pistons to death—causing the airliner to make an unscheduled landing.

The stubborn problems with the R-3350 didn't go away. It was ironic that the unreliable engine so disliked by the airlines resulted in mechanical mysteries that Paulson enjoyed investigating. "To be successful in anything you have to love it," he declared about his work. "And I've been in love with aviation from day one."[27]

He never missed an opportunity to peruse job postings on the bulletin board in the break room. He felt ready for a job in the cockpit, rather than languishing as a foreman in the shop for the rest of his career. He had plenty of mechanical expertise but few hours logged in the air as a pilot of small airplanes. The airline posted occasional pilot openings, but gave priority to applicants who'd flown during the war. Aware of the strong competition, he put his name on the list for a flight engineer position. Four-engine Constellations and Douglas DC-6s were each crewed by two pilots and a flight engineer. The latter kept a watchful eye on the aircraft's often-temperamental engines. The engineer was a mechanic rather than pilot; someone the airlines culled from the ranks of their senior mechanics. "He was a good mechanic and when openings in the program came along he applied right away," Lacy said.[28]

Paulson earned his stripes by having learned countless details about the Connie's innards, stemming from nose to tail, and dealing with the engine's mystifying quirks. Because TWA was short of flight engineers while it took delivery of additional airplanes, it was a no brainer for the airline to promote him. Completing training at the carrier's Kansas City base, he traded in a pair of oil-splattered coveralls for a snazzy uniform and began a job sitting at the side-facing flight engineer's instrument panel of a Connie. The engineer was an essential crewmember aboard the first generation of four-engine

Paulson serves as a flight engineer on Lockheed L-049 Constellations at Trans World Airlines from 1947 to 1953 (H. M. Davidson via American Aviation Historical Society, reproduced with permission).

piston-powered airliners. The job was considered more important than the copilot because the engineer served as a master of the airplane's complex systems. He was the busiest member of the crew. On rare occasions, the engineer might roll up his sleeves and pick up a wrench—but only while stewards from the machinist union weren't looking.

The occasion when flight engineer Paulson cared for a sick TWA Connie was remembered by Lacy.

"They landed at Salt Lake City for a mechanical problem," he began. "An engine had blown a cylinder. All Al had to do was leave the airplane because it would be grounded for two days to get mechanics there and change the bad cylinder. Al took a look at the engine and said 'I can fix it.' He got some tools, found a spare cylinder, took the bad one off, and put the new one on. The airplane left in six hours rather than two days. Al went way beyond his duties as a flight engineer to get the airplane going."[29] Replacing a cylinder wasn't as simple a task as it might seem. He had to shove his hands into a dark, confined space between two adjacent cylinders and thread steel safety wire through a series of cylinder hold-down bolts. It meant enduring scraped knuckles and palms from having to press against the sharp edges of air baffles and ends of the wire used to secure the bolts.

In the world of organized labor, then or now, for a pilot or flight engineer to pick up a wrench and turn a bolt on an aircraft is a no-no. There are unions for pilots, flight attendants, flight engineers, and mechanics to oversee who does what—and to make sure that the respective union members are the employees benefiting from the work. Paulson gingerly ignored the rules. If an airplane got stuck on the ground he'd dive in and fix it—and damn the consequences in doing so.

3

Plane Peddler

You might think that a man with a stable job at a leading airline and a loving wife at home with three young children would be enough to satisfy him. Paulson was the exception. Although he enjoyed flying and family life, he was obsessed with doing more to elevate his career.

Repairing automobiles brought in cash, but not much. After crisscrossing the country as a flight engineer in Constellations for two years, he dreamed up another venture to boost his income. Making liberal use of TWA's free travel privileges during the winter months, a valuable employee perk, he commuted as a passenger between Los Angeles and Chicago. Arriving in the Windy City, he bought automobiles from private parties at depressed prices. In the Midwest, many cars remained parked in garages during the snowbound winter months, while commuting Los Angelinos were addicted to them on a year-round basis. Some of the cars needed minor repairs, but Paulson the mechanic, easily remedied the shortcomings. He drove the cars to Los Angeles, selling them for cash to eager buyers. Initially operating on a shoestring, a rising postwar demand for reliable used cars caused the venture to prosper. It wasn't long before he bought a van to transport several cars across the country at a time. "The whole time I was flying I had this business going," he said.[1]

When not wheeling and dealing in the part-time automotive business, Paulson and his fellow crewmembers coped with the Connie's temperamental Wright R-3350 engines. For flight engineers, it wasn't unusual to have to feather the propeller of a burning engine, hoping for the best outcome. Lubrication problems continued to plague the monstrous power plants. The thought of an engine exploding, followed by a wing bursting into flames, was enough of a recurring nightmare for flight crews to plan for the worst.

Paulson said that he "kept trying to figure out what was wrong. I'd fly, have a fire, and we'd land the airplane. The engines were experiencing a lot of cylinder failures."[2] It took an alert flight engineer to keep a watchful eye on the Connie's ignition analyzer, checking for indications of *both* spark plugs in a cylinder failing at the same time. It signified that the electrodes of the plugs had been hammered by a disintegrating valve or piston. To prevent a fire, the engine had to be shut down immediately and its propeller feathered.

Sadly, the incidents were becoming routine, if not predictable, but pinning down a cause remained elusive. The engineers at TWA and the engine's manufacturer, Curtiss-Wright Corp., remained confounded.

The early models of the R-3350 had the scary habit of "swallowing" cylinder valves. The mushroom-shaped head of a valve would break off from its stem and batter around inside the cylinder. If the engine weren't shut down quickly, the unattached valve head would beat a hole in the aluminum piston, finding its way into the bowels of the crankcase. More often than not, the resulting damage required mechanics to replace the entire engine. All moving parts in the engine were lubricated by oil under pressure—except valve stems, piston rings, cylinder walls, and crankshaft main bearings. These were lubricated by splashing oil against their surfaces. The tremendous amount of heat built up on the parts called for more effective lubrication—not only to oil the parts but also to remove more of the scorching heat. An expanded pressure lubrication system was what was needed. "Oil pressure lubricated the upper cylinders but didn't get to the lower cylinders," Paulson observed about the existing form of lubrication. Unfortunately, the engine's manufacturer never offered a definitive solution.

The engine failures were bad enough for TWA, but other issues were playing out in its corporate office. The price of the airline's stock plunged from $53 a share to $10 in 1946, due to a pilot's strike and the government grounding of the Constellation fleet. On a positive note, TWA's routes were expanded, flying to every corner of the globe. Its tripletail Connies could be seen on airports from Los Angeles to Cairo.

The Korean War ended on July 27, 1952, offering optimism that peace might stimulate the economy. It was also the time when Paulson became a part-time entrepreneur in the aircraft parts business. Strangely, the problematic 3350s failing so frequently is what created an opportunity for him to start a business. An improved lubrication system was a *must* for the highly stressed, hot running engines. He came up with a bright idea to cure the problem.

"As an employee I tried to give them the solution but they wouldn't listen to me," he said, running headlong into the oft-heard phrase, "not invented here." The college-educated engineers in TWA's engineering department, having little or no hands-on mechanic experience, weren't interested in the opinion of a lowly mechanic turned flight engineer. "For someone who was not in the engineering department to tell them how to fix their engine, they just didn't want to listen."[3]

Receiving no help from the airline to develop his idea, Paulson found a military version of the R-3350. He needed an engine to determine if his solution would actually work. "I went and bought it from a pilot who invested in surplus B-29 engines," he said.[4] Having kids to feed, a mortgage to pay, and not much cash on hand, he borrowed $1,500 from the TWA credit union to pay for the purchase.

Over dinner, he told Irene that he wanted to tap into whatever money they had saved to rent a small shop and carry out the mechanical work. It wasn't a popular idea with her. But lacking other options, he withdrew the money to rent the shop. He equipped it with enough tools to undertake the backbreaking, greasy tasks involved in taking the engine apart. The eighteen-cylinder, 2,670-pound monster was disassembled, piece-by-piece. The R-3350 was among the largest piston aircraft engines built. "I tore the engine down and really learned about its innards to figure what it would take to fix it," he recalled. His theories about the cause of the lubrication failures would prove correct.

Paulson's relationship with the airline's engineering department didn't improve. The engineers considered that he, an independent-thinking outsider owning a part-time business, competed with their work—yet he still wore a TWA employee badge. They showed little interest in talking with him about anything to do with the engines. He decided to visit the maintenance chiefs in Kansas City. Mechanics were first responders when it came to dealing with engine problems and seemed eager to listen to what he'd discovered. "I modified one of the parts, put it on an engine, and showed them how it worked. It really got them interested."[5]

In short order, he made his first sale. He would hit the mother lode by modifying the lubrication system to remedy its major shortcoming. The modified part came from the B-29 engine he bought. To turn his bright idea into a full-fledged business he needed to buy more R-3350s. "They gave him $25,000," said Mary Lou Paulson in recalling what TWA paid him for the solution. "That's how he got the money to start buying more engines."[6]

Busy in the shop, he continued to maintain a full flight schedule at TWA, the steady employment needed for bread-and-butter income. Returning from a transcontinental trip in a Connie, he devoted day and night to working in the crowded shop aided by a couple of helpers, disassembling newly purchased engines to retrieve the parts he needed to modify and sell.

"As time went on, the side business I had while flying for TWA just kept growing and growing," he recalled. "I'd work the business during the week and fly on Saturday and Sunday. I used to go from Los Angeles to New York and back, which took about twenty hours round trip. I only had to make four and a half trips a month to get my thousand hours in."[7] Airline flight crews were restricted to flying no more than 85 hours a month. Assigned to TWA's Transcontinental Division, it operating domestic flights, the arrangement assured that he wouldn't be away from California for long stretches as were the crews working in the International Division.

To spend time with Irene and their sons, he squeezed in whatever hours were left between working in the shop and flying. He was seldom at home. In spite of his best efforts, he'd become a stranger around the house. He pondered whether to quit the airline.

"Irene was upset as he had a solid job with TWA," Clay Lacy said about the time Paulson brought up the idea of quitting. "It was a good company. She wondered how much business he could do by going out on his own."[8] The family was fortunate to have a home in the San Fernando Valley and a steady salary to pay the bills. However, any extra money was earmarked for investing in the part-time business. Leaving a good paying job, especially one with an airline posting the best year in its history, remained disconcerting for Irene.

Convinced that he had a solid handle on the moneymaking potential of the parts business, Paulson lost interest in working for the airline—in spite of its stellar financial performance. He had flown as a flight engineer on Connies from 1947 to 1953, amassing thousands of hours. The job combined his love of flying with a sharp mechanical aptitude. In August 1952, his supervisor had presented him with a ten-year service pin. Little did the man know, or anyone else for that matter, that this would be Paulson's final year on the airline's payroll. He couldn't live three lives anymore: airline employee, business owner, and family man. Something had to give. He couldn't wait to devote full-time to his business. Mary Lou offered a different explanation: "TWA made him quit. They said it was a conflict of interest. He needed to do one thing or the other. So he chose to go into business for himself."[9] Regardless of the reason, he was about to embark on a time-consuming journey with no turning back. During the spring of 1953, Paulson resigned from TWA, starting a regimen of working seven days a week to expand the fledging business. Naming the entity California Airmotive Corp., a lawyer drew up incorporation papers.

Through relentless effort on his part, the engine-saving devices he invented turned into best sellers. "I went and sold enough parts to modify the whole TWA fleet," he said, stressing the airline's new opinion of him as a *former* employee and president of a corporation. "Then I sold them to every other airline," at least those flying airplanes powered by Wright engines. What he was selling wasn't newly a manufactured item, but consisted of components removed from surplus engines and modified in his shop. "While tearing them [engines] down, after I took out the parts that I needed, I could sell the rest of the parts for more than what I paid for the engines," he said.[10] Whatever pieces remained were sold for a profit. It was like a butcher selling everything—meat, bones, and fat.

"Al was told that TWA didn't buy military surplus engines like what he had in stock," Lacy said. The 3350s were similar to their civil variants but carried a military specification part number. Paulson expected such a response from TWA and approached the sale process from another angle. Rather than selling them assembled engines from his warehouse, "he started selling parts to TWA. He'd take an engine, tear it down, and sell them the parts," Lacy continued.[11] It made no difference if the parts were manufactured for a commercial or military engine because they met identical specifications. The scenario resembled a junkyard where the parts stripped from a car prove more valuable than the intact car.

"I got enough from the parts to buy two more engines, and then I got enough [money] to buy five," Paulson recalled. "From one engine, the business grew to several thousand. Things just mushroomed."[12]

He went on to develop an improved oil pressure relief valve for the engines. The existing valve gave mechanics fits at both the airlines and the military. "I came up with a new relief valve since there were a lot of oil pressure fluctuation and low pressure problems," he said. "I sold them for all Wright engines."[13] The man with no engineering degree outsmarted the engineers working for the engine's manufacturer.

To build up a large parts inventory he continued buying surplus engines. The Air Force had mothballed many of its B-29 bombers, relegating thousands of unused engines to storage. The L-049 and L-749 Connies were powered by the same basic type of engine. He'd tear those engines down, stock their valves, cylinders, pistons, gears, and bolts in his warehouse, and sell the parts to airlines at prices cheaper than the engine manufacturer. It helped that he'd paid pennies on the dollar for the engines at government auctions.

"Al spent twelve hours a day working," Lacy recalled of Paulson's days in the shop. "When things were really tough, it was nothing for him to spend fourteen hours there. When at home, he thought about the business all the time."[14] More than ever, his absence at home was taking a toll with Irene. For much of their marriage she spent the days functioning, in essence, as a single parent. He would travel to see customers or become immersed with work in the shop, and she'd deal with household tasks, whether a leaky faucet or helping the children with homework. The work at California Airmotive consumed his life except for the infrequent hours spent with the family. All his mental and physical energies were devoted to the business. He gradually acquired a reputation as a kingpin in the aircraft parts business, although some people called him a junk dealer. One year he posted sales of $100,000. The next year they grew to more than a million. "From then on the engine parts business just kept building up," he said. "That was the little acorn that grew into a big oak."[15]

During 1955, a tall, handsome pilot dropped by his warehouse to say hello. It was Clay Lacy. "I met Al through Jack Conroy who knew everybody in town who had anything to do with aviation," he recalled. "I was twenty-three when I met Al, and just out of the Air Force. I'd flown for United for two years, went into the Air Force, followed by coming back to the airline."[16] Enjoying each other's company, the men began to build a friendship with Lacy beginning to work for Paulson on an occasional basis.

Thirty-five-year-old Conroy came to know Lacy when they were assigned to the same California Air National Guard unit in Van Nuys. Returning home from the war after flying missions in B-17s over Germany, and getting shot down on one of those flights, Conroy flew for several non-scheduled airlines in Southern California. Missing the allure of military flying, he joined the guard unit. Along with Bill Lear, Jr., and test pilot Herman Salmon, each man lived to fly airplanes. Whether sipping a frosty beer in a bar, or relaxing around a backyard barbeque, they never stopped swapping flying tales. A dapper dresser, Salmon sported a flinty crew cut and thin mustache, not unlike a Hollywood version of a test pilot. Nicknamed "Fish" by friends, apparently attributable to his surname, the one-time barnstormer and race pilot moved up the corporate ladder at Lockheed to the chief engineering test pilot post. Lear became an accomplished pilot who people expected to be the alter ego of his famous father, inventor of the car radio and later the business jet bearing his name. The role of being the industrialist's son was never comfortable for him.

Following stints in the cockpit or working on an airplane in a hangar, the men could be spotted tucked away in a booth of the dimly lit Flight Room Lounge at Johnny's Skytrails Restaurant, a convenient watering hole at Sherman Way and Hayenhurst Avenue bordering the Van Nuys Airport. Eclectic freethinkers, they didn't hold much back in conversation, could be a bit loud at times, were adept at poker, and relished taking risks, whatever they may be. There existed a thread of camaraderie between the men, a result of the common challenges they faced as aviators.

Paulson's workdays at California Airmotive continued without letup. "Early in life, I discovered there is no such thing as a lazy, lucky guy," he was fond of saying when people asked why he worked all the time. Competitors considered him unorthodox, chalking up successes by running a company that benefited from cheap rent, a limited number of employees, and luck. They did concede that Paulson had brains and gumption, two attributes he possessed in abundance. His optimism concerning the future could be termed obstinate.

In both his personal and business lives, Paulson avoided discussing anything in a negative vein, always focusing on the positive. An important influence shaping his vision of how one should live his or her life evolved from reading *The Power of Positive Thinking*, authored by minister Norman Vincent

Peale, a spiritual icon of the 1950s. Paulson encouraged each of his employees to read the book, live a spiritual life, and adhere to the philosophies that Peale espoused concerning work. A prolific writer, Peale's book became his most famous work. First published in 1952, it stayed on the *New York Times* bestseller list for 186 consecutive weeks. According to its publisher, Simon and Schuster, the book eventually sold five million copies.

"Religion had something to do with it. The truth in it is so obvious," Paulson said of the book's message.[17] As a Christian, Paulson attended services at Presbyterian churches. "He's [Peale] been one of the biggest inspirations I've ever had." On the job, Paulson "preached" the gospel of Peale blended with the advice of President Theodore Roosevelt: "Think positively, walk softly, and carry a big stick."

Paulson believed that *all* organizations, including his own, were populated by a small minority of disgruntled employees. They were people who, for whatever reason, criticized their company and its management—and tried to convince new employees that they'd never succeed. It was tempting for a new employee to adopt a negative attitude while trying to fit into such a culture. Once headed down a path of negativity it could become an ingrained way of thinking. His advice was to avoid participating in such behavior by remembering: "I plan on being the exception, not the rule." Positive-thinking individuals succeeded over time and negative ones stayed in the same job, or if they left, ended up in the same cynical role at a different company.

Fast-forwarding fifteen years, after much success in the aviation business; Paulson directed his secretary, Kathy O'Sako, to order thousands of the Peale books and present one to each employee. "It was a small paperback book that could be kept in a desk drawer, purse, or tool box," she recalled. "All new employees for the following year also received the book in their new employee package. After that year, Mr. Paulson told me to donate the rest of the books to the Boy Scouts."[18]

At the same time Paulson was working exceedingly long hours, Irene carved out the best life she could at home, tending to the needs of sons Richard, James, and Robert. On October 6, 1955, John Michael was born to the couple.

While Paulson's life was often strained at home, Lacy remained at his side as a friend and part-time employee. He recalled accompanying Paulson on an important business trip in the early 1960s. "We flew down to Mobile, Alabama, in Al's Twin Bonanza," he began. "They were going to have a government surplus sale." The auction would be conducted for the benefit of the Defense Logistics Agency. "We walked around and saw some turbine wheels. There were boxes of them. Al asked a guy what they were and he said he didn't know."[19]

Paulson knew exactly what they were—and how much they might be

At home in the San Fernando Valley during the mid–1950s, Paulson family members pose from left, sons Robert, James, Richard, along with Irene and Allen holding baby Michael (Paulson family archives/Crystal Christensen).

worth to the airlines. They were power recovery turbine wheels (PRTs) for Wright R-3350 turbo-compound engines. If he could buy the hundreds of boxes of PRTs at a rock-bottom price it could turn into a big payday for him.

During the mid–1950s, the airlines demanded an uptick in performance from their latest Lockheed and Douglas airliners, increases in both speed and range without consuming more fuel. Achieving the goal required an upgraded engine from Curtiss-Wright: the turbo-compound R-3350. The "compound" label came about because the engine produced power through the action of both pistons and turbines.[20] It developed 20 percent more horsepower than earlier 3350s with no increase in fuel consumption. Although the PRT-equipped engines *appeared* to be a godsend for the airlines, they created reliability problems, failing mainly due to high exhaust gas temperatures weakening the turbine wheels. Pilots and flight engineers coped with a dramatic increase in engine failures. Mechanics joked that PRT stood for "parts recovery turbine." Failure of the PRTs was a nagging concern, not only due to fatigue of their turbine wheels, but something as simple as the hardware securing them. "Overheated shafts will stretch, causing the nut that holds the entire assembly to lose its tightness," reported an article in *Aviation Week*. "This causes the wheel to jiggle on the spline and results in a breakage."[21] The PRTs weren't alone in causing problems. Wright's old nemesis, the cylinders and cylinder heads, continued to top the list of culprits. The highly stressed compound engine was a maintenance nightmare, worse than the 3350s on the original Connies.

"The PRTs had a military part number," Lacy said. "Al looked at them while we were standing in the aisle. He said he could modify them and put on a civilian part number. It would really change their value." Paulson knew that the military and civilian specifications for the wheels were identical.

Paulson decided to try sniffing out a customer for the PRTs before putting money on the line to bid for the entire lot. Departing Mobile in the Twin Bonanza, the men headed for Kansas City to visit TWA. "We went to see the vice president of engineering," Lacy said of the visit, which initially involved Paulson making a pitch for the thousands of engine parts he had stockpiled in California. "Al tried to sell him some engine cylinders. The man said they had plenty of them. Al then said, 'How about buying some PRT wheels?' He knew they were hurting for them.

'Would you buy a thousand?' he asked.

'Yes, we'll buy a thousand,'" said the vice president. It might have been the easiest sale of Paulson's career.

"Al hadn't even bought them yet. We left and headed back to California. As soon as we got in the airplane he told me his thinking. He planned to bid $35 for each wheel. It would cost money to rework them, but not much."

When it came time for the auction they flew back to Mobile. "A guy named Miller showed up at the surplus sale," Lacy recalled. "The bidding jumped to $65 apiece. Miller went to $80 and bought all of them. But Al ended up buying the wheels from him for about $120 each. He then sold them to TWA for $750 apiece. To buy new ones [from Curtiss-Wright] would have cost TWA $2,000 a wheel. Miller made a little money but Al made a lot of money."[22]

Closing the deal with TWA, Paulson's profit amounted to more than $500,000.

The California Airmotive office and warehouse at 7139 Vineyard Avenue in North Hollywood kept abuzz with ringing phones and rustling papers. Orders for parts, some large and some small, were processed daily. The austere concrete block building would serve as Paulson's command post during the decade to come. He also set up satellite parts warehouses in Mobile, Alabama, and Shreveport, Louisiana.

By the late 1950s, Paulson began shifting from selling parts to entire airplanes. They weren't Piper Cubs, although it began that way. "Al had a little airplane and took a guy up to sell it to him," Lacy said. "All the fabric came off one side of the fuselage. They got back down and Al told him, 'This is your airplane, you're so lucky to get this one.' The guy ended up buying it."[23] Lacy's friend was a crack mechanic—but an even better salesman. If Paulson had embarked on a career selling furniture or fertilizer he may have failed. It was his consuming passion with aviation that impressed prospective customers and helped close sales.

Some of his customers were tiny startup airlines operating south of the border. Others were air carriers in the United States formed after the war by ex-military pilots. They were known as charter, supplemental, or nonscheduled airlines—most of them simply nicknamed "non-skeds." The major airlines considered such upstarts to be unreliable and undercapitalized shoestring operations, but their founders thought of themselves as pioneers. For the first time in history, they provided nationwide air transportation for economy-minded travelers.

Before they could take to the air, the carriers needed government approval, pilots, mechanics, and a source from where to buy second-hand planes and their spare parts at reasonable prices. Paulson had all the parts they'd need. And now he could supply the airplanes as well. He recalled the day in July 1959 when he bought his first airliner from TWA with the intention of selling it. "They had an order for parts from me worth over a million dollars," he said. Looking to conserve cash they asked: "Why don't you take some of our surplus airplanes?" He took five cargo door equipped Douglas DC-4s in payment for the parts. Among four-engine airliners, the DC-4 was considered the equal of the workhorse DC-3—and in similar demand. He bought the planes by trading the roughly million dollars' worth of parts, each airliner valued at $250,000. "I sold those airplanes and continued to buy more airliners," he said. "I was in business."[24] What he meant was that he had moved beyond serving as a spare parts supplier to becoming a businessman who bought and sold airliners.[25]

"I knew Al for two years before he got into the airliner business," Lacy said. "As a pilot I loved having the opportunity to fly the different airplanes he owned. As a young kid I was having a ball."[26] His experience could be compared to being an eight-year-old boy running wild in a candy store.

Paulson needed a hangar large enough to house the airliners. "Al leased old Hangar 2 at Burbank," Lacy recalled. Until the mid–1960s, two hangars stood alongside the passenger terminal at the Burbank airport. Hangar 2, built in 1929 of Spanish revival architecture, sat adjacent to the terminal's south side, just east of Runway 33.[27] For Paulson, it was a business decision that caused him to locate at the airport, although there was a sentimental reason as well. Lockheed's plant buildings dominating the airport property saw every Constellation in existence built—and Paulson spent his career at TWA flying many of those airliners. It was nostalgic for him.

His next deal had to do with buying twin-engine Convair 240s from

Western Airlines. The forty-seat airliners were for sale at bargain prices as the carrier was anxious to replace them with four-engine Lockheed L-188 Electra turboprops. "Al called me on a Friday night and asked if I'd go with him to take a look at one of the 240s the next day," Lacy said. "The following week Al made a deal to buy them. I flew the airplanes to Burbank over a week's time."

After refurbishing the Convairs, Paulson's plan was to sell them to corporations and entertainers. He thought that an industrialist by the name of Elton MacDonald might be a hot prospect. "Al told MacDonald to drop by the Palm Springs Airport to see the Convair," Lacy said. "We landed in Palm Springs and MacDonald told us that 'bringing me a Convair was a waste of time. I'm not interested. They're too damn noisy out back.' He said, 'If you have a Martin 404, I'd be interested. They're much quieter.'"[28] It was back to the drawing board for Paulson to find a crème puff Martin and bag the sale with MacDonald.

The Martin-built airliners had a checkered history. The 202, forerunner of the 404, featured a wing structure fabricated from an aluminum alloy that was susceptible to cracking from stress corrosion. The weakened wings couldn't withstand turbulent flying conditions, leading to structural failure that caused several fatal accidents. The planes were grounded until the wings were strengthened. When production of the 202 ceased, Martin developed the 404, a variant with a beefed-up airframe. There was another reason for the upgrade. The 202 had an unpressurized cabin, uncomfortable for passengers. Martin's competitor, the Convair 240, offered pressurization. So the 404 debuted with a new wing, a fuselage lengthened to carry forty passengers—*and* pressurization. For convenience, an air stair door beneath the aft fuselage could be lowered to speed passenger deplaning. TWA operated forty 404s between September 1950 and the last flight of the type in April 1961. However, even with the refinements, the Martins eventually lost favor with TWA's passengers and the airline's management. Starting in February 1958, TWA offered its 202s and 404s for sale.

"Al knew that TWA was going to sell their 404s," Lacy said. "He flew to Kansas City and talked with them about the Martins. He made a deal to buy airplanes over a two-year period." Closing the deal, the first ship was ready for delivery in three weeks. "I went to Kansas City to fly it back to Burbank. I'd never flown a 404 but it was a lot like the Convair."[29] It was an era when FAA regulations governing a pilot's experience in a given type of airplane were less rigid than today. Arriving in Burbank, the aircraft were stored outside Hangar 2. Although the hangar was a spacious enough structure to accommodate most types of airplanes, the 404s posed a problem. "We couldn't fit the Martins inside the hangar as their tails were too high," Lacy recalled about the airplane's 29-foot-high vertical stabilizer.

Declared surplus by Trans World Airlines, its Martin 404s are acquired by California Airmotive Corporation in the 1960s (R. Hufford via American Aviation Historical Society, reproduced with permission).

TWA was anxious to rid itself of the remaining Martins. Paulson bought eight of them during 1959 and 1960. He continued to bid for more, although other companies did likewise. A handful of local-service airlines, today called regional airlines, bought what he didn't buy. The sales effort continued until the end of 1962.

"When we got the first Martin, Al called MacDonald who bought it right away and used it for years until the jets came along," Lacy said. Another buyer was Essex Productions, a company owned by Frank Sinatra. The entertainer bought a 404 from Paulson in June 1961. The airliner, which he named *El Dago*, was modified with a plush interior, including a piano.

"The big airplanes were all for sale, but there was always one sitting around to take on a pleasure trip," Lacy said. "We had everything from Lodestars and Beech 18s to Martins. We'd fly to Acapulco, Idaho, and Kansas City in them. "When Al got the 404s he set up trips for his friends to fly to the Indianapolis 500 race."[30] When an unsold airplane was parked on the ramp, and they felt like flying somewhere for the heck of it, the adventuresome duo would hop in with family and friends and go.

Paulson enjoyed his limited amount of leisure time in sun-drenched Palm Springs, a two-hour drive from the hustle of smoggy Los Angeles. Relaxing at a vacation home in the desert became a welcome respite. He especially enjoyed playing a round of golf on the manicured courses of nearby country clubs. The golf course was where he struck up a friendship with fellow Midwesterner Dwight Eisenhower. The desert resort's population was still modest and culturally informal in the late 1950s, enabling Paulson to easily cross socio-economic lines and cultivate friendships. Vacationing in the desert during 1959, the president and wife Mamie were guests of Allen and Irene at their home. It was an exciting time for the Paulson sons, watching the moves of Secret Service agents guarding the family home with machine guns. During his two terms in office, Eisenhower set a "record" by playing 800 rounds of golf, a fact publicized by his detractors. Whether in Georgia at the Augusta National Golf Club, or the Eldorado Country Club in Indian Wells, Ike enjoyed the company of people

President Dwight Eisenhower joins Paulson for a game of golf on the links in Palm Springs, California (Paulson family archives/Crystal Christensen).

he considered successes in their chosen careers. Included were Hollywood celebrities, sports figures, and industrialists. Eisenhower and his friends rose early in the day to play golf. At noon, they'd break for lunch, following by strolling around town in the afternoon. After dinner there were card games. Bob Hope and Arnold Palmer were two of his best-known acquaintances. As time ran out during his second term in the White House, the presidential couple escaped the harsh winters of the east as much as possible and stayed in a home at Eldorado.

Following World War II, Eisenhower continued to socialize with the officers he came to know from his decades in the Army. But in an unusual turnabout, upon leaving the White House he preferred to socialize with businessmen. Growing up on the poor side of the tracks in Abilene, Kansas, he began cultivating friend-ships with the wealthy. In doing so, an important distinction was that most of the people weren't born into wealth. They were self-made. Their rise to the top is what intrigued Ike, such as what Paulson accomplished in the avi-ation business.

"Al and Eisenhower were great friends," Bruce McCaw recalled. "They'd play golf together and Al flew him around, too." Although golf was a con-suming pastime for Ike, he enjoyed fishing and hunting as well. Having dozens of airplanes at his disposal, Paulson flew him to Baja California to fish. There were other pleasure trips as well. Secret Service men were never far behind.

"For a guy who was so quiet, Al sure made a lot of connections," McCaw added.[31] Cementing friendships in high government circles were always done in a quiet, circumspect fashion. Never beating on doors to win friends, Paul-son developed friendships on a long-term basis, and not with any sense of urgency.

Paulson again visited the TWA chiefs at Kansas City in March 1962. The airline was accepting bids for its entire fleet of L-049 Connies, the transports first seeing scheduled service in 1945. He ended up buying twenty-five of them. With no space available in Burbank, he stored the planes at his "bone yard" in the desert. If they didn't sell in a reasonable period of time, "teardown crews" would dismantle the airframes for parts, piece-by-piece. Most of the Connies were scrapped by 1964. The survivors were sold to small airlines for a few more years of service.

Approaching commercial bankers to borrow money for buying such air-craft was not in the cards. They couldn't fathom why he'd want to buy scores of worn out airliners and take chances trying to sell them. It ran afoul of their established lending practices. Luckily, Paulson connected with Bill Murphy, a wealthy automobile dealer in Los Angeles who appreciated what he was doing and agreed to serve as his occasional "banker."

Leasing and selling airliners was a lucrative endeavor—but also pre-sented a downside. California Airmotive's customers were primarily upstart airlines. Limited working capital crippled their ability to buy aircraft or make timely lease payments. "There is considerable interest in used transports from airlines without the cash to pay for them," reported an article in *Aviation Week*. "The field is a money market more than an aircraft market in many cases. Extremely flexible arrangements for pay-as-you-go financing and other services will have to be made to tap this demand."[32] Most of the customers were non-scheduled carriers shuttling military troops between bases, deliv-ering gamblers to resorts, or flying freight around South America and Alaska. Some of the airliners were used to whisk entertainers to their next venue. Paulson worked with them all. But the monthly checks for the sales and leases didn't always arrive. A case in point involved Standard Airways, Inc.

Burbank-based Standard was a longtime California Airmotive customer, the airline winning contracts to transport military personnel. Along with non-sked carriers Imperial Airlines and President Airlines, Standard came under scrutiny by a House Congressional subcommittee after an Imperial L-049 Connie crashed on November 8, 1961, killing seventy-four Army recruits on their way to boot camp. A Civil Aeronautics Board investigation revealed that twenty of the twenty-two non-sked airlines in existence during the early 1960s were in precarious financial condition.

On May 28, 1963, a Standard Airways L-1049G Super Connie crashed during an approach to the airport in Manhattan, Kansas. The airplane suffered an unexpected reversal of the Curtiss electric propeller on its number three engine—a result of sloppy maintenance. Although the airliner was packed with sixty-three military personnel, only one soldier suffered serious injury when the plane burst into flames following an off-airport landing. The Civil Aeronautics Board pinned the cause on "bad maintenance, servicing and inspection." Paulson had owned the Connie for less than four months before selling it to Standard on July 30, 1962.

Six days after the Kansas accident another Standard L-1049G experienced a different type of propeller problem, the flight engineer unable to control the blade's erratic pitch. Fortunately, the airplane landed safely. These and other incidents caused the military to poke into Standard's maintenance methods with a fine-tooth comb. The carrier's series of government contracts to transport military personnel were cancelled. California Airmotive incurred no liability as it sold the airplanes in an "as-is" condition. It was the responsibility of the airlines to maintain them properly.

In September 1963, Paulson repossessed five airliners that Standard had bought from California Airmotive. Three other aircraft, under lease from him by the airline, ended up on the repo list for Lacy or other pilots to pick up. Heavily in debt, Standard filed for bankruptcy on June 4, 1964, an expected outcome. Paulson had sold and leased airliners to the carrier over a four-year timeframe. When the checks stopped arriving, the relationship soured. California Airmotive was owed $160,000, a considerable sum at the time.

Associated Air Transport, a Miami-based non-sked air carrier, was another California Airmotive customer—it too was running out of money. In September 1961, its liabilities exceeded assets by $202,000. The airline was declared unfit to operate by the Military Air Transport Service, the agency severing all contracts with the airline "for financial inadequacy, substandard maintenance and substandard quality of service."[33] It appeared there was a lack of safety oversight on the part of the government as the carrier had suffered three accidents during the preceding four years. Because Paulson was owed money that the airline didn't have, he wanted something in lieu of it: the carrier's CAB operating certificate. By assuming its debts, California Airmotive acquired a controlling interest in the line during July 1962, Paulson planning to move its headquarters to Burbank. His idea was to equip the fleet with L-749 and L-1049G Connies to run charter flights over Puerto Rico-Miami-Chicago and Burbank-San Francisco-Hawaii routes. The idea was short-lived. Complications arose and the concept fizzled, causing the airplanes to remain parked in the desert to await buyers.

The time came when buying and reselling airliners, engines, propellers, and their parts wasn't enough for Paulson. Within the cavernous hangar in Burbank, his mechanics switched to tackling repair and modification projects. They thought nothing of removing a wing from an airliner and grafting its fuselage onto another ship, or cutting fuselages in half to insert cargo doors. Converting piston-powered aircraft to turbine engines would become routine. Other facilities passed up the business when it came to such monumental work. California Airmotive mechanics reveled in assuming the challenges. In the middle of the hubbub on the hangar floor, and never far from his mechanics, could be seen Paulson, delving into every detail of the work. He'd lean against a fuselage sketching solutions for structural or electrical problems holding up progress. It wasn't unusual for him to spend more time in the hangar than in his sparsely appointed office.

The maintenance, repair, and overhaul of older airliners turned into a godsend for California Airmotive's bottom line. By May 1960, its business had grown to a point that Paulson leased Hangar 27 on the northwest side of the airport in Burbank. Located at 3000 North Clybourn Avenue, the hangar's domelike span could easily accommodate the Martins and Convairs with their tall tails. Slick Airways built the maintenance hangar in the 1940s, and later an identical one next to it with an adjacent office building. By 1960, the airline opened other maintenance bases around the country and offered to lease one of its Burbank hangars, with California Airmotive signing up for it.

When Paulson's airliner sales and leasing activity overtook his other endeavors, he decided to exit the aircraft overhaul and maintenance line of business. On January 29, 1962, he sold that portion of California Airmotive's operations to PacAero Engineering Corp.; it a subsidiary of Pacific Airmotive Corp. PacAero took over Hangar 27. It sought space to eventually convert 170 Convair 340s and 440s to turboprop-powered Convair 580s for regional airlines. Slick Airways had vacated the remaining hangar at approximately the same time that Paulson handed over the keys to PacAero, the latter taking over the entire site, upgrading the facility with additional hangar and ramp space, and building an executive aircraft terminal.

Selling airliners was profitable, but Paulson hadn't stopped selling aircraft engines and their parts. He kept in mind that the Wright R-3350 is what started him in business. In July 1962, he bought Aircraft Engines and Metals

Corp., based at the Long Beach Airport, about an hour's drive from the San Fernando Valley. The price was a reported $2 million. What Paulson focused on were the engines that were included in the deal. They were sealed in olive drab painted steel containers at the company's storage yard: 1,600 Wright and Pratt & Whitney piston engines.[34]

Lacking adequate space to store his thousands of airframe and engine parts, many of them sold to the same airlines that bought airplanes from him, Paulson rented satellite warehouses. Business was brisk, requiring his unrelenting involvement, but on the home front, things weren't going so well. In 1963, at the age of forty-one, Allen's marriage to Irene crumbled after more than two decades. The relationship produced four sons: Michael, Robert, Richard, and Jim. "My grandma was married over twenty years, he loved her and she loved him, but he was gone all the time," Crystal Christensen said. "With four kids at home it wasn't easy for her."[35] Irene's residue of bitterness continued for some time as Paulson embarked on the most productive decade of his career.

4

Checkered Flags

Wikipedia has this to say about Clay Lacy: "His professional resume includes airline captain, military aviator, experimental test pilot, air race champion, world record-setter, aerial cinematographer and business aviation entrepreneur. Lacy has flown more than 300 aircraft types, logged more than 50,000 flight hours and accumulated more hours flying turbine aircraft than any other pilot."[1] A number of those experiences took place because of his friendship with Allen Paulson.

Raised in Wichita, Lacy caught the flying bug early in life. At the age of seven, his father died from tuberculosis, the lengthy illness indirectly cultivating the boy's interest in aviation. "Before he died, my father was sent to a sanitarium located about a mile from Wichita Municipal Airport," Lacy said, "but they wouldn't allow me in because I was too young."[2] While mom visited his dad, young Clay would sit in the car watching airplanes take off and land. When he finally bummed a ride in one, it was memorable enough for him to want nothing but a future in aviation. "I knew for sure that's what I wanted to do."[3] By the age of sixteen he'd earned a flight instructor rating. By nineteen, he logged a remarkable 2,000 hours by giving flying lessons and ferrying small airplanes.

In 1951, he spotted a pilot recruitment ad placed by United Air Lines. He applied for the job but knew that his chances of getting hired were slim, competing with ex-military pilots. An unexpected surprise came his way when the airline made him a job offer. His first flight as a twenty-year-old DC-3 copilot occurred in April 1952. Based at Los Angeles International Airport, he continued to log extra hours as an instructor at flight schools on the Torrance and Van Nuys airports.

Taking a leave of absence from United in 1954, Lacy joined the California Air National Guard. It was his opportunity to fly jet fighters, something new for him. As a member of the 146th Air Fighter Wing in Van Nuys, he found himself in the cockpit of North American F-86s. When the guard wing transitioned from fighters to transports, changing its name to the 146th Air Transport Wing, he flew Boeing C-97 Stratofreighters. During the Berlin Crisis in 1961, he was called up for active duty. After a year overseas, he went back to flying full-time for the airline and part-time for Paulson at California Airmotive.

In January 1964, thirty-one-year-old Lacy found himself in Reno during a brief layover between flights. He noticed a poster announcing the National Championship Air Races. Curiosity caused him to stop by the chamber of commerce office to learn more. Bill Stead, a local rancher and promoter who organized the race, happened to be there. Chatting with Stead for a few minutes, Lacy made a quick decision to attend the race—and hopefully compete in it. The only obstacle was that he didn't own a North American P-51 Mustang or comparable race plane. He didn't own any kind of airplane.

A wealthy rancher, Stead had developed a passion for fast boats and faster airplanes. Passed down from his family, he owned the Stead Hereford Ranch, located northeast of Reno in Spanish Springs Valley. As a teenager who learned to fly on the ranch, he became a seasoned pilot by the age of sixteen. During his adult years, Stead went on to race hydroplanes. He retired from boat racing in 1959 after winning the world title and surviving two near-fatal accidents while jetting across the water. "It's getting too dangerous," Stead half-jokingly told a reporter. "The last few years, I've spent more time in the hospital than in the boat."[4]

It took Stead ten years of steady effort to introduce air racing to the Reno area. Stressing the safeguards instituted to mitigate the possibility of accidents, he gained sponsorship of the chamber along with local businesses and civic organizations. "There is no reason why aviation can't be as safe and sane and as successful as other motor sports such as sports car racing if it's done properly," he said.[5] It made sense for the merchants to be supportive as the races would bring in tens of thousands of visitors to the Northern Nevada gambling mecca.

Returning to Burbank after meeting Stead, Lacy couldn't hold back his enthusiasm about the race. He called Paulson. "I told Al they are going to have an air race in September. 'Why don't you buy a P-51 and California Airmotive can sponsor me?'" Paulson thought about it for a minute. He owned a five-seat, twin-engine Cessna 310 that he didn't want to keep. Owning dozens of aircraft, it wasn't one of his favorites. By coincidence, a customer living in Montana heard about the unwanted Cessna and called him about the plane a day before Lacy suggested the racing opportunity. The man asked Paulson if he'd take a P-51D in trade for the Cessna. The answer was a quick "yes."

"[Al] figured the Cessna was worth seventeen-thousand-five hundred," Lacy said. "He picks up the phone, calls this guy and says, 'bring that P-51 down here to L.A. with ten thousand and I'll give you the Cessna.' He basically bought the P-51 for seventy-five hundred."[6]

Paulson agreed to sponsor Lacy for the inaugural event in Reno and loaned him what would become his race plane for most of his racing career.

As a fighter plane in World War II, the P-51 earned an enviable reputation with Army Air Force pilots. A range of 1,000 miles, combined with nimble maneuverability, made it popular for escorting bombers and attacking ground targets. Its twelve-cylinder Rolls-Royce Merlin engine (built by Packard in the United States) produced 1,695 horsepower, an enormous amount of power for a flying machine weighing less than 10,000 pounds. Boasting a top speed of 437 miles per hour, it could execute the most extreme maneuvers. After the war, the airplanes were declared surplus by the government with most of them ending up scrapped. Wealthy collectors and race pilots snapped up some of the few hundred P-51Ds remaining of the 8,200 built. The rest were melted into aluminum ingots.

Following a wartime hiatus from its heyday in the 1930s, close-circuit air racing was re-established in Cleveland and other venues around the country. There were also transcontinental races flown at high altitude where the P-51's performance shined, a credit to its supercharged, 1,650-cubic-inch engine. Realistically, in common with NASCAR racing, the dangerous nature of the sport is what drew many fans to the events. Closed-course races, where pilots jockeyed for position, were fraught with risk. Accidents were commonplace and fatalities were bound to occur. During the Cleveland National Air Races in 1949, celebrated pilot Bill Odom crashed while flying near the town of Berea, killing himself as well as a mother and young child trapped in a house. His radically altered P-51C, owned by celebrated aviatrix Jacqueline Cochran, veered off the racecourse, the uncontrollable machine smashing into the house and catching fire. In the accident's aftermath, community activists in Berea and surrounding cities were relentless in their efforts to ban the races. For this and other reasons, 1949 was the last year that air races were held in Cleveland. Nationwide, all air racing ceased until revival of the sport at Reno in 1964.

Paulson had sold a few Constellations to a group of men wanting to start an airline. When they failed to finance the ambitious undertaking, he repossessed the aircraft. Coming into play after a buyer misses a few payments, the repossessing of automobiles is big business. In aviation, the same practice takes place, although it's little known to the public. "Repo" actions involve retrieving aircraft when buyers stop paying and abandon them somewhere. Whether it's a helicopter, light plane, or jumbo jet, repo work is an everyday happening. At California Airmotive, when the checks stopped arriving for a purchase or lease, Paulson dispatched Lacy or another pilot to find the airplane and ferry it back to California.

As his "fleet" of airliners grew, Paulson thought he might start an airline. Sitting on the sidelines, "Fish" Salmon and actor Dale Robertson told him they'd be willing to run the airline—or at least *help* him run it. The L-1049Gs he planned to use, the best all-around Connies built, had enough range to reach Hawaii from California. Salmon was a legendary test pilot while Robertson was well known to television viewers by playing rough-and-tumble cowboy roles. Following service with the Army combat engineers in World War II, twice-wounded Robertson started an acting career. In the 1960s, he appeared in Western movies and television shows, best known for starring in the TV series *Tales of Wells Fargo*.

The Orchid Line was envisioned as offering low fares for flights between California and Hawaii. Because the route would take the planes to the tropics, Mary Lou suggested naming it "Orchid." To distinguish the Connies from those of other carriers, he planned to have purple stripes painted along the sides of the fuselages. His purchasing agent ordered the paint, but rather than receiving the 50 gallons he wanted, a shipment of 1,500 gallons arrived. The supplier said he could keep the extra paint, a custom color, at no extra charge. To prepare Paulson's 1944-vintage P-51D for "unlimited" class racing, meaning only the fastest airplanes, a snazzy paint scheme was concocted. The Mustang, along with ladders, toolboxes, and anything else in sight, ended up being painted purple. Legend has it that the widespread use of purple accounted for Federal Express founder Fred Smith to select the color for his many jet freighters.

Before the Orchid Line venture got off the ground, or even much beyond the talking stage, the project fell by the wayside. The Connies continued to gather dust in the desert until sold or scrapped—but Paulson's purple P-51D was ready to race.

The inaugural championship race at Reno got underway on September 20 on the airfield at Sky Ranch, adjacent to the Pyramid Lake Highway. The runway consisted of a pebble-strewn dirt strip barely 2,000 feet long. Owing to a pent-up demand for racing action, thousands of fans watched as the former fighter planes were about to twist their way through a nine-mile, pylon-defined course. Positioned on the starting line, with their throttles opened full bore, airframes shook as their pilots held the machines stationary with locked brakes. Lacy was ready to do battle in the P-51D. When the starting flag dropped, the airplanes lurched forward on a short takeoff roll, zoomed upward, and headed into the first of eight laps around the course. The 25-foot-high pylons created two long straightaways and six tight turns. Cutting a pylon (flying inside of it) would cause a pilot to suffer a penalty of one lap, easily resulting in a last-place finish.

Screeching around the pylons at an average speed of 354.74 miles per hour, Lacy came in third—a respectable showing for his first race. Paulson sat in the stands watching his friend's every move. Although hoping that Lacy would win, he was afraid the engine might blow, an expensive proposition for him as the airplane's sponsor. A Grumman F8F Bearcat, piloted by Mira Slovak, got the checkered flag. He didn't cross the finish line first, but won the race by racking up more points than the other planes. Bob Love, in a P-51D, was the first to actually cross the finish line.

The race took about the same time it takes to brew an urn of coffee. But in the cockpit, it seemed far longer. "You live more than eight minutes during a race because it's the culmination of months of this," race pilot Jack Hall said.[7]

Lacy went on to enter the P-51D in every unlimited class air race in the nation. He became so enamored of the sport that he was elected president of the Professional Race Pilots Association from 1966 to 1970. His purple airplane had a "Snoopy" character emblazoned on its tail, the idea borrowed from the *Peanuts* cartoon series concocted by Charles Schulz. The artist gave his permission to adorn the airplane with the unique design.

Following years of racing under the California Airmotive banner, and spending more money for the aircraft's upkeep than it won, Paulson decided that the cost of racing made it unprofitable and pulled out. For $12,500 he sold the airplane, along with its spare engines, to Lacy so he could continue racing. The package was worth $30,000. A rebuilt Merlin engine cost $8,000

Paulson, Clay Lacy, and Jack Conroy (from left) pose alongside Lacy's P-51 Mustang at the Reno Air Races, circa 1970 (Clay Lacy archives).

and the fee for competing in a race added another $4,000. Professional air racing called for being wealthy or finding a rich sponsor.

Lacy placed third in every unlimited class race at Reno from 1964 to 1969, but never captured first place. In 1970 he finally did—screaming around the pylons at an average speed of 387.34 miles per hour to claim victory as that year's national air race champion in the unlimited class. He took home a purse of $7,200. His last race at Reno was in 1972, flying the P51D repainted with *Miss Lois Jean* adorning its side. He placed fourth. The airplane's name had special meaning: it represented his romance with Lois, a flight attendant he met on a United 727 flight. They would marry in 1973.

Bill Stead continued to defy death. But on April 28, 1966, his luck ran out while racing an 85-horsepower Goodyear Racer at St. Petersburg, Florida. As thousands of spectators watched in horror, a pin connecting a push-pull rod to the airplane's elevator control surface came loose. Stead lost all pitch control. He struggled to make a "controlled crash" onto the runway, but the severe impact killed him. Stead stayed a gambler to the end by flying a high performance midget racer after logging a total of only 3 hours in the airplane—and not ensuring that its airworthiness was up to snuff. Tempting fate ran in his family. Stead Air Force Base north of Reno was named for brother Croston Stead, who died in 1949 during an Air National Guard training flight. Following deactivation of the base in 1966, it became a public airport with the yearly races relocated there from Sky Ranch. To this day, the National Championship Air Races are held each September at what is now called the Reno-Stead Airport.

It wasn't easy for Lacy to squeeze in time for racing while adhering to his flight schedule at United. During off-duty days, he worked for Paulson, ferrying airplanes from sellers to California and to buyers wherever they might be located. At the controls of everything from DC-3s to DC-7s, he crisscrossed North America and flew deep into South America. Paulson sometimes accompanied him when he ferried the airplanes. "During our flying time together I always put Al in the left seat," he remarked. "I don't know if I ever flew in the left seat while I was with him. I wanted to give him all the flying time."[8] During the workweek, Lacy commuted between California and Colorado, spending four days instructing pilots at United's training center in Denver, and setting aside the other three days to attend to his duties at California Airmotive.

During his first few years in the airliner sales business, Paulson parked airplanes in distant corners of the Burbank and Van Nuys airports. As his number of aircraft increased, a larger parking area became essential. The answer: lease 40 acres of land at General William J. Fox Airfield, situated in an isolated stretch of the Mojave Desert 7 miles north of Lancaster. The airport was a short hop by air and an hour's drive from his operation in Burbank.

Best of all, the rent was cheap, as the wartime pilot training airport was mostly abandoned. The airport's namesake, one-time movie stunt pilot William J. Fox, served as the first chief engineer for Los Angeles County. Fox Field was one of several airports he supervised the construction of during the 1950s. He doubled for Errol Flynn as a stunt pilot in the 1941 film *Dive Bomber*. In World War II, Fox flew bombers and served as a base commander in the Marine Corps. Although Fox Field looked like an aircraft bone yard, it was more of a winged bazaar for Paulson where he eventually sold and leased hundreds of airliners.

The arid climate at the half-mile-high airport turned into a blessing for preserving his growing collection of airline transports. Corrosion, the killer of aluminum airframes, didn't have a chance to take hold as it would have if the airplanes were stored near the coast battling salt spray from the ocean. But ever-present gusty winds did create havoc, blowing sand and sagebrush into wheel wells and air scoops that weren't sealed tightly. During the spring months it wasn't surprising to spot a rattlesnake coiled alongside a tire seeking shade from the sun.

Paulson continued to sell, lease, and scrap airliners—whatever outcome brought the most money. As the major airlines ditched their older airplanes, they became his. After mechanical reconditioning and a coat of paint, they ended up with airlines having names that weren't exactly household words. Among them were California-Hawaiian Airlines, Modern Air Transport, American Flyers Airline, and Zantop Air Transport. None of them exist today. Many of the hastily organized carriers suffered from cash flow problems. As a result, Lacy did a fair amount of flying devoted to repossessing airplanes— after Paulson did some detective work to figure out where they might be abandoned.

During 1968, thirty-two Super Constellations, twenty-two DC-7s, and assorted other types were stored on the field. By the early 1970s, Paulson had bought and sold three hundred airliners: DC-3s, Convairs, Martins, Connies, DC-6s, Viscounts, DC-7s, and Electra turboprops. In one transaction, he scooped up Eastern Air Line's entire fleet of piston-powered ships. He then bought more airplanes from United. The dusty "parking lot" at Fox Field filled up.[9] Considering that the wingspan of a Super Connie is 123 feet with a fuselage length of 114 feet, it was a tight squeeze to fit all the ships on the windswept plot of ground.

To increase the profit potential of Paulson's buying and selling activity, a bit of repurposing was undertaken by stripping the airliners of their passenger seats and installing cargo doors. In the case of the Eastern purchase in 1965, he bought forty-two DC-7Bs for a total outlay of $2 million—about $48,000 per ship. The airline threw in spare parts, tooling, and engineering data. The same year, after converting seven of the DC-7Bs to freighters, he sold them to Zantop Air Transport for $2,250,000—about $321,000 per airplane. It was almost *seven times more* than what he paid Eastern.

It took six years for TWA to phase out its piston-powered fleet. First to go were the Martin 404s, the last of the type bowing from service on April 29, 1961. Next in line were the elderly L-049 Connies, all of them pulled from scheduled service by January 1, 1962. TWA's era of flying any type of piston airliner ended on April 6, 1967, when the last Connie in passenger service, an L-749, was parked for good.

California Airmotive supplied aircraft parts that were most in demand by the airlines: components for engines, propellers, and airframe systems. Once the parts were disassembled from an airliner, mechanics ripped out the remainder of the airframe's innards, comprising miles of wiring, control cables, and plumbing lines. Some of the material went to the dump but much of it was recycled. The stripped airframes, sans landing gear, were hoisted atop huge wooden blocks to support the fuselages so giant grappling hooks and shears could devour what remained. A crane lifted the shards of aluminum into oversize trailers for transport to smelters for melting the metal into ingots. The final step in the recycling process involved recasting the aluminum into car wheels, transmission housings, lawnmower engines, and hundreds of other products. It was ironic that the cylinder head of a power lawnmower sitting in a suburban garage could have once been a section of a Connie's wing. Paulson could be called an early "environmentalist," although he didn't recycle the materials to save the world. He did so to make an acceptable profit.

Not content to sit on the sidelines while others basked in glory, Paulson and Lacy raised the bar for air racing exploits on November 15, 1970. They competed in the California 1000 Mile Air Race, held 50 feet above the sagebrush at the Kern County Airport in Mojave. It was the first unlimited class, closed-course *endurance* race in the nation's history. The airport, situated 80 miles east of Los Angeles, opened in 1935 as a rural airstrip to enable operators of the area's gold and silver mines to land small airplanes. The Marine Corps acquired the field in 1942 to conduct airborne gunnery training. Kern County obtained title to the airport in 1961 and opened it for public use.

The California 1000 race was reportedly dreamed up in the cafeteria at the Lockheed plant in Palmdale by test pilots Darryl Greenamyer, Chuck Hall, Tony Levier, and Fish Salmon. Spending many of their workdays flying in and around Edwards Air Force Base, the pilots agreed that the isolated Mojave airport would be a logical place to hold the event. Hall was chief test pilot on Lockheed's L-1011 TriStar jetliner program and a veteran of air racing, having flown a P-51 in the Reno races. Greenamyer, Levier, and Salmon were longtime Lockheed test pilots and seasoned air racing participants. The outcome of the discussion saw the men form a company to sponsor the race. Lacy was a witness to what they were planning.

"I told Al about wanting to race a DC-7," Lacy said, knowing that Paulson was receptive to trying offbeat ideas. Lacy had his eye on entering the airliner at Reno.

> "Yeah," he said, "I've got some DC-7s. One we just repossessed."
>
> It was supposed to be in really good shape, parked at Burbank alongside the runway. I went there with another guy to look it over and run up the engines. While the engines were running I saw a DC-6 land. As it rolled by, the flight engineer opened the door and waved. Fifteen minutes later he came over and we started talking. He'd been the engineer on the DC-7 for the people who leased it from Al. He really cleaned that airplane up; it was looking almost new. He asked me what was going on. I said we're going to fly it.
>
> He asked where I was going to fly. I said in an air race.

The conscientious mechanic didn't like the idea. Although his former employer failed to keep up the lease payments, he still felt a bond with the airplane.

> He asked, "How much power are you going to put on?" I said, whatever power it has to go fast. Actually, I wouldn't have to pull takeoff power. Redline was 310 knots. And it would do that with about METO [maximum except takeoff] power.
>
> He was kind of startled and said, "I've spent a lot of time working on this thing." He was worried about it. I said we're not going to hurt it. We're only going to fly about four and a half hours and then bring it back here.[10]

Before the Mojave race, Lacy wanted to enter the big Douglas in the unlimited class at the annual championship race in Reno. The organizers wouldn't let it compete there but did give him a green light to try its wings at Mojave. They waived a 21,000-pound gross weight limitation for race planes in the unlimited category to allow the 70,000-pound airliner to enter. Lacy's longstanding relationships in the upper echelons of professional racing circles may have helped prompt the go-ahead decision.

Mojave would be an unusual race because the rules called for the airplanes to remain airborne long enough to travel 1,000 miles around a racetrack-shaped course. Ten pylons were set up with a spacing of 15 miles between them. The pilots would need to finish sixty-six laps roaring around the 40-foot high pylons.

Shocking the other race pilots, Paulson and Lacy announced they would enter the DC-7 at Mojave, without passengers or cargo, of course. It's worth noting that on March 29, 1954, an American Airlines DC-7B flew from Los Angeles to New York City in 6 hours, 10 minutes—an official transcontinental speed record at the time. When pushed, the DC-7 could be a speedster.

The repossessed airplane began life with American Airlines. DC-7s were promoted as the airline's flagships for less than ten years, a short lifespan for any transport and a money loser for the carrier. When it came time to retire them, the going price for each formerly million-dollar Douglas was $175,000—

the fastest depreciation rate in commercial aviation history. By the time Paulson became interested in buying them, even that price was too high. He proceeded to buy seven DC-7Bs from the airline. The airliner he chose to race was actually a DC-7BF, the "F" signifying it was a passenger transport converted into a freighter by Douglas Aircraft Co. Both men knew that the "seven" wasn't a match for the speed of P-51s and P-38s, but it could fly the *entire* race without stopping to refuel; after all, this was an endurance race. Some of the contestants decided to tuck in refueling stops. Others installed auxiliary fuel tanks under the wings. The precious time wasted by the fighters to refuel was the key to why the big Douglas would shine.

The DC-7 was adorned with Lacy's usual "64" race number painted on its vertical stabilizer plus "Super Snoopy" emblazoned on the nose. He would serve as pilot with Paulson as copilot. Omni Aviation Managers was recruited as a co-sponsor to offset the costs of participating. Aviation entrepreneurs Michael Eisenstadt and Bill Woodard headed that aviation insurance company in Van Nuys. They believed that an airliner, by dwarfing the size of the other airplanes, would cause thousands of spectators to take note of their company's sponsorship painted in big letters on each side of the fuselage. At the Reno races two months earlier, Omni had sponsored Lacy's P51D, it winning for the first time.

Eleven P-51 Mustangs, two F8F Bearcats, two Hawker Sea Furies, two F4U Corsairs, a P-38 Lightning, an A-26 Invader, and the DC-7 made up the field at Mojave.

The race started differently than the traditional protocol at Reno. The airplanes were lined up on the runway with their exact spacing determined by earlier qualifying times. The DC-7 was forced to stay out of the lineup due to its immensity. It would be the last plane in the field to depart. Minutes before the start flag fell, the race announcer blurted out on the public address system, "Starting positions are according to qualifying times except for the DC-7, which will start last to avoid blowing the other planes off the runway."

The two friends took turns at the controls, Lacy handling the majority of pilot duties over an exhausting 3 hours. He occupied what was the customary first officer seat. Because the racecourse was set up requiring clockwise turns around the pylons, he needed to be on the right side to judge his distance from the desert floor. They sat in relative comfort, having simple refreshments at their disposal, while the pilots in the cramped, hot cockpits of the fighter planes sweated every mile. Having two pilots share the workload was a relief. Making sure that the R-3350s didn't miss a beat, a flight engineer, the only other person aboard, monitored the engine instruments with an eagle eye, worried about overheating. They were going all out to beat the other guys.

"Lacy was an experienced race pilot and didn't climb on the turns where

I might sneak under him," Howie Keefe said, a veteran air racer flying one of the P-51s. "And he had enough fuel on board to fly the entire race without needing to make a pit stop."[11]

A Hawker Sea Fury piloted by Sherman Cooper, a Merced, California, orthodontist, went on to win in 2 hours, 52 minutes, 38 seconds, at an average speed of 344.08 miles per hour. The 35-ton DC-7 sped around the pylons at an average speed of 325. It flew faster than a former A-26 light bomber, the airliner hugging the ground closer than some of the fighters. It finished sixth in the field of twenty airplanes. Considering that they were running against star-studded competition, Lacy and Paulson didn't turn in a bad performance. "The g load was limited to 2.2 and we used an average of sixty to seventy degrees of bank," Lacy told a reporter upon landing. The thirsty Wright R-3350s consumed 4,100 gallons of high-octane aviation gasoline and eighty gallons of oil.

"Even though I was going about 390 miles per hour, the straight-aways weren't long enough to pass them," Keefe said of the DC-7's maneuvering. "At each pylon, that giant 117-foot wingspan went sky-high and pylon-low at the same time with four engines churning the air. Flying behind that air-mass was frustrating to say the least."[12]

An earlier concern about the engines overheating never materialized. "They ran perfectly," Lacy said. "In fact, they ran so cool that we couldn't warm them up. You try to run the head temperatures at about 200 degrees but they were running about 140 or 150. When you have 310 knots of air blowing through them, the heads cool like crazy."[13]

Posing for photos, an exuberant Paulson stood next to Lacy and the women in their lives. Mary Lou and Lois were attired in customized white flight jackets like their men, with race number 64 emblazoned on the front. Free publicity was always welcomed, even expected. In the stands, celebrities watched the action. "The competition at Mojave was remarkable," said Academy Award winner Cliff Robertson, keeping an eye on his friends as they roared around the pylons. "Clay, with Al as copilot, flew that great big four-engine aircraft and beat fifteen of those other guys flying fighter aircraft," he said.[14] Robertson was a lifelong aviation enthusiast, harking back to the age of thirteen when he washed airplanes in exchange for rides. He entered a balloon race in 1964, drifting 26 miles from the Southern California coastline on the way to Catalina Island. The adventure ended abruptly when the balloon sprung a leak that immediately grew into a gusher. Radioing in a distress call, it was fortunate he didn't spend much time in the chilly Pacific before his rescue.

Bruce McCaw recalled one of the Mojave races. "Al rented this motor home," he began. "Gordon Israel was drunk, making the chili he was famous for in a big stewpot outside the motor home. It was eleven in the morning

After Paulson's Douglas DC-7 finishes sixth in the California 1000 race at Mojave on November 15, 1970, are from left, Clay Lacy, future wife Lois, along with Mary Lou and Allen (Clay Lacy archives).

and everyone had already gotten into the sauce. Ed McMahon [Johnny Carson's TV sidekick] was flying high. Everybody was laughing. Al decided to fix something on the motor home and ended up accidentally hitting the dump valve for the potty. A flood started flowing down the hill. He hit the wrong valve. Downstream, it ruined everybody's morning. McMahon remarked, 'You always want to stay upstream with Paulson.'"[15] McMahon served in the Marine Corps during World War II flying F4U fighters, later promoted to brigadier general in the California Air National Guard. Israel, a talented aircraft designer, established an unwanted reputation as a heavy drinker, but was considered a genius when it came to aeronautics. He gained fame in the 1930s by designing winning race planes. While he worked with Bill Lear on the Learstar and Lear Jet projects, synergy existed between the men. "Gordon was an absolutely brilliant aerodynamicist, even though he had a serious relationship with John Barleycorn," Bill Lear, Jr., wrote in his autobiography. "The old man [his father] fired Gordon hundreds of times during the Learstar program, but Gordon simply wouldn't leave, so he was kept on the payroll doing what he so ably did—even when half smashed."[16]

The DC-7, and each of its engines, survived Mojave without a hitch. Its former caretaker in Burbank breathed a sigh of relief. "I saw it five years later in Panama," Lacy said. "I was flying a DC-8 that Al bought from Varig Airlines in Rio. I landed in Panama City to get a little fuel and the DC-7 was sitting there. It still had the big snoopy on the rudder and sixty-four, my race number, painted on it. I walked over and talked to the guy who'd been flying it for two or three years and asked how much time the engines had on them. He said 2,400 hours." It's unusual for the engines of a four-engine airliner to run all the way to overhaul together. "The man said they ran like a champ. The airlines didn't know how to run them while flying 175 knots. If you go 310, you have much more cooling."[17] Even during his days at United, Lacy believed in flying fast.

In 1971, Greenamyer promoted an event called the United States Cup, to be held in July at Brown Field near San Diego. It would be another 1000-mile race. Once again, Paulson and Lacy planned to enter the DC-7 as it had not been sold or leased yet. To net the most publicity for California Airmotive, Paulson planned to enter a second plane: an L-1049G Super Connie pulled from Fox Field. The ex-Qantas airliner was named the *Red Baron*. Fish Salmon and Paulson were expected to handle the Connie's piloting duties while Lacy would fly the DC-7. As a pilot at Lockheed, Salmon tested early models of the Connie for Civil Aeronautics Administration certification. For the first flights of other airplanes, he was at the controls of the L-188 Electra, P-3 Orion antisubmarine aircraft, and F-104A Starfighter.

For the San Diego event, the thousand-mile course involved completing 100 laps. By carrying extra fuel, Sherman Cooper's Hawker Sea Fury had beaten the other airplanes by several laps at the California 1000. For this race, the rules were altered to require each competitor to make at least one refueling stop—a crucial difference.

Paulson's crew looked forward to entering the DC-7 and Connie in the same race. Both airplanes qualified, but on race day, pilots of the competing fighters complained that turbulence created by the wings and propellers of the airliners would render the racecourse too dangerous. Shortly before race time, the "pilots voted to have a maximum altitude on the race course of 200 feet, which automatically eliminated these giants," Keefe said.[18] The concern

The former Eastern Air Line's L-1049G Super Constellation Paulson intended to race in the United States Cup at San Diego in May 1971 (Neil Aird collection).

over turbulence became the publicized issue, but there was another reason why Paulson had second thoughts about competing. The organizers were forcing each airplane to make the required refueling stop and take on at least 100 gallons. Requiring a pit stop for the DC-7 and Connie would have consumed too much time and negated their non-stop flying advantage. Paulson, Lacy, Salmon, and their crewmembers elected to stay on the ground that day and watch the race from the grandstand.

Cooper won the race in his Sea Fury. Unfortunately, the event was marred by the fatal crash of a Grumman F8F Bearcat. Keeping the tragedy in mind, it may have been fate that the airliners didn't race. They would have been stuck in a crowded field of fast fighters. It could have been a dicey scenario with an increased possibility of a midair collision. Unlike *Super Snoopy*, which went on to haul freight south of the border, the *Red Baron* saw little use after the race. In July 1974, Paulson told his mechanics to scrap the airliner in a corner of the Burbank airport.

Salmon continued to live life on the edge until his luck ran out on June 22, 1980. He died in an accident while ferrying an L-1049H Super Connie from Columbus, Indiana, to Seattle. The plane crashed immediately after takeoff and caught fire; five of the eight people aboard were lucky to survive, including Salmon's son, who had served as copilot.

The first endurance race at Mojave attracted many thousands of sun loving fans. Its success caused the organizers to sponsor another long-distance event at the airport on November 14, 1971. The only problem was that the original race was too tiring for pilots sandwiched in the cramped cockpits of the fighters. This time, the distance flown was shortened to about 600 miles and 44 laps, rather than the previous 1000 miles and 66 laps—although the race was still publicized as a "1,000." Paulson decided to not enter his airliners.

"The race promoters wanted to again use the '1,000' catchy number, but the two '1,000 milers' we had, one at Mojave and the other at San Diego, proved tough on the planes, pilots, and crew," Keefe said, "and tended to get boring for the spectators who often didn't have a clue as to what was going on. The thought of turning to the metric system's 'kilometers' to be able to still call it a '1,000' was a bit of marketing genius."[19]

The event gained steam with great expectations. During qualification trials in October, the Hawker flown by previous winner Cooper blew its engine. He crash-landed in the sagebrush about 5 miles from the airport. The airplane was damaged but Cooper escaped injury, forcing him to pull out of the lineup for the race. Cooper's luck was not to last. On May 10, 1972, his Pitts Special sport biplane suffered an in-flight structural failure, causing his death.

On the day of the race the weather turned windy, with the temperature barely reaching 40 degrees. Because the venue was held 95 miles from downtown Los Angeles, it was inconvenient for people to drive so far out of town on a wintry day. The turnout was disappointing. Only 6,000 diehard fans bought tickets, the event losing money. A few weeks later the partners exited the air racing business.

In spite of the sparse head count at Mojave, the air-racing bug would prove far from dead. Picking up the slack, Lacy along with two fellow racers formed Air Race Management to organize an event called the California Air Classic. Held at Mojave, it ran from 1973 through 1979. The races were patterned after Reno with everything from 3,000-horsepower fighters to biplanes. Returning to the sport indirectly in 1975, Paulson allowed Greenamyer to use his facilities in Van Nuys to prepare a much-modified Grumman Bearcat for the Reno unlimited class race. Greenamyer won six times at Reno before he donated the airplane to the Smithsonian National Air and Space Museum in 1977.

Throughout his years of involvement with racing, Paulson kept several hats in the air and worked long hours. His dedication to work was understood by Mary Lou. No matter where or when he flew, she could be seen alongside him. As for Paulson's best friend, on March 30, 1973, in Los Angeles, Lacy married Lois Carnagey, his longtime lady friend. To appreciate their obsession with aeronautics both men came to realize that it was best to marry women who had more than a passing interest in airplanes.

Yearning for more adventure, Lacy got involved with a crazy stunt flight sandwiched between heats at the California National Air Races in Mojave. It was the summer of 1976, a time to do something to knock everyone's socks off.

"When I wanted to fly a guy on top of a DC-8, Al told me it was 'no problem,'" Lacy said. "He had three DC-8s that he bought from Japan Air Lines."[20] Friends for a quarter-century, he was accustomed to Lacy's out-of-the-box thinking, although this idea did seem extreme. Paulson seldom hesitated in going along with his schemes. This was especially true if he thought the publicity might result in his company selling something. "Al was a practical thinker," Lacy continued, "and he had lots of nerve to spend money on ideas that he believed in. He had a lot of guts." This particular stunt would reap *plenty* of publicity.

The proposed flight involved a twenty-nine-year-old stuntman from Montreal named Rick Rojatt, calling himself "The Human Fly." He kept his identity a secret at the time. His plan was to stand upright on top of the jet's fuselage, strapped firmly in place, barreling through the air at more than 200 miles per hour. His benefactors included two brothers in Canada who owned a meatpacking company. They contributed $200,000 to promote shocking events such as the Human Fly—to be followed by a 1,800-foot dive off a Toronto skyscraper into a 20-foot-square water tank. Rojatt was reported to have been the victim of an automobile accident in North Carolina six years earlier, in which his wife and four-year-old daughter were killed. He underwent thirty-eight operations over a four-year period before he was able to walk again. To condition his body for the upcoming flights, he awoke at 3:00 a.m. each day, ran 6 miles, and "plunged into a bathtub full of ice cubes." Asked if he had any fear of dying, he replied, "I don't have a death wish. I have a life wish."[21]

For a chunk of the Canadian's money, Paulson supplied a former Japan Air Line's DC-8–32, a long-range version of the Douglas-built jetliner, from his storage yard in Mojave. The well-traveled machine, powered by four Pratt & Whitney JT4A turbojets, was built in 1960, before the widespread introduction of fanjet engines. Emitting an ear-shattering roar and clouds of black soot on takeoff, the jet had seen better days after innumerable ocean crossings. Rather than the 4,600 nonstop miles it was capable of traveling, the plane would need to fly no more than 50 miles at Mojave. The action-hungry race fans would love it.

With Lacy doing the flying and Jack Conroy as copilot, the DC-8 took off and orbited the field in Mojave, sometimes little more than 50 feet over the sagebrush. Keeping in mind that the jet's wing spanned 142 feet, Lacy's keen eyesight and razor-sharp reflexes were needed to keep the wing tips from striking the ground.

Atop the DC-8, to withstand 3,000 pounds of air pressure pressing against Rojatt, a thick helmet, steel-reinforced leather jumpsuit, and metal chest plate encased his body. Covered with a flowing white cape, the masked daredevil remained airborne for 15 excruciating minutes, enduring a 220-mile-per-hour blast of air. The first flight took place in front of a large crowd on June 18, 1976, interspersed between the pylon races in Mojave. Following Mojave, the next flight was planned for Texas with the final one taking place back at Mojave.

The area in Texas selected to conduct the stunt was about 20 miles south of the Dallas/Fort Worth (DFW) Regional Airport. The flight was planned for a television show but the jetliner hit a violent rain shower, causing the day's videotaping to get "washed out." On Lacy's return flight to DFW, heavy water droplets pounded Rojatt as the jet approached the runway. After landing, pain resulting from the buffeting and rain became so extreme that he passed out. It was fortunate that the fail-safe safety harness restraining him to the fuselage had withstood the violent storm or the outcome would have been fatal. Rojatt spent six weeks recovering from his injuries.

Lacy described how the final flight at Mojave was aired on national television. "We flew at noon, which was 3 p.m. in New York," he began. "The segment was scheduled to air at 4:15 p.m., just over an hour after we landed."[22]

The "Human Fly" is strapped atop Paulson's Douglas DC-8, piloted by Clay Lacy in 1976 (Clay Lacy archives).

The broadcast schedule was so tight that the network had positioned a mobile unit alongside the taxiway to quickly edit the videotape and beam a signal to the network's facility on nearby Mount Wilson for relaying to New York. Time running out, the producer in New York wanted to kill the story. Persevering, the editor in Mojave pushed to prepare the tape post haste and transmit the segment, it occupying a minute on the evening news.

During the summer and autumn months of 1976, Rojatt made the rounds of prime time television shows, including *That's Incredible* and *Headline Hunters* in Canada. He even appeared in a TV movie, *The Beach Boys: It's OK*, alongside John Belushi and Dan Aykroyd. Rojatt eventually dropped out of sight by his own design, and his fate remains a mystery. As for the elderly DC-8, Paulson converted it into a freighter in 1979, the plane serving with at least one airline before ending up on the scrap pile in the early 1980s.

Lacy considered his aerial exploits as nothing more than adventure, enjoying the rush of adrenalin brought about by the experiences. Paulson felt that he benefited from racing in a different way—to let the world know about his company, and in the process, maybe sell something.

The DC-7s and Constellations were well on the way to becoming yesterday's flying machines. The world of aviation had advanced to encompass magic carpets called jetliners and business jets. Paulson decided to join the "jet race," working with noted inventor and industrialist William P. Lear.

5

Jet Setter

The prototype Lear Jet Model 23 was poised on the runway ready for its maiden flight. It was late afternoon on October 7, 1963, Wichita Municipal Airport the place. More than a thousand spectators waited at the fence alongside the airport's perimeter. Many of them had followed the airplane maker's progress through newspaper and television coverage. There were retirees, employees who left their jobs early, and children who set aside homework. The patrons of neighborhood bars and cafes joined in to watch. Even skeptics from the executive offices of Cessna and Beech were there, all eager to see the revolutionary jet fly.

As dusk approached, they began to think the flight might be scrubbed for the day. Meanwhile, sixty-one-year-old Bill Lear worried about a minor mechanical delay. But postponing the flight was out of the question for him. Not a patient man, his anxiety escalated by the minute. He couldn't relax until his brainchild made a successful flight. Even a short hop before dusk would do.

"At five-forty, with fifty minutes of sunlight left, the Lear Jet taxied out for its first flight," recalled John Lear, Bill's youngest son. "The entire length of the runway was lined with employees, visitors and Wichitans."[1]

Completing a taxi test to check the nose wheel steering and brakes, these among dozens of ground tests conducted over the preceding weeks, there was no doubt that the jet was ready to fly. Lear radioed the pilots to get going. Bob Hagan and co-captain Hank Beaird lined up on the runway's threshold, anxious to depart. Hagan pushed the thrust levers forward. As the twin General Electric CJ610 turbojets spooled up, the resulting acceleration pushed the men against the headrests of their seats.

The jet roared down the runway, lifted off smartly, and climbed into a darkening sky. Hagen handled the controls for the takeoff. "I was standing with Bill out on the ramp," remarked Lear's wife, forty-eight-year-old Moya. "We were holding hands. He was gripping mine hard. When the Lear Jet went up, both of us were weeping. It took off like a rocket."[2]

In what seemed like seconds, the airplane turned into nothing more than a speck in the sky, climbing to 5,000 feet, landing gear still extended. After cycling the gear up and down to make sure its hydraulic actuators worked properly, the crew climbed to 10,000 feet, where Hagen began a series of gentle turns to check the control responses. All went well. Descending and soon swooping low over the boundless Kansas cornfields, he turned the controls over to Beaird. Lear Jet N80lL made a straight-in approach to the airport and a faultless landing. The men were in the air for half an hour—and aviation history had been made.

Hundreds of hands were heard clapping as the tires contacted the runway. First to exit the plane in front of Bill and Moya was smiling thirty-eight-year-old Beaird, a lanky, soft-spoken test pilot from Alabama. Without batting an eye he said, "The airplane performed better than I expected, and I was optimistic before it flew."[3]

Plenty of emotion was evident that evening. The city's faith in the project was affirmed. The company's lenders relaxed while Wichita's workers didn't doubt that Lear Jet Corporation would hire hundreds of employees to build the airplanes. To celebrate the milestone, an all-night party followed at the Diamond Club, a watering hole tucked inside the Diamond Inn motel a mile from the plant. As the evening progressed, most of the talk revolved around how "stormy genius" Bill Lear was slowly moving to the front of the race to build business jets and revolutionize aviation. The Lear Jet 23's first flight came nine months after the maiden flight of the Jet Commander 1121—its direct competitor. Lear had a lot of catching up to do.

William Powell "Bill" Lear, born in 1902, became best known as the father of the Lear Jet. To his credit, he earlier invented the first radio for automobiles, and decades later, the eight-track cartridge tape player. Lear bought his first airplane in 1931, but finding it difficult to navigate during cross-country flights, he invented one of aviation's first radio direction finders. Inventing and manufacturing aircraft instruments became his ticket to become a major force in aviation. The late 1940s saw him develop the first all-electronic autopilot for jet fighters, causing him to win the prestigious Collier Trophy. In 1960, he moved to Switzerland to form the Swiss American Aviation Corp. The company's sole purpose was to design a small business jet. Lear's next home became Wichita, where he set out to manufacture what would become the Lear Jet 23.

A showman in promoting his business interests, one couldn't escape Lear's name while perusing the pages of aviation magazines. He was a member of a select circle of pioneers that stretched back to a time when any technological advancement in aviation was lauded. Journalists gravitated to his side, knowing that he offered futuristic, and often entertaining, quotes for their publications. Lear never stopped selling. It's been said he had the fattest

Rolodex in existence, keeping in touch with hundreds of acquaintances, some of them turning into customers for his products.

At the same time that Lear courted the reporters in Kansas, Paulson took a less publicized approach to his work in California, selling refurbished planes to airlines that few people had heard of. Some of the planes found homes with entertainers and corporate titans. But with his jet, Lear was about to render each of those propeller-driven airplanes obsolete.

Industrialist Elton MacDonald bought a Martin 404 from Paulson for personal and business transportation. He telephoned Clay Lacy toward the end of 1961 to ask if he'd be willing to fly him in the plane from Los Angeles to Palm Springs. He told Lacy that Bill Lear, a longtime friend, had contacted him and wanted to talk about a new aviation project. Lear wanted to see him in person and wouldn't discuss details over the phone. The next day, the men arrived at the Palm Springs airport and drove to the industrialist's vacation home in Palm Desert.

MacDonald had started a firm in 1922 called the E.F. MacDonald Company. Decades later, he latched onto the idea of creating customer incentive programs to grow the sales volume of retail chain stores. By 1961, he expanded into offering "Plaid Stamps" to customers whenever they bought anything in the stores. The merchants paid MacDonald for the stamps and advertised to customers that they were a reward for making purchases. Customers pasted them in pocketsize books and trekked to any one of 675 MacDonald-owned redemption centers to trade the books for household merchandise. Flush with cash from the stamp business, MacDonald went on to acquire a supermarket chain, a finance company, a mail-order house—and the Martin 404.[4]

Lear was anxious to talk with MacDonald and another part-time desert dweller he invited—Justin Dart, chairman of the board at Los Angeles–based Rexall Drug and Chemical Co. Consumers were more familiar with that enterprise as the corner Rexall Drug Store. An admirer of Lear and friend of his family, Dart lived in the ritzy Pebble Beach enclave along the central California coast, but enjoyed the desert way of life during mild winter months. He ran Rexall by trial, error, and a forceful personality—mimicking Lear's style. An avid enthusiast of anything to do with aviation, Dart joined the board of directors of United Air Lines and made sure that Rexall operated its own fleet of airplanes to shuttle executives wherever they needed to go. He was the bluntest and most outspoken member of what became known as the "kitchen cabinet"—a select group of close friends and unofficial advisers to President Ronald Reagan during his years in office.

MacDonald and Dart were all ears when Lear spoke up. Broaching what he wanted to say as soon as they were comfortable, he described how work was underway on the design of a small jet to fly executives around at twice the speed of existing planes. He made it clear that the converted Martin and Lockheed airplanes the men flew in were relics.

Lear told them he was about to depart for Switzerland to work on the project, but before leaving, he wanted to nail down purchase commitments. He was taking orders to the tune of $275,000 per airplane. For a $10,000 deposit, a customer would get a guaranteed early delivery position. Dart ordered two of the jets and MacDonald another. Thus began the birth of Lear Jet, about to get underway in Switzerland and enter production in Wichita two years later.

By the time Lear wrote up orders for twenty of the planes, he realized that the price would have to increase by almost $200,000 to cover the cost of building them. Not understanding the reason for the jump, MacDonald asked another favor of Lacy: visit Lear in Wichita and determine the rationale for the steep price increase. Arriving at the Lear Jet plant in 1963, Lacy did a bit of checking. After meeting with Lear, he determined that the increase was justified. This kind of aircraft project had never been attempted before. There were many unknowns and unforeseen costs lurking in the future. While Lacy was forming a friendship with Lear, Paulson didn't have a clue that he'd play a pivotal role in the future success of the airplane.

Although the Lear Jet wasn't close to reaching the production stage in 1963, Lear planned to market the plane using factory-direct salesmen. Further into its development he changed his mind. His largely self-financed project had eaten up far more money than he first imagined. It didn't take much coaxing for him to realize that appointing independent distributors, rather than hiring factory salesmen, might bring in immediate orders. The distributors could have hot prospects already in mind, and cash deposits coming in from each distributor would help meet the payroll in Wichita.

"Bill determined that five distributorships with initial deposits of $250,000 each would be a huge help," said Lacy. "Soon after, Elroy McCaw visited Lear in Wichita and loaned him $250,000 to complete certification and start deliveries."[5] McCaw was a magnate in the broadcasting industry, buying and selling radio and television stations in the 1960s. As a friend of Lear, he knew all too well how seriously the plane maker needed the money. One of his four sons, Bruce, became immersed in the aviation industry and a close friend of both Lear and Paulson. The son formed an aviation insurance brokerage; it later becoming Forbes Westar, Inc. Following his father's death in 1969, Bruce and his brothers expanded the family's cable television subscription business into a cellular communications giant. In 1994, they sold McCaw Cellular to AT&T for $12.6 billion. McCaw, Joe Clark, and two other friends co-founded Horizon Air, a regional airline that became the sixth largest regional carrier in the United States at the time it was sold to Alaska Airlines in 1996.

Lear was fortunate to have a favorable national economy on his side when he introduced the jet. In 1964, the Gross National Product (GNP) totaled $635 billion. Corporate profits after taxes were expected to reach a record-shattering $31.9 billion for the year. For 1965, economists forecasted a GNP of $660 billion. Lear marketers targeted companies and individuals that were expected to receive the greatest benefit from such economic expansion.

Following another visit to Lear Jet Corp., Lacy returned to Van Nuys and called on Paulson. He told him about an opportunity to get in on the ground floor. "I talked to Al about a distributorship and tried to get him to the factory," he said. Paulson didn't have time to make the trip and put the idea on the back burner. "I'd been trying to get Al to fly back to Wichita for three or four months. The distributorship program was one helluva deal. I told him that I sure as hell would like to see him get it and make me manager of sales." Lacy was a capable pilot having logged thousands of hours in jets—something Paulson didn't have in his logbook. In addition to Lacy's flying experience, it helped that he had a pleasant sales personality.

"Rushing around all the time was standard operating procedure for Al," Lacy said. In a surprising move Paulson phoned Lacy and said, "Why don't we fly to Wichita in the P-51? We can get out there and back fast." Taking advantage of the impromptu decision, Lacy got the two-seat P-51D ready to fly. "We took off the next morning, landed at Albuquerque to refuel, and flew on to Wichita."[6]

They taxied up to the brand-new Lear Jet plant built along a newly constructed taxiway. Spotting the second jet off the assembly line on the ramp outside Lear's office, Paulson's interest perked up immediately. "It got him excited," Lacy said. "Bill arranged for Al to get a flight in the number two Lear. We spent a day and a half in Wichita. Al was really pumped up. He wanted to get into the jet business. We came home after Bill offered him the distributorship for the nine western states."[7] Paulson's first flight in the speedster convinced him that the plane would be a winner. A cruise speed of 500 miles per hour and an initial rate of climb of almost 6,000 feet per minute is what sold him. The propeller-driven airplanes were lucky to go half that speed and could never climb so fast. It flew like a jet fighter.

At Paulson's Vineland Avenue facilities in the summer months of 1964, he organized the distributorship as a division of California Airmotive. He told Lacy that he could become sales manager if he wanted. There was no need to ask because Lacy loved the airplane. But flying 727s for United Airlines and C-97s at the California Air National Guard consumed much of his time. Burdened with too many responsibilities, he resigned from the guard. Lacy became one of the first pilots to earn a Lear Jet type rating from the FAA. "We got our first Lear Jet demonstrator, serial number twelve [which

Lacy, at the age of eighty-six still owns], and I went to work for Al as manager of Lear Jet sales," he said.[8]

Taking delivery of the jet in October, Lacy or one of his salesmen kept it ready to show anyone at the slightest hint. Paulson was thrilled to be selling such a revolutionary product, but Bill Lear was even happier setting up the distributorships. Each of them paid a franchise fee and handed over a sizable deposit for a jet to use as a demonstrator. The money helped pump up Lear Jet's shrinking checking account at a critical time in its short history.

Needing to shelter the airplane from the elements, Lacy found an empty hangar along the east side of the Van Nuys Airport. "I rented the hangar on Stagg Street, an old wooden building that could hold about six Lear Jets," he remarked.[9] The jet's exterior won accolades for its sleek design. But its interior was another story. "We had the demonstrator for a couple of months and I told Al that he had to get an interior installed. It looked like hell and took from December to March to get it put in."[10] Interior or no interior, the sleek Lear Jet was about to take the world of aviation by storm.

Jack Conroy set a coast-to-coast round trip speed record in 1955, flying an Air National Guard F-86 jet fighter. On May 21, 1965, Lacy, Conroy, and the latter's three teenage children, took to the air in California Airmotive's Lear Jet to retrace the earlier dawn-to-dusk flight. The trip from Los Angeles to New York and back spanned 5,005 miles. To confirm they hadn't cheated, an official from the National Aeronautic Association tagged along in the cabin. Three world records for business aircraft were set: Los Angeles to New York (5 hours, 8 minutes), New York to Los Angeles (5 hours, 44 minutes against strong headwinds) and round trip (11 hours, 36 minutes, including over an hour on the ground for refueling).

"We were the first to fly a civilian aircraft coast-to-coast between sunrise and sunset," Lacy said with aplomb. Paulson felt that the money spent for fuel was inconsequential as the flight yielded a ton of publicity for the Lear Jet and his distributorship. Few people had seen or even heard of the new airplane. Wherever it landed, particularly at smaller airports, it attracted a crowd of curious onlookers. It was the start of California Airmotive going forward to become Lear's most successful marketer of the aircraft.

Between making demonstration flights, Paulson and Lacy enjoyed taking their one-and-only jet on personal trips, such as a jaunt to Mexico to go fishing. Some of those trips turned into unwanted adventures. "The Lear had great range, like Van Nuys to Acapulco nonstop," Lacy said about one of those flights. "Al and I flew it there but the windshield defog wasn't working. After landing, I tried to taxi the airplane but I couldn't see the taxiway. Al got out of the airplane, and with a flashlight, guided me for three-quarters of a mile to the parking area without hitting anything."[11]

Separated from Irene after twenty-one years of marriage, it was an

Clay Lacy and Paulson disembark from California Airmotive's Lear Jet demonstrator in 1966 (Clay Lacy archives).

opportune time for Paulson to meet other women, particularly those who shared his passion for aerial adventures. He was going through a protracted divorce process, needing a break from both business and the courtroom. In the early 1960s, he dated actress Donna Douglas for about a year. She came across as a true Southern Belle, not unlike her most memorable role, Elly May Clampett on *The Beverly Hillbillies* television sitcom. Douglas was raised in the Baton Rouge, Louisiana, area. She married after high school, had a child, got divorced, won a couple of beauty contests, and moved to New York City where she appeared in several television shows. *The Beverly Hillbillies* series made her a star. It was the most popular sitcom on television.

In 1963, once the relationship with Douglas had run its course, Paulson met twenty-eight-year-old Mary Lou Cox. Unlike the other women he'd dated, she was no stranger to aviation. At age nineteen, she quit college to work as a flight attendant. Returning to college and starting work in a downtown Los

Angeles office, the boredom of the job caused her to realize how much she missed the allure of flying. She returned to the airlines as a flight attendant until meeting Ralph W. E. Cox, Jr., marrying him on January 30, 1959. A colorful entrepreneur who began his career as a dentist, the former Navy pilot started United States Overseas Airlines (USOA) in 1946. He acquired a fleet of twelve DC-4 and six DC-6 airliners. Along with other supplemental air carriers, USOA pioneered low-cost coach passenger service—a progenitor of today's Southwest Airlines. But his success was not to last. The Civil Aeronautics Board grounded his airliners in 1962, followed by the carrier filing for bankruptcy in 1964. Prodded by the nation's major airlines, the CAB shut down USOA and other independent airlines, citing safety and service violations.

Mary Lou divorced Cox on November 16, 1964. Ironically, it was Cox who introduced her to Paulson. The airline owner had made purchases from California Airmotive. Allen's own divorce from Irene became final the day after Mary Lou went on a date with him. "He called and invited me to dinner," she said. "That was the beginning of it."[12] On December 23, 1965, the couple tied the knot in Las Vegas. Prior to meeting Mary Lou, Paulson had built a home off Laurel Canyon Boulevard overlooking the San Fernando Valley. It would serve as their first of several homes.

Mary Lou experienced her own share of flying adventures with her husband, most of them fun, but at least one downright hair-raising. On a trip to Mexico in the Lear Jet a couple of months after Paulson bought the demonstrator, all hell broke loose. "We had a double flameout over Mexico City," she said about a flight that would not be forgotten. "We flew to Acapulco and were starting to fly home when an engine quit. Allen and Hank Beaird were flying. I could see Allen was getting upset. All of a sudden, the other engine quit. It got really quiet. We circled over Mexico City." Thinking her life might be measured in seconds before crashing into hills surrounding the airport, the uncomfortable environment in the cabin did nothing to calm her nerves. Having little experience flying the Lear, Paulson's anxiety may have equaled hers. It was fortunate that test pilot Beaird accompanied him in the cockpit. "The airplane didn't have an interior," she said. "When we were up at altitude, water froze on the metal ribs. As we descended, the ice melted and began to drip on us."[13]

A credit to Beaird's skillful handling, the powerless jet landed in Mexico City without further incident. Known to be unflappable while working as chief test pilot for Lear Jet Corp., it was just another day in the air for him.

Popular music changed in the mid–1960s and the way entertainers flew to concert engagements changed, too. Jetting around in a Lear Jet became the new "in thing" to do. When it came time to market the airplane, Lear harped on his distributors to offer celebrities, politicians, and top-level executives free rides. The practice was similar to taking a test drive in a new car at a dealership: try it, enjoy it—and you'll want to drive the car home. In this case, it meant buying a half-million-dollar jet. Paulson got this message from Lear very early during his time as a distributor, directing Lacy to offer rides to Hollywood entertainers. A camera was always on hand to snap photos of the VIPs they took up. Publicity and word-of-mouth praise is what helped sell the airplanes.

Bill Lear knew that California Airmotive was the linchpin to close sales on the west coast. "Allen took Frank Sinatra on a demo ride. And he took Kirk Kerkorian on a demo ride," recalled Mary Lou. "He was a wonderful salesman. He would persevere and close sales."[14] The men learned the value of involving celebrities in their endeavors. "In those days, when Bill wanted to make the name [of the jet] a household word, he thought the way to do it was to get celebrities in it," Lacy remarked. "Many were friends like Danny Kaye and Art Linkletter, as well as Frank Sinatra, Dean Martin, and Sammy Davis, Jr." Sinatra bought one of the first Lear Jets from Paulson, registered as N175FS with the FAA. Lacy said, "Just about everybody in Hollywood flew in the demonstrator. We got a lot of free publicity, like with Sinatra."[15] Some of those flights resulted in selling a jet.

"We sold serial number 31 to Frank in May of 1965," he recalled. "He

Posing alongside a Lear Jet with Paulson are from left, entertainers Yul Brynner and Frank Sinatra (Paulson family archives/Crystal Christensen).

wanted the jet to go to places faster. Sinatra began a love affair with the "little Lear," as Lacy affectionately called the jet. "He was in New York for an hour-long television program when he came over to LaGuardia. There were several airplanes parked there. Sinatra walked by the nose of one of them and said, 'This one can go from New York to Los Angeles with one stop in eight hours flying time.' When he walked up to his Lear, he patted it, and said, 'With this baby we'll get to Los Angeles in five and a half hours flying time with one landing for fuel.'"[16] Sinatra called his Lear Jet the *Christina II*, named for daughter Tina.

The crooner's company, Sinatra Enterprises, formed an aviation subsidiary to furnish jet charters for studio moguls and entertainers. Cal-Jet Airways owned not only the Lear Jet, but also a five-seat Alouette helicopter and a three-passenger Morane-Saulnier MS.760 Paris personal-size jet. Sinatra's best-selling rendition of "Come Fly with Me" described his jet-setting personal life. During the time that Sinatra owned the Lear, his pilots shuttled his Rat Pack buddies between Burbank, Las Vegas, and his desert compound in Rancho Mirage. To the entertainer, owning a jet was the same as being the only kid on the block to own a car in his hometown of Hoboken, New Jersey. From the time Paulson handed him the key, to when he sold the plane two years later (after buying a much larger Grumman Gulfstream II), Sinatra and his friends logged 1,500 hours in the Lear.[17] "If you want to get Sinatra in a movie, give him a role where he gets to sit in a cockpit," it was said.[18] The crooner wasn't a pilot, and not always an enthusiastic passenger, but he did love getting to wherever he was headed as fast as possible.

Bill Lear's brainstorm about offering rides to prominent people worked. Besides the pro bono flights, the jet appeared on television programs like *The Dating Game*, where winners were whisked off in the plane to Las Vegas or San Francisco for a holiday. The Lear Jet name was well on its way to becoming a part of popular culture.

Wherever the Lear landed, an inquisitive crowd gathered. The sexy jet had star power, an instant hit. A partial list of celebrity users included Johnny Carson, Richard Nixon, Steve Lawrence and Eydie Gorme, Joe E. Brown, singer Roger Miller, the Smothers Brothers, and Bob Cummings. Even broadcast journalists Howard K. Smith and Peter Jennings flew in it. Paulson's distributorship was responsible for much of this activity.

Between the hours flying for United and handling the demo flights, Lacy didn't spend much time on the ground. "Al and I got a little bit crosswise during the Lear period because I was flying all the demonstrations," Lacy said. "He told me he was getting jealous as I was having all the fun flying Hollywood people around—including some good looking gals." Of course, Lacy was the man with a Lear Jet type rating from the FAA. It meant that he had to fly most of the demonstration flights. "Al finally got a type rating in

Actor Forrest Tucker with Paulson following a flight in the Lear Jet (Paulson family archives/Crystal Christensen).

the Lear but it was restricted to visual flight rules. He could only fly below 24,000 feet."[19]

Outside of the demonstration flights, they made use of the jet for flights at air shows. Sometimes they took mini vacations with the airplane.

"Al and I took a trip with the Lear during the summer of 1965," Lacy recalled. They needed to be at an air show on Sunday in Pendleton, Oregon, to display and demonstrate the jet. Saturday was available to do whatever they wanted. "I suggested to Al that we fly the Lear to McCall [Idaho]. We had a cabin on the middle fork of the Salmon River not far from there."[20] It was a remote place called Pistol Creek. Mary Lou and the couple's children were often companions on such trips.

Lacy continued the story:

We could rent a little airplane at Pendleton and have someone bring it to McCall. The same guy could fly it back. So we rented a Cessna 182 and the guy flew it to McCall while Al and I flew there in the Lear. From McCall, Al flew the Cessna to Pistol Creek and I flew there in a Bonanza we rented [to transport family members]. Coming back to McCall, Al flew the Cessna ahead of me. The runway's direction is north south. He was going to land to the south. I'd land to the north. We both made short approaches and landed head on.

Lacy had a friend aboard the Bonanza who yelled, "*Hey, there's a plane coming right at us.*" Lacy replied, "that's Al's airplane. He'll land on his half and we'll land on our half. Al didn't see us until we got closer, although we weren't about to hit. He chomped on the brakes and blew out the tires. The airplane tilted to one side and he said, 'Gosh, my tire is flat.' Mary Lou looked out the window on her side and said, 'So is mine.'"

"When we went into McCall with the Lear, Al landed it. We landed in 2,500 feet—it being the first time a jet had landed at the airport." The airport had a 5,000-foot paved runway but was situated at an altitude of 5,000 feet, the thin air making it tricky to land a jet. "When we were ready to leave we went inside the FBO [fixed base operation] when someone said, 'Wasn't that amazing, the Lear Jet turned off in 2,500 feet.' Al was listening and about to say something when another guy said, 'Just a few hours ago there was a dummy that blew out both tires in a 182 halfway down the runway.' Al just kind of smiled and looked away."[21]

At Pistol Creek, "Allen owned the cabin with Clay and another man," Mary Lou remarked. "It was pretty primitive. That's where her mom and dad had met. They were kids growing up together."[22] Mary Lou was referring to Crystal Christensen, the daughter of Robert Paulson, Allen's son who would perish in an airplane crash during 1970 when she was three years old. Pistol Creek was one of the few "fly-in" communities located in a true wilderness area. Christensen's grandparents, Marvin and Barbara Hornbeck, built the ranch after owning another spread in the area called the Sulphur Creek Ranch. The 2,500-foot private airstrip at Pistol Creek offered the ultimate in seclusion for families owning vacation cabins there. By air, it was 45 minutes from Boise and 20 minutes from McCall. The Pistol Creek Ranch development covered 220 acres, with a dozen or two cabins built near the dirt airstrip, a short walk from the rapids of the Salmon River's middle fork. A unique place, the ranch sat in the midst of 2.3 million acres of protected wilderness. If a resident didn't own an airplane or horse, the only way to reach Pistol Creek was by chartering a small aircraft.

Landing on a backcountry airstrip presents a unique set of challenges. On the website for Sulphur Creek Ranch, pilots are cautioned to "overfly runway before landing—livestock and animals in vicinity ... first 300 feet during

California Airmotive's Beechcraft Twin Bonanza after landing at Idaho's Pistol Creek airstrip, circa 1959. From left are Paulson, Marvin Hornbeck, and Clay Lacy (Clay Lacy archives).

spring can be mushy ... while taxiing stay on the gravel surfaces and beware of gopher holes."

Christensen remarked: "My mother's mom was a commercial pilot and a member of the 99's organization that Amelia Earhart belonged to. Marv Hornbeck was a John Wayne kind of character, but well respected for being a fantastic pilot." Christensen lived her life with a family of Idaho aviators. "My family did some pretty hairy flying in those days and my grandma was right in the thick of it."[23]

Paulson met Hornbeck at a sports show in the late 1940s and began visiting Sulphur Creek, a property Bruce McCaw would later buy, on vacations. The cabins were not for sale. Christensen's family moved up the river and built Pistol Creek Ranch where the cabins could be purchased. Paulson and Lacy were among the first owners.

On October 16, 1965, Hornbeck and a friend were killed in the crash of a single-engine Stinson while shooting touch-and-go landings at the Boise airport. "That's when my grandma sold Pistol Creek and new owners took over," Christensen said.[24] Hornbeck's death came five years and one day before her father died in another Idaho airplane crash. Mountainous terrain and inclement weather in the region often made for treacherous flying conditions.

Christensen enjoyed a close relationship with Paulson throughout his life, more akin to the experience of a daughter than granddaughter. It may have resulted from losing her father at such a young age. Paulson made every effort to be a resource for the young woman, providing repose and guidance when asked. She flew in his airplanes to points far and wide, rode horses with him around Pistol Creek, and joined him for dinners with politicians and celebrities. For a Democratic, middle-class mental health therapist working in Idaho, being around conservative Republicans was an unusual addition to her lifestyle.

McCaw joined Paulson for frequent visits to the rural area. "I used to go to Pistol Creek with Al in blue jeans, flying around the backcountry and doing simple stuff," he remarked. "We'd have a barbeque, a few drinks, and tell stories. Mary Lou wasn't crazy about Pistol Creek, preferring something a bit more refined. The place was dusty and dirty."[25]

When not flying somewhere for the weekend, life at home with Mary Lou and the children was fairly quiet. "He just liked to fly. It all had to do with aviation," she said of her husband's passion. "He did like boating, so we had a boat and enjoyed water skiing. We played tennis and he'd play golf. We had season tickets to Dodger games and attended the World Series. And we went to all the children's football games. His son Jim was an all-star pitcher in the valley. With five boys we kept pretty busy." She had brought a young son into their relationship from her marriage to Cox.

Paulson had a religious bearing, although he wasn't a regular churchgoer. "Except when my son was in a Lutheran school," Mary Lou remarked about her husband's stepson, "and it was mandatory we go or he wasn't going to graduate."[26]

6

Let's Make a Deal

Bill Murphy, a wealthy Los Angeles automobile dealer and acclaimed sports car race driver, financed airliner purchases for California Airmotive in the 1960s. It was a mutually beneficial relationship: Paulson needed working capital and Murphy wanted more involvement in aviation. In 1938, Murphy opened a DeSoto-Plymouth dealership on Vermont Avenue in downtown Los Angeles. Ten years later, he opened another store in Culver City, operating it until 1997. The business earned him the distinction of selling more Buicks than any dealership in the world from 1962 to 1967. But he was best known as a sports car racer in California in the 1950s. Driving a Kurtis roadster powered by a 400-horsepower Buick engine, he became a consistent front-runner at races up and down the state. "The Buick engine that Bill had in his Kurtis was more powerful than any of the engines built for Ferraris, Maseratis, or anything at the time," said Murphy's friend and racing icon Carroll Shelby.[1]

Murphy and Paulson had much in common, both down-to-earth, rags-to-riches "gear heads." As young men, they earned money buying, repairing, and selling older cars. Each loved fast machinery, in the air or circling a racetrack. Murphy owned a cattle ranch in San Obispo County where he raised thoroughbred racehorses. Visiting the property, Paulson enjoyed hanging around the animals, kindling an old interest with its origin dating back to his days on the dairy farm in Marin County. He was also appreciative of Murphy's investment in California Airmotive, especially when Murphy financed the purchase of Paulson's first Lear Jet. During the years to come, he encouraged Paulson to pursue ventures ranging from raising thoroughbreds to selling luxury cars.

"Murphy would go along with most anything Al wanted to do," Lacy remarked.[2] In addition to horses and cars, the men had something else in common. They didn't talk much in public and tended to blend in with a crowd. A columnist for the *Los Angeles Times* interviewed Murphy, calling him the "quietest Irishman in captivity." He continued: "His frugal use of words leads to the assumption that he thinks he's sending a telegram when he talks and has to pay for his statements by the word."[3]

Murphy was all business. "He would write a check [to buy airliners] and then split the profits with Al, so he really was a banker," Bruce McCaw said. "The banks wouldn't handle the airliners because they didn't understand the business."[4] When Paulson sold an airliner, life was good. But when he had to repossess airplanes and they sat in desert storage for a while, he needed a shot in the arm to keep the company afloat. It was the same when the sales of aircraft parts dipped. Murphy would come to the rescue. "Bill had a lot of money and in the parts business it is feast or famine," Joe Clark remarked. "Al came close to the edge. I recall sitting in Clay's office one day and Al asked Clay if he had thirty grand sitting around because he couldn't make the payroll."[5] It wasn't an unusual occurrence. "When I handled Al's insurance, I went through this all the time with him," McCaw said. "I went to see Al when he owed me quite a bit of money. He showed me a Beech Baron and asked if I'd like to take it home. Instead of paying for the insurance premiums he offered me the airplane."[6]

Bill Murphy Buick, Inc., evolved into more than an automobile dealership. It served as a nerve center for handling its owner's investments in real estate and aviation. In addition to Lear Jets, he financed purchases of many DC-7s and Connies for California Airmotive. He functioned as a silent, crucial business partner of Paulson's enterprise. He had the money, and Paulson sold the airplanes. After closing the deals they'd split the profits. McCaw remarked: "Bill Murphy was really Al's back door banker."[7]

Inspired by Murphy's success as a car dealer, Paulson formed the Paulson Automotive Group in Beverly Hills during 1992. The firm acquired seven dealership franchises for Rolls-Royce, Bentley, Lexus, Infiniti, Cadillac, Lincoln-Mercury, and Ford brands. He monopolized the sale of luxury cars on the affluent west side of Los Angeles. "The opportunity just came up and it seemed like a good bargain, so I made a personal investment," he said of entering the world of high-end automobile retailing.[8] Ensconced in aeronautical ventures, he wasn't involved in day-to-day management of the stores. Ultimately, he lost interest in a line of business he knew little about, didn't see the profits materialize as hoped, and sold all the dealerships. "The real trick [in business] is knowing when to get out," he said. "I had to do that with the car dealerships in L.A. If you keep things too long, they can drag down the rest."[9] Gaining the friendship of the right people, such as Murphy, to make deals was crucial to Paulson's success. "Al was very good at surrounding himself with well-heeled people who could help in his business," Clark concluded.[10]

Along with Murphy, entertainer Danny Kaye was another Angeleno who invested in California Airmotive. Lacy also joined in, buying about a 5 percent stake. Several investors now involved, Paulson reorganized the distributorship as Pacific Lear Jet Sales Corp.

Kaye had established a sterling reputation as an actor, singer, dancer, and comedian. An excellent golfer, he gave up the game at the age of forty-eight upon catching the flying bug. Unlike most student pilots, Kaye learned to pilot a twin-engine airplane before a single engine one. Six years after earning a private pilot's license, he finally earned a single-engine endorsement. At that point he was authorized to fly everything from small Cessnas to multi-engine planes. The first airplane he owned was a PA-23 Piper Aztec, followed by a Beech Model 80 Queen Air, both twin-engine, piston-powered planes used primarily for business trips.

"I introduced Danny to Bill [Lear]," Lacy said. "Danny and I had just flown back from Portland in the Lear. It was a demonstration flight for him as he was thinking of buying one. Bill had just arrived and pulled up behind us. They hit it off right away. Danny told Bill that he'd like to get involved with our distributorship, saying how much he loved the airplane. Bill told Al to take care of it and Al got him involved."[11]

Lear was ecstatic about Kaye's participation, appreciating the value of celebrity endorsements. In addition to becoming a partner in Pacific Lear Jet, Lear boosted the entertainer's visibility by appointing him as a vice president at the manufacturer. It was a part-time job, carrying a business card and scheduling appearances to talk about the benefits of owning the jet. His association with the manufacturer reportedly helped sell airplanes. "Danny Kaye's profound interest in aviation is a well known facet of this amazing man's talents," Lear was quoted in a news release issued by his company. "We are delighted he has chosen to pursue this interest in an active way."[12]

The entertainer's movie career was largely in the past, but he remained a star on television. In 1963, his career experienced an uptick with his show. It became so successful that the network built an apartment for him on the top floor of Television City, the west coast CBS headquarters on Beverly Boulevard in Los Angeles. Judy Garland and Red Skelton broadcasted weekly shows from the studio but didn't rate an apartment as Kaye did. By the end of the 1963–1964 season, The Danny Kaye Show was doing fine, winning two Emmy Awards. The next season went okay, too. But the euphoria didn't last: in 1965 the ratings plummeted to eightieth place among network shows. Kaye went on to do another year of the show before CBS cancelled it. Having less entertainment work scheduled, he intensified his activities in aviation.

After Lacy checked out Kaye's competency in the Lear Jet, they flew hundreds of hours together. "This is such an incredible airplane," Kaye told a reporter. "It's alive. It wants to fly."[13] With a salesman like Kaye talking up the product wherever he traveled, Paulson and Lear couldn't do any better.

Kaye's aviation exploits included charity flights to benefit the United

Nations Children's Fund, known as UNICEF. "They called Danny the ambassador at large for UNICEF," Lacy remarked. "I said to him wouldn't it be great if you took a trip in the airplane for them? He said, 'Let's do that, it's a good idea.' We talked about going to a bunch of cities." A 17,000-mile journey would take them across forty states and three Canadian provinces, all within 120 hours. Kaye enjoyed entertaining the kids at each stop, but didn't neglect to perk up his waning status as a star.

"Each time we landed somewhere there were maybe a hundred kids there," Lacy said. "Danny would get out, sing a song, and talk to them. We'd spend about twenty minutes on the ground during each stop and go to as many as twelve cities a day." There was more than one of the globe-girdling trips. "On the last trip, we went to sixty-five cities in five days. The first night we visited Pierre Trudeau and then flew on to the White House to see President Ford."[14] Gerald Ford was a Paulson friend. The flights were a winning move for UNICEF and for Lear: word was spread about the charity, the children met a famous comedian, and the jet began to get known on an international scale. Another reason for stopping in as many as sixty-five cities per trip was to give Kaye the opportunity to make that many takeoffs and landings. He hadn't flown the Lear much and wanted to log as many hours as possible to maintain his proficiency. In Van Nuys, the trips turned into a moneymaking proposition for Paulson: UNICEF paid California Airmotive $22,000 for its use of the jet.

Kaye loved hanging around the kids, yet it would be naïve to think he was oblivious to how the exposure enhanced his image as a performer. There were cynics who viewed the trips as nothing more than a calculated scheme to promote his status as a celebrity and to sell airplanes. Presenting a happy-go-lucky attitude before millions of fans, people closest to the entertainer knew him as someone with an occasional crass, temperamental personality. He could be solicitous and remote; the mood swings often wide and unpredictable.

As a seasoned marketing executive, Alex Kvassay had no use for the man. "One evening, when sales were not exactly going like gangbusters, we were summoned to Bill's office and had to listen until midnight while Danny Kaye preached to us why we were not selling enough airplanes and how to go about selling more. I was outraged, though very quietly, for having been told by a clown how to conduct my business."[15]

It was predictable that levelheaded Paulson would tangle with Kaye at some point. "Al and Danny didn't get along too well," Lacy said without being specific.[16] Their strong personalities clashed. It wasn't serious at first—just collisions between two men having vastly different temperaments. But as time went by, it turned into more than an occasional quarrel. It didn't surprise Paulson's employees when Kaye exited the Pacific Lear Jet partnership. Adding

insult to injury, Kaye later sold the Lear Jet he bought from Paulson and purchased a competitive Jet Commander. "Danny wasn't the easiest person to
get along with," Mary Lou Paulson added. "He wasn't as kind and nice as he
appeared to the public. Allen had to ask him to clean up his language whenever his mother came around."[17]

As 1965 got underway, a plethora of new business jets began to appear
on airports across the country. It was the advent of general aviation's jet age.
Besides "heavy iron" airplanes like the Lockheed JetStar and North American
Sabreliner, the medium-size Hawker-Siddeley HS.125 and Dassault Falcon
20 arrived from Europe. Each of the planes made a favorable impression and
garnered sales. But compared to the Lear Jet, all of them were larger and
more expensive.

"We sold fourteen of them [Lear Jets] the first year, which was kind of
unusual," Lacy said. "In the New York area there were 33,000 potential buyers.
In our area there were only 3,300, but we sold more airplanes than the New
York distributorship. We had a different kind of clientele. Back east, I think
people felt better dealing with bigger companies. A new company scared
them."[18]

The one airplane that competed directly with the Lear Jet was the Jet
Commander 1121, designed by Ted Smith, a brilliant engineer at the Aero
Commander division of Rockwell in Oklahoma. Smith was the visionary
founder of the company. Born in 1906, he graduated from an aviation trade
school, learned to fly, and built his own small planes. Hiring into Douglas
Aircraft Co. in 1935 as a trainee tool designer, his talents eventually landed
him a project engineer post on the Douglas A-20 Havoc light bomber program. Dreaming of manufacturing an airplane of his own design, he quit
Douglas in 1945 to start a venture with fourteen former Douglas engineers.
They proceeded to design a plane with the sole purpose being to transport
business executives. The shirtsleeve leader pushed his team to develop a full
line of popular business airplanes, culminating in the Jet Commander. Bill
Lear was touted as a genius by developing the Lear Jet, but Smith was already
known in aviation circles as a preeminent aircraft designer of the twentieth
century. Unlike Lear, he avoided publicity and didn't relish owning luxuries,
preferring to live a sedate lifestyle characteristic of many engineers.

Lear kept a close eye on the Jet Commander's development—and the
people who planned to buy the planes. "It was really a race between this aircraft [the Jet Commander] and the Lear Jet," Bill Lear, Jr., said.[19] Although
the Jet Commander didn't have an especially long range, pilots liked its flying
characteristics. Many of those pilots had moved up from their company's
piston-powered aircraft and made an easy transition to the jet. More important to the CEOs and celebrities who wrote checks to buy the airplanes, a key
selling point was the spacious passenger cabin situated forward of the wing.

The engines were positioned well behind the cabin. The layout provided plenty of cabin space, unobstructed views through panoramic windows, and little noise. The airplane represented stiff competition for Lear.

The Jet Commander sold for $475,000 when introduced. For that money, customers received a finished interior, buffet, and a lavatory—a toilet being something that Bill Lear didn't plan to offer. He felt it was an admission that an airplane took too long to get to its destination. After a few VIPs flew on his jet and needed to use a potty, he changed his mind and installed a semi-private toilet. That is, one with a small privacy curtain surrounding it.

"Some of these guys think they want hot food, stand-up bar, sit-down toilet, lie-down couch, walk-around headroom, everything up to and including hot and cold running bidets in an airplane," Lear told a writer. "Who the hell needs it? In my plane, it takes one hour from Detroit to New York, two hours from New York to Miami. After two hours, even wall-to-wall girls are no substitute for getting there."[20]

The angst existing in the Lear Jet and Aero Commander camps escalated. Bill Lear, Jr., wrote in his autobiography that Aero Commander executives referred to his father's jet as a "boob tube," because its fuselage was round and smaller than the Jet Commander fuselage, "and they thought that only a 'boob' would buy one." At the annual National Business Aircraft Association convention, Jet Commander salesmen handed out long-handed shoehorns, "for those considering the purchase of a Lear Jet."[21] Retaliating, Lear aficionados praised their airplane's ear-popping climb and cruise performance. But its FAA certification in the general aviation category, rather than in the Jet Commander's transport category, was considered a negative.[22] Salesmen pushing the Jet Commander were quick to identify this and other shortcomings to anyone who would listen.

There were challenges ahead for Lear Jet Corp. Following much initial success; unsold jets could be seen parked on the ramp outside the plant in Wichita. They were waiting for buyers—as do slow selling cars sitting on an automobile dealer's lot. Worsening the dampened sales picture in 1966, a rumor was circulating that the Lear took a tender touch to fly. If a pilot let the aircraft slip too far out of bounds, it could be difficult to regain control. On the other hand, many Lear pilots having no previous jet experience managed to fly the airplanes without difficulty. But the rumors persisted.

In spite of the Jet Commander's presence, Lear Jets continued to set flight records. Its pilots were unofficially smashing speed records during daily business flights. Lear and Paulson soaked up every bit of the glory.

~ ~ ~

Robert Paulson, the industrialist's twenty-four-year-old son, was killed with his flight instructor in an airplane accident on October 10, 1970. He was nearing completion of a training program to earn a commercial pilot's license. The NTSB accident investigation report stated that his thirty-year-old instructor had "exercised poor judgment," resulting in their deaths. He flew a single-engine Cessna 150 into a boxed-in canyon near Eagle, Idaho, didn't maintain sufficient flying speed, and stalled the plane at too low an altitude to recover. A witness on the ground watched as the plane flew over wooded terrain before descending in a steep nose down attitude, slamming into tall trees.[23]

"Bob was getting his commercial pilot rating," Mary Lou Paulson said. "He had an instructor with him for his final hour of instruction. They were heading back to the airport and went down low to look for chucker's [game birds]. They were flying at 500 feet when the airplane did a whipstall[24] and went into the ground. The crash mangled his face badly. They [investigators] said he had a candy bar in his mouth so he was not expecting what happened."[25] Robert left behind twenty-one-year-old wife, Patti, and three-year-old daughter, Crystal.

Each of the industrialist's sons expressed an interest in aviation from an

Daughter Crystal with her father Robert Paulson shortly before his death in an airplane accident on October 10, 1970 (Paulson family archives/Crystal Christensen).

early age, but only Robert and Richard became pilots. The accident troubled Paulson for the rest of his life; Robert had perished in an accident that was so preventable. Understandably, his death stunned Patti and Crystal. A native of Idaho, mom needed a change of place to grieve and recover from the tragedy. Devastated, and not knowing what to do, Allen and Mary Lou opened their home to them in the San Fernando Valley for as long as they wished to stay. "We went to California so we could get back on our feet," Crystal said of what she remembered as a child. The stay in California helped her mother regain enough strength to return to Idaho "and get going again."[26]

Paulson's recurring thoughts about losing his son caused him to reprioritize his life at home. "It distracted me many times in my life," he said. "It's something you just don't wipe off real quick. In fact, you never do."[27]

Mary Lou was a party to his pain. "Prior to the time his son died, we always had business people with us during the weekends," she said. "When Bob died, Allen said, 'no more weekends for business.' That's when we began to visit with the Conroy's, Lacy's, and other friends. During vacations, we traveled the world together. We had children and a shared interest in aviation." She continued, "Every weekend, six of us, and whatever children there were, would do something together. We'd go to their house or they'd come to ours. Or we'd go on a trip. We'd spend Easter in Cabo San Lucas or go water skiing in Lake Havasu. We all had homes in Lake Arrowhead. Everyone had an airplane. Sometimes Jack [Conroy] would take everybody in his DC-3."[28]

Apart from the experience of losing Robert, the industrialist was aging comfortably in his middle years, projecting a calm demeanor that conveyed success. Slightly balding with riveting blue eyes, he polished a longtime skill at bringing people around to his way of thinking. It was the power of positive thinking he said, ignoring the ills of the past and moving ahead with life.

Lurking in the shadows was an event that would cause the Lear Jet bonanza to fizzle for Paulson and the other distributors of the airplane. The company manufacturing the fastest-selling business jet in the world began losing money. The deficit deepening, Wall Street analysts awaited Lear Jet's demise. A recession, hit-and-miss marketing, and an overzealous push to diversify into unrelated businesses were principal reasons for the woes. In particular, the distributor system was proving ineffective for selling expensive jet aircraft. The factory was unable to enforce sales territories and prevent price-cutting enacted by the distributors. Bill Lear faced the inevitable: shut the manufacturer down or sell his stake to an entity having sufficient financial resources to restructure the company and weather the recession.

Grudgingly, he chose to sell the company. Denver-based Gates Rubber Co., a major manufacturer of automobile tires, was the buyer. On April 10, 1967, Gates assumed control of Lear Jet. The new management's first order of business was to cancel the distributorships and replace them with a factory sales staff.

"They came in and cancelled all the distributorships," Alex Kvassay recalled, Lear's vice president of export marketing at the time. "They notified the distributors by sending a telegram stating that their contracts were cancelled immediately. Nobody [at Gates] had read the distributorship contracts, which said that either party could cancel the contract by giving thirty days' notice. If they had waited thirty days, it would have cost them nothing."[29] Instead, the distributors filed lawsuits citing breach of contract.

The distributorship era passé, Paulson ramped up his involvement in buying, reconditioning, and selling secondhand airliners. "All told, I've got about seventy-five," he told a reporter in describing his oddball collection of airline transports, worth upward of $10 million. The piston-powered airliners, selling for up to $2.5 million apiece when new, were sold to smaller airlines and individuals for $95,000 each. Or whatever the market would bear when he wanted to sell. California Airmotive's annual sales topped $14 million in 1969.

A 1973 article in *Newsweek* magazine described Paulson as the "used airliner king." It went on to report that his airplanes were "the propeller-driven flagships of the 1950s, the rejects in the rush to the big jets with mini-skirted stewardesses."[30] In a sense, the airplanes may have been "rejects" from major airlines, but those same aircraft turned into gold for a wheeler-dealer like Paulson. Rather than operating from a lot filled with used cars, he ran one packed with used airliners. The *Newsweek* article continued: "During the last decade he has sold about 300 airplanes, including 110 Constellations at $35,000 to $95,000 each, a hundred DC-7s, also at $35,000 to $95,000 each, scores of the old DC-3 workhorses at $10,000 each and an assortment of Electras at nearly $1 million each."[31]

Visiting Fox Field and staring at the rows of airliners, another stunned reporter wrote, "Allen Paulson has more airliners than El Al and Continental airlines put together. He's crammed most of them onto a dusty, windblown weed-covered lot."[32] The parked aircraft were as jam-packed as cars sandwiched into parking spaces at a stadium hosting the World Series.

"When Al had forty acres up at Fox he had dozens of Connies up there," Clay Lacy remarked. "They came from almost everywhere in the world, from TWA, Eastern, and a few from Qantas and other airlines,"[33]

Paulson bought and rebuilt all kinds of damaged airplanes. On one occasion, he bought two Lear Jets that suffered severe damage as a result of hard landings. The landing gear struts had punched holes through the aluminum skin panels atop the wings. Repairing them would take Kvassay's help:

Bill Lear was gone and the Gates Aviation people refused to do business with the former distributors. They wouldn't sell Al those wing panels—and the Lear Jet factory was the only source for them. Al came to me and said, "Alex, do you think you

Minus their valuable Wright R-3350 engines, a row of Douglas DC-7s owned by California Airmotive gathers dust at Fox Field in the Mojave Desert during the 1970s (Neil Aird collection.)

can help me?" I went to the spare parts department at Gates, ordered two of the panels, and shipped them to a fictitious address in Tijuana, Mexico. When the panels came in, the freight forwarder delivered them to Al in Van Nuys. I didn't think I'd get caught selling something to Al because the paperwork showed that I sold them [to an address] in Mexico.[34]

California Airmotive continued to operate from offices in the austere, concrete block building at 7139 Vineland Avenue, a stone's throw from Burbank's Runway 7. The facility served as a nerve center during his years as a Lear Jet distributor, although he actually housed the airplanes in a hangar on Stagg Street at the Van Nuys Airport. He also rented additional warehouse space. Each warehouse and storage yard was packed with parts dismantled from the aging airliners. Stacked in piles could be found everything from pumps and actuators to instrument panels and control surfaces. The best sellers were items that airlines wore out frequently—engine components, electrical accessories, and mechanical parts. Slower-moving items sat in the dusty warehouses for years, causing him to occasionally retain auctioneers to conduct sales and pull in whatever cash they could. The auctioneers considered the material to be aeronautical junk. At one warehouse in the east valley, Paulson posted a handmade sign next to a telephone used by his employees: NO PERSONAL CALLS ALLOWED."[35] He could be frugal when it came to the simple things in life, reflective of a childhood when every dime was needed to survive.

Many of the parts didn't sell quickly, but some of the airplanes didn't move either. "We used to turn over our whole inventory in two or three months," he said about a normal year. "Now, some of these planes stay around for years." Recessions, combined with political calamities in the United States and elsewhere, had a direct effect on how fast the airliners moved and for what prices. "When one is sold we have it reconditioned to the specifications of the buyer," he continued. "Once they finish cleaning and painting them, the planes look like new." Not every deal was consummated. "I had one completely overhauled and ready to go, and no buyer. That's what you call a loser."[36] If an airplane didn't sell or get leased in a reasonable period of time, wrecking crews came in to remove its most saleable parts, and scrap the remainder of the airframe to reuse its valuable aluminum. The parts and scrap metal often pulled in more money than what the intact aircraft was worth.

Of all the airplanes he owned, the Constellation meant the most to him. "Al bought the first Connie from TWA that became surplus," Lacy remarked. "It was an emotional thing for him because he was a former flight engineer at the airline."[37]

Disappointing economic news caused California Airmotive's business to hit an occasional sales slump. During such dry spells, Paulson stopped drawing a salary. During good years, corporations bought business jets, obsoleting the piston airplanes they owned. The same thing happened with the piston-powered airliners. Obscure companies that Paulson counted on to purchase parts for their planes stopped buying. They moved on to flying jet transports. At one point, Paulson was awash with warehouses packed with thousands of parts for DC-7s and Connies. There were no buyers in sight. He considered bankruptcy when an unexpected cash infusion from outside the company landed him back on track. The piston airliner parts inventory was liquidated as he switched to sales of turbine-powered airplanes. He successfully transitioned the company from the Lear Jet distributorship to airliner modification work and spare part sales for jet transports.

Typecast as a junk dealer within the aviation industry, Paulson dreamed about doing more than selling used airliners and running a parts warehouse. What he really wanted to do was to notch up his career by manufacturing aircraft of his own design. Development of the Lear Jet served as an inspiration—if Bill Lear could create an airplane so could he. He decided to mimic what Lear did by building and marketing his own airplanes. But rather than sell another business jet into an already crowded market, he resurrected a military jet trainer project abandoned by its manufacturer, albeit prematurely.

Unlike vociferous Lear, Paulson came across as soft-spoken. But in common with the Lear Jet's father, he was restless and relentless in seeking opportunities showing promise. The idea of getting an airplane into mass production is what excited him the most. If successful, such a project would yield millions in profits—the acquisition of wealth representing a principal measure of success to him. "For better or worse, money is how we keep score in this society," he would say.[38]

The early 1950s saw the United States at war with North Korea. For the first time in the nation's history, jet fighters performed most of the aerial sorties during that conflict. The jets rendered obsolete the piston-engine fighters that proved instrumental in winning World War II, the planes now idle and deteriorating in the desert. Recognizing the blazing performance that the first-generation of subsonic jets offered, the Air Force and Navy pressed ahead developing more advanced fighters to fly at supersonic speeds.

A concern in the minds of planners in both the services was how to best train their young pilots to fly the new jets in a reasonable period of time. All primary flight training then took place in piston-powered airplanes, much the same as civilian pilot instruction. It would be a risky leap for inexperienced student pilots to advance from puddle-jumpers directly to the cockpits of supersonic jets. The solution became obvious: build a simple, jet-powered basic trainer to prepare student pilots to fly the latest fighters. Assuming that the pilots would fly nothing but jets during their military careers, it made sense to teach them to fly a jet soon after enlisting and not start them off in an airplane with a propeller hanging on it.

On April 15, 1952, the Air Force solicited the nation's airframe industry to submit proposals for a small jet trainer. Anticipating a major contract, Cessna Aircraft Co. responded. After eliminating other bidders, the service awarded Cessna a contract to develop the airplane, later designated the T-37A. The twin-engine, turbojet-powered trainer, featuring side-by-side seating for instructor and student, first took to the air on October 12, 1954, with Bob Hagan at the controls. Nine years later, Hagan would fly the Lear Jet on its maiden hop. Entering production, the T-37s replaced a fleet of piston-powered Beech T-34 Mentors the Air Force had used for primary flight training.

While the Air Force locked up the contract with Cessna, the Naval Air Training Command pressed ahead with its own all-jet training syllabus. The Navy had also made use of the T-34 Mentor to train its pilots. "The Navy wanted some of what the Air Force had, but all-jet training takes a lot of money, and it didn't fit the Navy's pocketbook," said Lewis Shaw, an Air Force instructor pilot who flew T-37s.[39] The T-37's twin turbojet engines made the plane too expensive for the Navy. At the Beech plant, across town from Cessna in Wichita, the engineers sent a proposal to the Navy describing a jet-powered version of the T-34. Designated the Model 73 Jet Mentor, the plane first flew in December 1955. In Dallas, the Texas Engineering and Manufacturing Company (Temco) was another proposer. Its entry, called the Model 51, first flew on March 26, 1956. Competitors considered Temco an underdog in the procurement, but the company's executives showed unwavering faith in their product and expected to win. Developed with Temco corporate money, the plane was powered by a single turbojet engine, as was the Jet Mentor.

Both Beech and Temco eventually won development contracts. The Navy brass was nothing short of euphoric about the Model 51's potential at the outset of the program. On June 29, 1956, the Navy ordered fourteen production airplanes to evaluate. In 1958, the planes were stationed at the Naval Air Test Center in Patuxent River, Maryland, and the training command facility in Pensacola, Florida. The designation of TT-1 was assigned to the plane, it gaining the official name of Pinto. Purpose of the dual evaluation was to compare the Pinto's performance with that of the Jet Mentor. "A turbojet powered trainer with the capabilities of the Stearman of past years probably is the best nutshell description of Temco's TT-1," wrote Richard Sweeney in a pilot report for *Aviation Week*.[40] The jubilation was not to last.

During the exercises, Navy pilots discovered that the Pinto's "wave off" capability was dismal while executing aborted landings on simulated aircraft carriers. The cause was obvious: its J69-T-2 turbojet engine. Manufactured by Continental Aviation and Engineering, the engine produced a minuscule 920 pounds of thrust. Aware of the performance limitations caused by the small engine, Temco designed the airframe to withstand the stress of an engine in the 3,000-pound thrust range. The Continental J69, the license-built derivative of an engine built in France by Turbomeca, was the only small turbojet sold in the United States at the time. The Cessna T-37 used two of them. When a larger engine would become available, the Navy figured it could be retrofitted into the existing airframe at little cost. On the positive side, pilots enjoyed the Pinto's responsive handling, while technicians assigned to maintain it were in awe of the plane's mechanical simplicity.

"This is an affordable, flyable, and almost practical airplane," said Shaw. "The controls are smooth, easily coordinated, and trouble-free. You just get in and go."[41]

Unlike the T-37s in service with the Air Force, the Navy program ran into snags—the limited engine thrust continuing as the nagging technical issue. Combined with inadequate 90-minute flight endurance, stemming from the jet's meager 127-gallon fuel capacity, the training command stopped buying more Pintos. Another factor prompting the decision was that the students trained in the jet were judged to be only slightly more competent than their peers who learned to fly in the T-34. A report documented that any advantage gained by training in the jet disappeared after T-34 students had logged several hours at the controls. They caught up with the jet-trained students within weeks. Further complicating matters, the all-jet training program was costing more to administer than the piston one. Adding still more doubt, five of the fourteen Pintos built were involved in mishaps during the evaluation phase, dampening the Navy's early enthusiasm to manufacture the jet in volume. In the spring of 1960, the all-jet program was cancelled, grounding the TT-1 Pinto program. The Navy reverted to standardizing on T-34s for its training needs.

During September 1960, the surplus Pintos were ferried to a Naval air facility at Litchfield Park, Arizona, for disposal. Of the nine surviving jets, four were transferred to vocational schools to serve as training aids for students studying aircraft maintenance. A local salvage outfit, Allied Aircraft Sales, bought the remaining five. Over the years to come, all of the Pintos were either sold or traded for other aircraft. The new owners modified the Pintos for civilian use—the most pressing modification being to substitute a higher thrust engine for the anemic J69.

Paulson became one of those owners. He bought a Pinto from Allied Aircraft in early 1968 for little more than its scrap value. Before writing a check, he took nothing for granted, devouring performance data from the Navy's test reports. He knew there was one major shortcoming: the lack of power. He also knew that with a 23-pound increase in engine weight, a General Electric CJ610 turbojet from a Lear Jet could be retrofitted to triple the airplane's thrust. His engineers and mechanics got to work. Enlarged compressor inlet ducts for the bigger engine were an obvious need. The rear structure of the fuselage was lengthened, the vertical stabilizer swept, and the leading edge of the horizontal stabilizer modified. The new engine was located aft of where the Continental engine had been installed, the change moving the plane's center of gravity aft. Two hundred pounds of ballast was placed in the aircraft's nose to serve as a counterbalance. Eliminating the plane's original rubberized fuel cells, and changing the type of tankage to a "wet wing" configuration, boosted the available capacity by 72 gallons to increase the range.

Paulson's modified jet, designated the Super Pinto, first flew on June 28, 1968. At the controls was retired Air Force pilot Dick Hunt, now a Paulson employee. In the air, the jet was a pilot's dream—three times more powerful than its predecessor with only a negligible weight increase. The engine made a rocket out of a lead sled. Hitting a top speed of 518 miles per hour, the rate of climb jumped from less than 2,000-feet-per-minute to 10,000 with the CJ610 pushing it up. Hunt discovered that takeoffs in the Super Pinto were similar to catapult launches from aircraft carriers. He went on to fly the jet at aviation expositions whenever he could. Emphasizing its nearly unlimited vertical aerobatic ability, he'd execute *consecutive* Immelmann maneuvers—stacked one on top of another. At the National Championship Air Races in 1972, he demonstrated the triple Immelmann maneuver. It was performed so precisely that race fans talked about it for years.

Converting the Pintos into hot rods wouldn't be profitable because only a handful of the well-worn airframes existed. To develop a viable program would require manufacturing hundreds of aircraft from scratch. In the March

Paulson's T-610 Super Pinto jet undergoes testing along the Southern California coast in 1968 (Paulson family archives/Crystal Christensen).

1969 issue of *Air Progress* magazine Paulson said: "After we got the idea for the engine mod, we figured it wouldn't be a very smart idea to go ahead until we had a talk with the Ling-Temco-Vought people. It wouldn't be worthwhile to proceed unless we could figure on manufacturing the plane."

He ended up buying the TT-1 Pinto's manufacturing rights from Temco, the company in the throes of merging with conglomerate Ling-Temco-Vought (LTV). Its new board of directors had no interest in the project. The long-forgotten aircraft remained unpopular due to the small engine and the political climate existing in the Navy during the earlier years. Paulson proved that the engine's mounting structure was adequate to hold the CJ610 and solve the low power problem. By marketing the jet to the military services of foreign countries, as he planned to do, any remaining animosity in the Navy about Temco or the Pinto wouldn't be an issue, especially after ten years had elapsed.

In a contract dated January 9, 1969, Paulson bought the rights from LTV to manufacture and market the jet trainer. He acquired all rights to the project for the *total* sum of $10—and a promised future payment of 1.5 percent of gross sales after selling fifty of the planes.

Hunt continued to crisscross the country demonstrating the Super Pinto's gymnastic ability. During the waning years of the Vietnam War, the Air Force announced a program called Pave-Coin. Its purpose was to supply allies of the United States with inexpensive high performance aircraft incorporating light strike attack capabilities. Paulson proposed the Super Pinto to accomplish the mission, planning to equip the airplane with six hard points mounted under the wings to attach up to 3,200 pounds of ordnance.

Lacking sufficient production space at his San Fernando Valley facilities, Paulson sought a major aerospace company as a manufacturing partner. On July 15, 1971, he signed a licensing agreement with Aeronca, Inc., an airframe fabricator based in Middletown, Ohio, to build and market the aircraft for American Jet Industries, Inc.—Paulson's new name for California Airmotive Corp. Aeronca was a subcontractor to manufacturers such as Lockheed and Boeing. The agreement called for Aeronca to serve as prime contractor if the Super Pinto won the Air Force competition. It would be responsible for military sales of production aircraft in the United States. American Jet Industries would retain foreign sales rights. Along with Paulson, Aeronca executives were confident they'd win the Pave-Coin contract, even though several other

The light-strike, counter-insurgency (COIN) variant of the T-610 Super Pinto shows its muscle with an array of ordnance carried under the wings (Paulson family archives/Crystal Christensen).

manufacturers had entered aircraft in the competition. The Ohio company developed the necessary airframe modifications to meet Air Force specifications. Changes included the hard points under the wings and tanks on the wing tips to provide more fuel capacity.

To narrow the field, the Air Force decided to evaluate three of the most promising aircraft at Eglin Air Force Base in Florida: the Super Pinto, the Piper PA-48 Enforcer (a turboprop-powered conversion of the North American Aviation P-51 Mustang), and the twin-engine North American Rockwell OV-10 Bronco, the latter already serving in Vietnam. The Super Pinto emerged as winner in both the performance and maintainability categories. Hearing the encouraging news, Paulson anticipated a production go-ahead with a contract award expected by January 1972. It was not to be. Without explanation, the Air Force abruptly terminated the Pave-Coin program, leaving American Jet Industries and the other suppliers high and dry without a contract. It was later revealed that the cancellation came about because the airplanes were intended to equip *only* the Vietnam Air Force. President Richard Nixon ordered the Pentagon to cancel the program because the Paris Peace Accords called for ending direct military support to South Vietnam. He imposed a moratorium on the delivery of all weapon systems to that country.

Not giving up, there was another possibility for Paulson to pursue. In 1972, the U.S. Department of Transportation sponsored an event called Transpo 72 at Dulles International Airport outside Washington, D.C. The weeklong trade show resembled the Paris Air Show. Its objective was to attract representatives from other countries to interest them in buying everything from wide body jetliners to high-speed trains. American Jet and Aeronca made sure that the Super Pinto flew each day with Hunt demonstrating its capabilities. On May 27, he set a time-to-climb world record by reaching 9,843 feet in 1 minute, 46 seconds.

A credit to Hunt's flying ability, the Super Pinto almost crashed due to no fault of his during a high-speed pass. Tens of thousands of spectators watched in horror as the incident unfolded. Flutter of the right horizontal stabilizer caused the part to fail, followed by extreme buffeting that ripped off the cockpit canopy. Ready to eject, Hunt sensed that the aircraft was still controllable. He landed without further incident. The jet was repaired and flew again at the show. However, in spite of earlier hopes, no orders were received during Transpo 72, causing Aeronca to end its agreement with American Jet Industries.

Flying the Super Pinto to the Reading Air Show in June 1976, Hunt executed an emergency landing—in the middle of the night. The main landing gear had extended properly, but the nose wheel didn't. It was fortunate that the jet sustained nothing more than cosmetic damage. Although embarrassing, the mishap didn't turn into a showstopper. Towed off the runway, its scraped nose section was repaired and the plane soon went on display for showgoers.[42]

Paulson expected a stream of sales for the jet would develop from smaller countries. It caused him to continue spending money on marketing efforts. Distracted by concentrating on unrelated projects, he eventually lost interest in the project and sped up the process to sell it for whatever money it would fetch. He asked $1.25 million for the entire package, including the prototype Super Pinto, the fuselage of a TT-1, the original manufacturing drawings for the J69-powered version, modification drawings for the CJ610 engine retrofit, plus the manufacturing and marketing rights he'd bought from LTV.

The Philippine government expressed mild interest in the project during 1976. Paulson retained Inter-Best Enterprises, Ltd., a Hong Kong sales agent, to follow up on the inquiry. The agent's pitch centered upon expanding the aviation industry in the Philippines using the Super Pinto program as the nucleus. The agent's presentation must have been compelling because the military agreed to buy the program for Paulson's $1.25 million asking price. In 1978, the Self-Reliance Development Wing of the Philippine Air Force handed over a check. The aircraft's new name: the T-610 Cali. Although it was planned to build the planes in the Philippines, bad luck haunted the project for years to come. The sole Cali crashed during an evaluation flight, killing a high-ranking military officer. Lost in the chaos following the collapse of President Ferdinand Marcos' administration in 1986, the project was abandoned and never revived.

Without the Super Pinto project, Paulson went back to square one in his quest to develop and mass-produce an airplane. As usual, plenty of ideas were cooking in his head.

7

Hustler

To Paulson's way of thinking, airplanes were airplanes, whether large or small. They could be Piper Cubs, Lockheed Constellations, Douglas DC-8s, or helicopters. Any type of machine that could roam the skies intrigued him—particularly if it presented a possible business opportunity.

In 1962, he sold the aircraft maintenance portion of California Airmotive's business to PacAero Engineering Corp. But to convert passenger airliners into air freighters in the early 1970s, he again needed a spacious hangar for the work. In preparation, he merged the resources of California Airmotive into American Jet Industries, Inc. It was the same company, but sported a worldlier name offering added cachet. Paulson purposely made *American* part of the name, as he was a staunch conservative who espoused the value of America's entrepreneurial heritage.

As the airlines shifted from piston- and turboprop-powered airliners to fan jets for passenger service, American Jet emerged as a leader in converting passenger planes to air freighters. It obtained FAA supplemental type certificates to install cargo doors in Convairs, Fairchilds, Electras, and early jetliners such as Convair 880s and Douglas DC-8s. His future plans included lengthening the fuselages of three-engine Boeing 727 passenger jets by 20 feet, turning them into high-capacity freighters. He envisioned a lucrative market for stretched 727s. Almost 600 of the so-called "three-holers" were then in airline passenger service.

The Flying Tiger Line, the nation's pioneering all-cargo airline, moved into a spacious hangar at 2800 North Clybourn Avenue on the Burbank airport in 1947. Three years later it built an identical hangar immediately east of it. Following the purchase of Douglas DC-8 jet freighters in the 1960s, the carrier's headquarters and maintenance operations were relocated to Los Angeles International Airport. The hangars in Burbank, vacant for several years, caused Paulson to negotiate with the airport authority and take over their leasehold. From his office perch in former Flying Tigers Hangar 34, a large window overlooked the hubbub below, where fifty or more mechanics were dismantling airplanes to repurpose them for new lives as freighters. It was an era when airline work was seldom outsourced outside the country and jobs in aviation were plentiful. In 1973, cargo doors were installed in five turboprop Convair 640s bought from Hawaiian Airlines. Converted into freighters, they were sold to Zantop International Airlines in Michigan.

Freighter conversions of four-engine Lockheed L-188 Electras grew out of the experience American Jet gained by converting twin-turboprop Fairchild FH-227 airliners to freighters. The latter program continued for several years. The work was initiated when the company won a sizable contract from Fairchild. By the time the last FH-227 rolled from the hangar American Jet had switched to converting Electras.

The Electra conversion work showed no signs of a letup in spite of stiff competition from major service centers, notably Lockheed Air Service, located 50 miles to the south in Ontario. The increase in business outgrew Paulson's facility. The spacious work bays in the Burbank hangars were too crowded to accommodate any increase in business. In search of a larger facility, Paulson leased a former Lockheed complex at 7001 Woodley Avenue along the east side of Van Nuys Airport. Hangars 901 and 902 in Van Nuys were built in 1943, totaling 126,000-square-feet. They were sited on 38 acres where Lockheed operated a modification center during World War II, flight-tested P-80 fighters in the early 1950s, and developed the AH-56A Cheyenne attack helicopter in the late 1960s. No scheduled airlines operated out of Van Nuys, it serving mostly private and business aircraft, and credited as being the busiest airport in the nation serving general aviation. The move ensured that his workforce would have plenty of elbow room to tackle new projects. The ongoing Electra conversion work occupied one of the hangars, the immense structure capable of housing six of the transports at one time.

The powerful Electra was a Paulson favorite. He dubbed his converted aircraft the "Airlifter." It was an airliner that passengers loved—roomy, fast, and vibration-free, although not as smooth as a 707. But it was the Electra's payload capacity and spirited performance that sold Paulson. Seeking more Electras to convert, he took a bold step to salvage and graft together the airframes of two Electras that crashed on the Alaskan North Slope. Following months of reconstruction, a single, born-again Electra rolled from the Van Nuys hangar, pieced together from the airframe sections of the two wrecked airplanes. After a "maiden flight" in October 1976, the Electra was delivered to Great Northern Airlines in Anchorage to begin its new life as a freighter.

"There is a demand for the Airlifter because it is economical to operate when compared to a jet freighter, it is very reliable, and the L-188 has the capability of operating from a 5,000-foot unimproved airstrip," said Bill Boone, American Jet's director of marketing. "If American Jet could buy additional Electras to convert into cargo aircraft we would have no trouble selling them."[1]

Formerly a Lockheed facility, American Jet Industries occupies the forty-acre site at Van Nuys Airport during the mid–1970s (Paulson family archives/Crystal Christensen).

American Jet refurbished several French-built Nord 262 turboprop airliners for Swift Aire, a Los Angeles–based commuter airline flying schedules between a dozen California cities. Paulson bought the older, high-wing mini airliners from Philippines Airlines and Filipinas Orient Airways. Ferried from the Philippines to Van Nuys, the aircraft were overhauled before delivery to Swift Aire.

Paulson took on projects and assumed risks that other companies wouldn't touch. An example was a National Airlines Boeing 727-235 that crashed in Escambia Bay on final approach to Pensacola Regional Airport in Florida. The accident occurred on May 8, 1978. Out of the fifty-two passengers and six crewmembers aboard, three people drowned. For over a week, the jetliner remained floating off the coast of Pensacola, poising a navigational hazard to maritime traffic. Paulson won a contract to salvage the heavily damaged jetliner. But first, he needed to tow it to shore. The task was not a simple matter.

"Al always had some wild new project going," Bruce McCaw remarked, "like fishing the National Airlines 727 out of the sea." The complicated recovery required a barge. "The barge operator was drunk all the time," he continued, "and I was afraid he was going to run into a bridge and knock it down." Adventure was an integral part of many Paulson projects. As an insurance expert, McCaw got involved with insurance issues having to do with recovering the floating Boeing. "In 1972, I went into the aviation insurance business," he said. "I knew Al quite well by then and wanted his business. I started writing his insurance and gave him something that provided him significantly more coverage. It saved him a lot of money and it brought us closer together."[2]

Spending much time and money recovering, and then transporting, the largely intact 727 airframe to Van Nuys, Paulson re-registered the disassembled airplane as N58AJ with the intent to recondition and sell it. Unfortunately, much of the airframe was submerged in salt water for two weeks before the recovery effort could be started. A detailed inspection of its aluminum fuselage and wing structure revealed there was too much corrosion to make the project worthwhile. After sitting outside the Van Nuys hangar for almost four years, the 727 joined the scrap pile in 1982.

At its peak, 350 employees were involved in converting airliners to freighters and handling spare part sales. The warehouses kept more than 200,000 parts in stock, ranging in size from jetliner wings to cockpit switches. For airlines flying older airplanes, the company was a godsend—stocking parts no longer available from the manufacturers that originally built their aircraft. Paulson monopolized maintenance support for the Electra, buying the entire spare part inventories of Garuda airlines in Indonesia and Pacific Southwest Airlines (PSA) in California when those carriers disposed of their turboprop transports and bought jets.[3]

American Jet's offices and hangars in Van Nuys were anything but opulent. Utilitarian is a better description. Many of the furnishings came from second-hand stores or auctions. Some of the stuff came from Saturday garage sales. Paulson had no interest in impressing visitors with anything except the work underway in the hangars. The philosophy mirrored his insistence on a spartan, close-to-the-vest operation stressing economy without sacrificing quality. "He was a practical thinking kind of guy," Clay Lacy remarked. Paulson had always been an inveterate bargain hunter, managing to scrounge needed items at ridiculously low prices. Budget meetings could be difficult to attend, with him likely to challenge expenditures he considered padded, questionable, or not vitally necessary.

Paulson spoke on the campus of Lynchburg College in April 1983, telling the students that he'd been lucky in his career but had also worked hard to achieve success. His popularity at Lynchburg helped him earn an honorary degree at its commencement ceremony. When the usual honorarium check arrived at his office, he sent it back. A note accompanying the check requested that the money be used to help fund a scholarship for a needy student. "I met his white Gulfstream II jet at the Lynchburg Airport," said Peter Viemeister, an executive at Grumman Aerospace. "As we drove to the campus he noticed a yard sale along the way and suggested that after the ceremony we might stop there and see what they had."[4] As was often the case, Paulson sought bargains, whether airliners or lawnmowers.

A practical thinker as well as occasional joker, Paulson relished those occasions when he could pull a joke on his friends. One of his "victims" was Joe Clark. "I walked into Al's office one day," Clark recalled. "He had a cage on the left side of his desk. It was a wooden box with a little hole in it. You could see a tail sticking out of it. I said to Allen, 'What the hell is that?' He said it was a 'mean little mongoose' caged up. I leaned over it and he said, 'Let's see if I can get him to move around.' There was a spring on the back of the opening. It went *bang* and the thing flew out. I jumped on top of Allen's desk. But it was only a tail—he had pulled a joke on me. This thing flying across the room scared me to death."[5]

Employed to transport rocket sections for NASA's Apollo program, the Pregnant Guppy, a bulbous conversion of the four-engine Boeing Stratocruiser, was retired from service with the agency after it logged more than 6,000 hours. In 1974, after completing a short flight from Santa Barbara to Van Nuys, it taxied onto the American Jet ramp where Paulson welcomed the crew. Along with an even bigger Mini Guppy, he bought the well-worn airplanes in March from Aero Spacelines, their builder, with an unusual mission in mind: fly large sections of damaged aircraft to his Van Nuys facility for rebuilding. Over-the-road transport wasn't always possible. The mini featured a completely new fuselage—the first "wide-body" guppy built. "I think he paid twenty-five grand for the Pregnant Guppy," McCaw remarked, "and about a hundred thousand for the mini." Flown infrequently, the guppies remained parked outside the American Jet hangars. Languishing at Van Nuys for five years, Paulson ordered that the "pregnant" be cannibalized during 1979, its parts sold to a dwindling number of Stratocruiser operators, and salvaging what was left of the airframe. "Al then leased the Mini Guppy," McCaw continued. "An airplane represented money to him whether it was all together or in pieces."[6] Paulson later sold the mini to Aero Union, a Northern California outfit specializing in converting airliners into aerial tankers to fight forest fires. In succession, Erickson Air Crane bought it from Aero Union in 1988 to haul heavy equipment. In 1994, the monster was donated to the Tillamook Air Museum in Oregon, where it remains as the most prominent aircraft on display—in both size and maybe history.

In France, a turboprop-powered Super Guppy was converted from another Stratocruiser. It would transport fuselage sections of jumbo jets built

Upon completing the Pregnant Guppy's first flight on September 19, 1962, are from left, test pilots Jack Conroy and Clay Lacy being greeted by Paulson. The reporter is Stan Chambers from KTLA-TV (Clay Lacy archives).

by vendors of Airbus Industrie. A problem arose: there weren't any lower aft fuselages available from other Stratocruisers to complete the conversion. Paulson came to the rescue and sold Airbus a fuselage section from the dismantled Pregnant Guppy. Shipped to France, the section was grafted into what became the latest version of the venerable plane. It was ironic that the last guppy built contained a major airframe section from the first guppy.

Devoting decades to the aviation business, Paulson knew how to make smart deals, forget about losers, and more often than not, walk away from projects a wealthier man. An inquisitive mind caused him to investigate untried concepts. Even if they didn't morph into successful products, he did conceive fresh ideas.

An all-new aircraft called the Hustler was the next project coming from his mind. It would be his first *completely new* aircraft project—a unique design concept never commercialized before. Zeroing in on its development, he intended to revolutionize airplanes designed to transport business executives.

~ ~ ~

Paulson wasted no time to begin design work for the uniquely different type of airplane in 1974, but revealed little about it publicly. Transporting seven people, it was not a single- or a twin-engine aircraft. Instead, it could be said that it was a combination of both. Although there were two engines, the plane was intended to fly with only the one in its nose operating. The other, located in the tail, would be used on a standby basis to supply extra power on takeoff or during an emergency. "We hit on the idea of installing a small turbojet in the tail and using it as a standby engine," Paulson explained about his out-of-the-box thinking.[7] For aviation traditionalists, it would be a tough concept to swallow.

The Hustler program at American Jet Industries wasn't managed like the committee style that characterized operations in mega corporations. Paulson didn't delegate much, diving headlong into each aspect of the airplane's development from initial concept and engineering to production planning and marketing. Ignoring the fact that his formal education ended with high school, he served as de facto chief engineer. He oversaw detail design of the fuel, electrical, and other systems to gain the reliability he wanted. The systems aboard the original Lear Jet were undependable. There would be no repeat of those shortcomings with this airplane.

"Al was like Bill Lear," Clay Lacy remarked of his friend's attention to detail. "He had a lot of Bill's traits. Bill would walk through the factory every day. He knew what was going on. Al was the same way. He didn't come to the office and start shuffling papers. He would go out in the shop to see what the people were doing."[8] Paulson was similar to Lear in another way: he sometimes spread himself thin by working on too many projects at the same time.

In a patent application filed on September 29, 1976, Paulson documented what made the Hustler tick: "While a nose-mounted turboprop serves as the main power supply a tail-mounted turbojet with only a small fraction of the turboprop horsepower provides a supplementary power source on takeoff or optionally to enhance cruise performance. Should the turboprop fail in flight the turbojet is capable of taking over at a reduced cruising speed."[9]

In the airplane's nose sat an 850-shaft-horsepower Pratt & Whitney PT6A-41 turboprop engine. At the extreme tail end of the fuselage was a 98-pound Teledyne CAE J402-CA-400 turbojet. The engine was originally designed to power target drones for a single flight, being expendable and not FAA-certified to power manned aircraft. Although Paulson knew of this limitation, he remained adamant in using the engine. It developed 640 pounds of thrust and was cheap to buy at $13,000. From early on, however, the question from within the aviation industry was how his airplane could earn FAA certification with one of its engines not being FAA-certified.

The Hustler's compact wing spanned a mere 28 feet compared to the 35-foot span of a Piper Cub. It incorporated a supercritical airfoil section

United States Patent [19]

Paulson

[11]   **4,089,493**

[45]   **May 16, 1978**

[54] AIRCRAFT WITH COMBINATION POWER PLANT

[76] Inventor: Allen E. Paulson, 7701 Woodley Ave., Van Nuys, Calif. 91406

[21] Appl. No.:   727,950

[22] Filed: Sep. 29, 1976

[51] Int. Cl.² B64D 37/00
[52] U.S. Cl. .... 244/135 R; 60/39.28 R;
                         137/567; 244/55; 244/135 C
[58] Field of Search .... 244/135 R, 135 C, 55;
              137/567; 123/136; 60/39.28 R, 224, 243

[56]   **References Cited**

U.S. PATENT DOCUMENTS

B 508,940	2/1976	Risse et al.	244/135 C X
2,817,396	12/1957	Booth	137/567 X
3,419,233	12/1968	Wotton	244/135 R

FOREIGN PATENT DOCUMENTS

1,041,132	9/1966	United Kingdom	244/55

Primary Examiner—Barry L. Kelmachter
Attorney, Agent, or Firm—Harris, Kern, Wallen & Tinsley

[57]   **ABSTRACT**

By employing in-line gas turbine power plants in the nose and tail of a low profile highly streamlined aircraft, twin engine reliability is obtained with only a single engine frontal area combined with the employment of strakes rather than pipes for the nose engine exhaust, excellent fuel economy is obtained. While a nose mounted turboprop serves as the main power supply, a tail mounted turbojet with only a small fraction of the turboprop horsepower provides a supplementary power source during take-off or optionally to enhance cruise performance. Should the turboprop fail in flight the turbojet is capable of taking over at a reduced cruising speed. A fuel system common to both engines offers additional safety features and an improved method for effecting proper trim with either or both engines operative.

6 Claims, 2 Drawing Figures

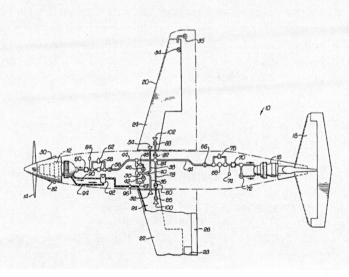

Allen Paulson as inventor, a patent for the Hustler reveals the airplane's design details (U.S. Patent Office).

fitted with full-span Fowler flaps. A novel feature was the elimination of ailerons common to other airplanes. Spoilers controlled the plane's banking.

On October 24, 1975, Paulson unveiled the Hustler 400 to the public. He stuck to the original concept of operating the tail engine strictly on a standby basis. Saving fuel was the prime selling point he stressed, as the nation remained stuck in an energy crisis. Jet fuel was costly and supplies were limited. The airplane was expected to travel 14 miles for each gallon of fuel burned—better than a Cadillac. "We felt the one who gets the most mileage out of a design is the one who will sell more aircraft," he told the press. "We will burn about one-third as much fuel as most twin turboprop designs and about one-tenth that of most twin jets."[10] Waiting in the wings were cynics who questioned the unusual engine configuration. Ignoring them, he continued to promote the unorthodox design.

In an article for *Flying*, writer Peter Garrison dismissed the Hustler as a side show compared to airplanes manufactured by Cessna, Beech, and Piper— the so-called "Big Three." The article infuriated Paulson, who expressed his displeasure in a letter to the magazine's editor: "If only the big three are capable of coming out with a newly-designed aircraft, why are the big three still building aircraft from 30-year-old designs? These companies won't come up with new and innovative ideas unless American Jet, Bill Lear, Ted Smith or some of our foreign competitors force them into it."[11]

When it became clear that Teledyne CAE had no intention of spending money to gain FAA approval for its engine, Paulson contacted Williams International, a manufacturer of small turbine engines. Headquartered in a suburb of Detroit named Walled Lake, the company's founder, prolific inventor Sam Williams, distinguished himself by proving that fanjet technology could be adapted to low thrust turbofan engines. His WR19, first run in 1967, was the

Paulson poses alongside a mockup of the Hustler at American Jet Industries in Van Nuys (Paulson family archives/Crystal Christensen.)

world's smallest turbofan. A version of the WR19 powered a Navy/General Dynamics cruise missile and the USAF/Boeing air-launched cruise missile. Paulson and Williams enjoyed each other's company, possessing like minds. "Sam Williams does not have a hierarchy of committees and boards to go through to make decisions or get products underway," wrote William Gregory in *Aviation Week & Space Technology*. "If Sam Williams decides he wants to do something, he can get started on the spot."[12] It was Paulson's hope that Williams would FAA-certify his small engine for the Hustler.

The Hustler 400 emerged as a star at aviation expositions in 1976, especially the National Maintenance and Operations Meeting in Reading, Pennsylvania. Paulson's mechanics had fabricated a full-size mockup of the airplane to woo the attendees. The method used to transport the mockup from Van Nuys to Pennsylvania created probably as much publicity as the mockup itself. Paulson now owning the Pregnant Guppy, the plane was called on to transport the mockup from California to Pennsylvania. Landing at Reading, following a night and day journey, the morning fog lifted. His mechanics pulled the guppy's tail open to reveal its cavernous cargo hold, giving "birth" to the mockup. Paulson made sure that a reporter was on hand to cover the unusual event and snap photos for the local newspaper.

"The workmanlike presentation of the American Jet Industries Hustler was a surprise for most visitors, many of whom had not previously been convinced that the project was more than a paper exercise," reporter Hugh Field wrote for *Flight International* about the plane's appearance at Reading. "The mockup, making its first public appearance, proved to be detailed and was frequently taken for the real thing."[13]

Paulson told visitors that 85 percent of the airplane's engineering drawings had been released to the shop. The jigs needed to assemble the plane were nearing completion. He planned to manufacture three Hustlers by December, two of them slated for flight testing with the third devoted to ground structural testing. FAA certification was predicted by the middle of 1977. He told reporters that up to $3 million would be spent to fund the airplane's tooling and testing phase.

"By the middle of the show, twenty-six customers had paid a returnable deposit of $10,000," Field continued to report, "knowing that this money would not be employed as working capital." The deposit money wasn't needed as a silent investor was waiting in the wings to bankroll the venture.

Fellow *Flight International* reporter Tom Hamill agreed with Field's appraisal: "Those who scoffed and said that the Hustler was a cardboard project which would never see the light of day must now prepare to changes their views."[14]

Before heading back to California a buoyant Paulson told the media, "You haven't seen anything yet."[15]

Jimmy Carter drove over to Peterson Field, four miles down the road from Plains, Georgia. He told Tom Peterson, the proprietor of the sleepy airport, "We are going to do some flying. I am going to be the next President of the United States."[16] Peterson had a second job as the peanut farmer's personal pilot. Rather than fly in a Boeing 737 during his presidential campaign, Carter preferred that Peterson transport him in a single-engine Cessna 172 Skyhawk. Carter liked the four-seat Cessna, remarking how economical it was to operate and how he could arrive at destinations with little fanfare.

Appalled Secret Service agents were aghast that a nominee for president would ride in such a minuscule airplane. They refused to fly in it, considered it dangerous, and something that wasn't required by their employment contracts. The Cessna continued to transport Carter even after his nomination. Upon winning the election, when cabinet members planned to visit Plains, Carter told Peterson to ferry the VIPs from Atlanta in the Cessna. The wife of one cabinet official said, "I'm not getting into that toy." The next day, Peterson began looking for a bigger airplane.

Enter Allen Paulson. At the time, he pitched the Hustler to anyone who would listen. "Al was trying to sell a Hustler to Peterson," Bruce McCaw remarked. "As president, Carter flew back and forth from Georgia to Washington D.C. in the Cessna. Peterson told me it took half the Marine Corps to escort him in the little bug smasher. He wanted to buy a Hustler to fly Carter back and forth."[17]

During the 1980s when Paulson lived in Georgia, he struck up a friendship with Jimmy and Rosalynn Carter. The industrialist was a founder of the Carter Center, organized by the former president and his wife in 1982 to advance peace and health on a global scale. Carter could identify with Paulson's childhood struggles on the farm. Early in married life, Carter, his wife, and their three sons lived in subsidized public housing in Plains. On their peanut farm, a drought meant there was a nonexistent first year's harvest. To prevent losing the farm, Carter borrowed heavily from local banks. Barely breaking even for years, his efforts finally grew the fledging agribusiness into a rousing success. "I think Jimmy Carter appreciated the fact that Mr. Paulson came from nothing," Kathy O'Sako remarked. "Carter was a peanut farmer, starting in government and working his way up. He had values and morals where they belong." For one of Paulson's birthdays, the presidential couple dropped by his office in Savannah to wish him happy birthday. "They were coming through town and came to see him for a social visit," O'Sako added. "We stood in his office and Jimmy Carter led us in singing happy birthday."[18]

In addition to its appearance in Reading, the Hustler mockup found its way to the Paris Air Show. "It looked like a real airplane," McCaw remarked. "It was pouring rain when this heavyset man saw the open cabin door and jumped in to get out of the rain. He broke the mockup, causing the wing to

President Jimmy Carter visits Paulson at Gulfstream Aerospace in Savannah (Paulson family archives/Crystal Christensen).

fold up at the root. It looked like a bird with a broken wing. Al wrote on a piece of cardboard, 'This is a mockup' and placed it on the windshield."[19] Broken wing or not, the show went on for Paulson. "The only reason Al would be in a crowd of people is if he was there for a purpose," Joe Clark added. "At the Paris show he would press the flesh with customers or meet suppliers. He was comfortable because he knew what he was talking about."[20]

None of the Hustler's original milestones were met. There were technical problems that consumed more time and money than Paulson anticipated. He brought in engineering whiz Gordon Israel during April 1977 to develop solutions. Israel had got to know Paulson from the early days at Lear Jet when the feisty self-taught engineer helped Bill Lear solve problems with the design of his jet's tail.

The first Hustler was pushed out of the Van Nuys hangar in November 1977.

Paulson's positive relationship with the aviation press paid off. Once news of the Hustler hit the pages of national magazines such as *Aviation Week & Space Technology*, it attracted the serious interest of readers. Girard "Jerry" Henderson, a short, tough-talking multi-millionaire aviation enthusiast, was one of them. He began to pay close attention to anything related to Paulson and his new airplane. "Jerry read about Allen Paulson developing the Hustler in Van Nuys," said Greg Henderson, his grandson. "He always was interested in anything innovative."[21]

Paulson needed an investor to subsidize the enormous cost of the Hustler's prolonged development program. Henderson showed up at an opportune time to offer a helping hand. In short order, he bought a 45 percent stake in American Jet Industries to provide the working capital needed for FAA certification of the aircraft. Not one to relinquish control, Paulson insisted on remaining majority shareholder, retaining 55 percent and continuing to manage the company's day-to-day operations. Their agreement stipulated that Henderson would remain strictly a passive investor.

Henderson had witnessed the evolution of aviation from its earliest days. "The streets were mobbed," he recalled in watching Charles Lindbergh's ticker tape parade along the streets of Manhattan in 1927. "It was exciting seeing people throw papers from the windows. Lindbergh was sitting in a car with the mayor of New York. It was at that time that I decided that I was going to get into aviation."[22] In 1929, at the age of twenty, he learned to fly at the Newark Airport. During the 1930s, he bought a single-engine Beechcraft Model D17S Staggerwing biplane and chartered it to wealthy business executives. During the next forty years, he owned dozens of airplanes, some large and some small, and knew how to fly each of them.

Considered to be more than a wealthy man who owned and flew airplanes, Henderson was best known as a major shareholder of the former California Perfume Co., a family owned business. The name was changed to Avon Products, Inc. in 1939. Following World War II, Avon became publicly owned, its stock trading on the New York Stock Exchange. The stock took off like a rocket in the 1960s when Henderson owned most of the company's equity. He became a millionaire many times over, providing him the wherewithal to invest in ventures he found offbeat or interesting.

Besides his investment in Avon, Henderson owned a company called Underground World Homes. He was convinced that diplomatic relations between the U.S. and the U.S.S.R. would collapse during the Cold War, both countries ending up destroyed by nuclear conflagration. He pitched the idea of living underground to escape the resulting inferno to anyone who would listen. At the 1964 New York World's Fair, he sponsored an exhibit titled "Why Live Underground." If Henderson had to wait out the end of the world underground, he decided to do it in a stylish subterranean home.[23]

Beyond his holdings in Avon and the underground living project, Henderson had no shortage of business interests. A side street in Monterey, California, is named for him, acknowledging his pioneering contributions to cable TV in that region. A staunch Republican, he formed the Alexander

Dawson Foundation, named for his father, dedicating its resources to furthering a politically conservative education for deserving students. In 1967, he established the Colorado Junior Republic School, beginning as a summer school to teach underprivileged kids. The school's curriculum later morphed into a year-round college preparatory program. The name was changed to Alexander Dawson School in 1980.

According to the Alexander Dawson School's website: "Jerry didn't like long hair on boys. He couldn't stand rock and roll, which he defined as any music written after 1945. He believed in freedom, hard work and self-reliance. He believed that America was the greatest country in the world that capitalism was the best economic system and together they offered astounding opportunity. While Timothy Leary was telling kids to 'Tune in. Turn on. Drop out,' Jerry was telling them, 'Work hard. Love your country. Get a haircut.'"[24] Henderson was blunt and outspoken, a man with strong beliefs who offered opinions on worldly topics to anyone within hearing range. "Henderson, like Paulson, is a loner," noted an article in the *Washington Post*, "part of a vanishing breed of sole proprietors who do not have to justify their actions to stockholders or anyone else."[25]

Unlike the routine activities normally associated with an airplane's first flight, Paulson orchestrated a carnival-like event at American Jet Industries for the Hustler's big day. "Van Nuys Airport was wild with personalities and three-piece suits, with half the crowd sporting promotional baseball caps made especially for the occasion," reported an article in *Flying* describing the turnout for the Hustler 400's first flight.[26] The caps had the letters *AJI* sewn on them. The airplane impressed journalists who followed its snail-paced evolution: "The Hustler 400 is built to draw crowds," *Flying* reported. "Gaze upon it and the word handsome does not come to mind as hardly do words like futuristic, unconventional, maverick, unique. It is all those and more." The Hustler 400 took to the air for a 40-minute initial flight on January 11, 1978. Paulson handled the controls with Joe Guthrie acting as copilot. During Guthrie's twenty-eight years in the U.S. Air Force he served as a forward air controller in the Korean War before moving into flying classified reconnaissance missions during the Cold War. Rounding out his career, he served as commander of the test pilot school at Edwards Air Force Base from 1972 to 1975.

Paulson and Guthrie took off from Van Nuys and landed at Mojave where the aircraft would be based for its first 10 hours of testing. All went well on the flight, except as Paulson noted after landing, the plane had a "slight rudder control problem."[27] The rudder's blunt leading edge disturbed the airflow over the empennage, requiring excessive rudder pedal movement to turn the airplane. It was back to the drawing board for what turned out to be an easy fix. The second prototype was expected to fly in March.

Encouraged by news of the long-awaited maiden flight, buyers lined up to place orders. Over the months to come, cash deposits came in for sixty-seven Hustler 400s. Cracking the whip to move the development program along, Paulson predicted that the aircraft would be FAA-certified in eight months. He hoped to manufacture seventy planes during 1978 and 1979. He held the $10,000 deposits in escrow and guaranteed buyers specific delivery dates. The first seventy airplanes were priced at $765,000 each.

He made an unexpected announcement in April 1978: the Hustler would be FAA-certified as a *true* twin-engine airplane. "The first idea was to put a small auxiliary engine in, a get-you-home type." he said in an interview. "The FAA wouldn't buy that. They said, 'No, you've either got to be a single or a true twin.' They put a restriction on: the engine would have to hack it if you lost the front one on takeoff ... so the second engine had to have enough power for that purpose."[28] Because the Williams engine didn't have sufficient thrust to keep the plane in the air if the front engine failed, Paulson had no choice but to switch to a larger engine or abandon the project.

He expedited the airplane's redesign to develop a version with an FAA-certified Pratt & Whitney Canada JT15D-1 turbofan installed in the tail. It developed 2,200 pounds of thrust. Other major changes included replacing the spoilers with ailerons and reducing the size of the plane's previous full-span flaps to two-thirds of the wingspan. In talking with prospective buyers, Paulson discovered that most of them wanted a true twin-engine aircraft and not what he originally offered. By changing the rear engine, it appeared like he nailed down the correct propulsion configuration. The design was about to be frozen. He expected to try for the FAA's blessing during the first half of 1979.

In September 1978, after the Hustler 400 had logged 120 hours in the air, he described its performance as "really good." It was a fast machine, offering a cruise speed of more than 400 miles per hour. After adopting a new low-set horizontal stabilizer, "stability and control, particularly in roll, is beautiful," he said.[29] The prototype's T-tail was originally positioned inside the arc of the propeller's airflow. The unwanted consequence was that any change in engine power would cause erratic changes in the airplane's pitch attitude. It was Gordon Israel who concocted a solution by moving the horizontal stabilizer to a lower position. The plane was re-designated the Hustler 500.

"There is strong customer interest for a true twin-engine Hustler, and with the Model 500, the pilot has the option of operating a twin or extending its range by shutting down the JT15 in flight," Paulson said.[30]

The only Hustler in existence started making the rounds of as many aviation exhibitions as possible. Anticipating military interest, he planned to build a version configured with a two-seat tandem cockpit using components from a Northrop T-38 Talon jet trainer. It would be marketed as a nine-g fully aerobatic jet to train student pilots. Competition included the turboprop-powered T-34C Turbo-Mentor built by Beech, an airplane that Paulson dismissed as "non-competitive." He went on to study special mission versions of the Hustler. He even proposed selling it to the Air Force with special modifications to replace aging Lockheed U-2s used as high-altitude photographic survey aircraft. None of these variants materialized.

Hustler 500 testing began in January 1981 at Van Nuys and continued in Mojave. The final design change was to replace the front-mounted PT6A with a more powerful 900-shaft-horsepower Garrett TPE331 turboprop. Although the design was supposedly frozen, studies to change the propulsion configuration continued, such as eliminating the nose engine and substituting two turbofan engines at the rear. As an inventor, Paulson found it difficult to resist tweaking the design.

The Hustler program continued to build momentum. The true test of its worth would come when the plane was readied for production. There would be future complications in doing so.

Paulson was pulled in many directions in the 1970s. His airliner sales and parts business continued to throw off cash. He dabbled in flying adventures with Lacy, Conroy, and Salmon. But the Super Pinto hadn't met expectations. He succeeded in selling it for others to dabble in, but was lucky in doing so. The Hustler was showing promise, but he remained unfulfilled about what he most wanted: to become a major aircraft manufacturer.

"He had nerve and guts to do things that were unusual," Lacy remarked. "He'd get an idea he believed in and went all the way, whether it was a success or wasn't a success. And fortunately, there were more successes than failures."[31]

At fifty-nine years old, Paulson had raised himself from poverty, a kid living in a farming town on the Mississippi, scrubbing floors and selling newspapers to survive, followed by climbing the ladder of business, rung by rung, truly a Horatio Alger story.

8

Golden Goose

Thirty-five miles east of New York City in Bethpage, Grumman Aircraft Engineering Corp. built fighter planes for decades; they became a mainstay of U.S. Navy operations aboard aircraft carriers. The airplanes proved so robust that the company earned a reputation as the "Grumman Iron Works." Its board of directors came to believe that Grumman products were indispensable to the Navy. In the mid–1950s, this proved to be a dangerous assumption. The military's emphasis was beginning to shift to buying more guided missiles and fewer airplanes. Exclusively a defense contractor, the aviation giant needed relief from the vicissitudes of Pentagon spending. Developing products for civilian markets seemed like a logical solution for the dilemma.

Old timers on the board recalled that building aircraft for civil aviation wasn't anything new for the company. It began manufacturing twin-engine amphibious planes in 1936, many of the versatile aircraft finding use in transporting business executives. The planes were named for feathered creatures such as Goose, Widgeon, and Mallard. By the time Grumman stopped producing the airplanes, it had built more amphibians than any other manufacturer. Production of the planes took a hiatus during World War II for enabling the company to concentrate on building warplanes for the Navy. Grumman named these and other airplanes for members of the cat family. The love of animals ran in founder Leroy Grumman's blood.

Under Leroy Grumman's coaxing, the board voted to authorize development of aircraft for commercial use. In late 1955, Grumman engineers began work on an airplane designed to fill a niche in that marketplace. Neither a light plane nor an airliner, it was designed for a single mission: crop pesticide spraying. Marketing research pointed to an expanding need for pest control application aircraft. Older aircraft, primarily Boeing Stearman biplanes, were then employed to spray agricultural fields but faced obsolescence. Grumman's single-engine G-164 AgCat made its first flight on May 27, 1957. The Bethpage factory chocked full of aircraft being assembled for the Navy, a production line for the "crop dusters" couldn't be squeezed in. To solve the capacity crunch, production was subcontracted to the Schweizer Aircraft Co. of Elmira, New York. The company would go on to build the AgCat continuously between 1957 and 1981, eventually turning out 2,455 of the odd-looking, purpose-built biplanes.

Douglas DC-3s converted into "offices of the air" dominated the business fleets of Fortune 500 corporations in the mid–1950s. Well on their way to obsolescence, Grumman executives pondered whether or not to develop a turbine-powered airplane to replace them and similar sized piston-powered transports. It would bring in more revenue than AgCat production generated. Market research substantiated the belief that manufacturing a turbine-powered "mini-airliner" to transport executives would be profitable. Grumman engineers began preliminary design work for such an airplane in early 1957.

The decision to develop a business airplane, albeit one selling for at least a million dollars, confused analysts on Wall Street. That is, until the doubters discovered that the nation's corporations owned more than a thousand large, multi-engine piston airplanes to fly their executives in. Most of the planes were of wartime vintage. Their owners would be logical customers for the aircraft taking shape in Bethpage. If only one-fourth of those corporations bought the airplanes, it would translate into an impressive return on investment for Grumman. The project got unanimous endorsement.

At the peak of the airplane's development program 250 employees worked on it, their efforts resulting in an eye-catching, nineteen-passenger, 36,000-pound transport powered by two Rolls-Royce RB53 Dart turboprop engines. Designated the Gulfstream G-159, later simply known as the GI, its name was derived from the Gulf Stream, an ocean current flowing along the Florida coastline. The GI's first flight took place on August 14, 1958, from a privately owned runway adjacent to the factory in Bethpage.

The GI could move along at a 350-mile-per-hour clip, covering an impressive nonstop range of 2,200 nautical miles. Unlike the older piston transports, it could undertake transcontinental flights without refueling. Inside its pressurized and air-conditioned cabin, a 6-foot-tall passenger could stand without the inconvenience of bending over. Unlike the DC-3 with its throbbing piston engines, the GI's smooth and powerful turbines meant it could fly over stormy weather. Once in production, the GI found itself in competition with Fairchild F-27 airliners and turbine-powered conversions of twin-engine Convair 440s. But the GI was the only executive transport on the market tailored to the specific needs of corporate users. The other planes were one-time airliners modified with plush cabin appointments. Grumman relied on its "one of a kind" sales strategy to sway buyers to its million-dollar product.

The first airplane of the Grumman Gulfstream family: the turboprop GI. First flown August 14, 1958 (©Gulfstream Aerospace Corporation, reproduced with permission).

On the military aircraft side of the business, Grumman scored a triumph in the early 1960s. It won a series of sizable contracts from the Navy to build A-6 Intruder attack planes and E-2 Hawkeye early warning surveillance aircraft. A satisfactory balance now existed between military and commercial aircraft production with the Gulfstream and AgCat in production.

The GIs became so popular with their owners that Grumman was asked to develop a jet-powered version of the airplane. Many owners were Fortune 500 companies having deep pockets and staffed by flight department managers who needed to whisk their executives to meetings at ever-faster speeds. Responding to an overwhelming demand, deciding what to do was an easy decision for the board. It gave the jet project a firm go-ahead on May 5, 1965.

On an accelerated schedule, Grumman engineers created the GI's successor. It was designated the G-1159—more popularly known as the GII. By the time a full-size mockup was fabricated, thirty firm orders were received. Based on the company's reputation producing warplanes, and because Rolls-Royce engines powered its civil aircraft, the GI and GII were branded as the "Rolls-Royces of business aircraft." Corporate pilots, many with military flying backgrounds, believed that any aircraft built by the Iron Works would be a winner. "Grumman Gulfstream, with the Rolls Royce image added, had the same cachet as Tiffany or the Waldorf Astoria," said George Skurla, president of Grumman Aerospace during the 1980s.[1] Graduating from the University of Michigan in 1944, Skurla began a forty-two year career at Grumman, starting as an apprentice mechanic in the factory.

The phase normally devoted to building a prototype was skipped to rush the GII into production. The first plane off the assembly line completed a 52-minute maiden flight on October 2, 1966. Its foremost requirement was to replicate the GI's ability to land at airports having short runways. The GII proved that it had a similar capability, coupled with significantly greater cruising speed and range. For propulsion, the GI's turboprops were passé—two Rolls-Royce Spey turbofan engines straddled the sides of the aft fuselage, similar to a DC-9 jetliner. Completing its test program with few surprises, the GII entered full-scale production.

"The lineage of the Gulfstream can be seen very clearly in this new project, which is indeed a very beautiful aero plane," reporter Michael Sutton wrote in the March 1964 issue of *Flight International*. "Carrying two jets in tail pods, it has all the grace and beauty of [what] one would expect from a thoroughbred born in the Grumman stable."[2]

Sutton was correct. Over the span of half a century the original GII

The first business jet built by Grumman: the GII. First flown November 2, 1966 (©Gulfstream Aerospace Corporation, reproduced with permission).

evolved into a series of upgraded Gulfstreams that continue to set a standard for performance, luxury, and safety.

Sprawled along the Savannah River, approximately 20 miles from the Atlantic Ocean, Savannah served as the first state capital of Georgia in 1733. The Port of Savannah, manufacturing, the military and tourism, have long constituted the city's major economic drivers. In spite of this apparent prosperity, the area's unemployment rate in the 1960s remained stubbornly high, even with a willing and trainable populace ready to work. The city's economic development director was tasked to pinpoint industrial companies in the northeast that might consider relocating. An established company like Grumman would prop up the city's anemic tax base.

After negotiating a relocation agreement with the city, Grumman moved its GII manufacturing operations from Bethpage to the airport in Savannah, dedicating a newly constructed facility on September 29, 1967. The city sweetened the relocation deal by selling $7.5 million worth of airport revenue bonds to pay for construction of the 260,000-square-foot assembly building leased by Grumman. Located on 110 acres of Travis Field, forerunner of today's Savannah/Hilton Head International Airport, the facility would house all GII production and flight test operations.

Seeking a refreshed corporate identity in 1969, the Bethpage manufacturer's name was changed to Grumman Aerospace Corp. But all was not well. Rising costs, combined with a recession, contributed to a financial stranglehold. On December 30, 1970, the picture worsened: the company's prototype F-14 jet fighter built for the Navy crashed after a failure of its hydraulic system. Test pilot Bob Smyth ejected safely—the same man who commanded the maiden flight of the GII. The F-14 had first flown only nine days earlier, casting doubts about its airworthiness. Adding to the stress felt by executives in Bethpage, Grumman was later forced to absorb losses of more than $220 million under its original F-14 contract with the Navy. The military made it adhere to the same pricing it agreed to under a fixed price contract signed in 1968. After endless arm-twisting that eventually resulted in the company pleading poverty, Grumman persuaded the Department of Defense to cover some of the costs.

Moving into the early 1970s, the financial condition of Grumman vacillated between solid and shaky. On a positive note, the Navy's EA-6B Prowler and F-14 Tomcat reigned as Grumman's top military products—the Tomcat featured prominently in *Top Gun*. The company became prime contractor for the Apollo Lunar Module that landed Americans on the moon in July 1969. As work on the Apollo program neared completion, Grumman competed to build the Space Shuttle, but lost the business to Rockwell International. The piggybank in Bethpage was nowhere full. Grumman's net worth and cash on hand had sunk to such low levels that it asked the Navy to pay in advance for the aircraft it ordered. The move was unprecedented. If the Navy wouldn't pay, Grumman made it clear that the company could easily end up in bankruptcy. It was a wake-up call for Pentagon procurement officials. After the Navy grudgingly approved the prepayments, the unusual action stirred up a hornet's nest on Capitol Hill. In Senate subcommittee hearings, a revelation surfaced about how Grumman executives had invested the cash advances in short-term U.S. government securities—and *didn't* use the money to pay the invoices of suppliers as earlier promised. Those investments produced $2.8 million of income, causing Grumman's critics to call the practice "illegal" and "improper." For the first time in Grumman's illustrious history, its corporate credibility was on the line. To shift public opinion away from the questionable practices, the company continued to explore markets outside of the defense industry.

As fast as the GII's sales trajectory shot up in 1967, it headed in the opposite direction within a few years. Following the initial slug of orders, many of them from existing GI owners, sales dwindled. A row of unsold Gulfstreams sat on the ramp in Savannah. "It was by no means selling like hotcakes," said Skurla.[3] A deepening recession did nothing to bolster sales at Grumman or other aircraft manufacturers. Rather than curtail GII production and reassert its dominance producing military aircraft, the company diversified into a field it knew little about—light aircraft production. Grumman found a manufacturer that was already producing such aircraft in volume: American Aviation Corp. Operating under the name Bede Aviation Corp., American Aviation started life in Cleveland, Ohio, owing to the inventive mind of designer and promoter Jim Bede. A short time after earning a degree in aeronautical engineering, he joined North American Aviation in Columbus as a design engineer. Bede's stay there was brief due to a youthful, restless nature, returning to his Cleveland roots in 1961 to form the aircraft company with his father. He knew that buying a light plane assembled in a factory wasn't affordable for most middle-class recreational fliers. Bede convinced the weekend pilots to assemble their own airplanes using the kits he sold. He explained that factory labor comprised the major cost of aircraft built by Cessna, Beech, and Piper. To eliminate the cost of the labor, Bede Aviation Corp. sold a kit-built airplane called the Bede BD-1. It could be assembled in a customer's garage as a so-called "homebuilt," permitted for flight only as an experimental aircraft with many restrictions.

A conventional, low-wing, single-engine, two-seat airplane best describes the BD-1. Following a first flight on July 11, 1963, further refinement of the do-it-yourself kits dragged on, causing expenses to soar over budget. In the midst of perfecting the aircraft, disagreements arose between the outspoken Bede and the company's principal shareholders. In 1965, several of them forced him to step aside and resign as board chairman. Although Bede still owned a sizable number of shares, he ended up serving in a powerless consultant capacity at the company he started three years earlier.

Bede Aviation's name was changed to American Aviation Corp in 1966. The manufacturer also gained a permanent president: Russell Meyer, Jr., a thirty-four-year-old former Marine Corps fighter pilot—and the lawyer for a group of shareholders that ousted Bede. As for Bede, he lost interest in the company's affairs and sold most of his stock to the other investors.

Rather than sell kits to homebuilders, Meyer's strategy centered upon manufacturing the plane's component parts as done before—but then assembling them into finished airplanes inside a factory and not in someone's garage. Under Meyer's direction, American Aviation kept the basic configuration of the BD-1 but dropped an expensive metal-bonding process used to fabricate the airframe. The change paved the way to simplify the FAA certification process for the plane. In acknowledgment of its certified status, the BD-1 was renamed the American AA-1 Yankee. The public's first look at the aircraft took place at the Reading Air Show in 1968. Over a two-year period, 350 of the two-seaters were sold to a mix of flight training schools and private pilots. Work began in June 1970 on a four-seat version. Two variants of it were introduced, named the AA-5A Cheetah and the AA-5B Tiger.

In 1972, Grumman made a move to buy the Cleveland firm's stock with the proviso that Russ Meyer remain as president. He had pulled the company onto its feet following the missteps of Bede, causing the board in Bethpage to take note of his leadership.

Paying American Aviation's shareholders for their equity presented a problem. Plagued with a diminishing backlog of defense contracts and slow sales of the GII, Grumman didn't have enough cash on hand. "We didn't have any money to buy anybody," John Carr said, Grumman's vice chairman.[4] Because Grumman couldn't afford to make a cash buyout, it gave the Ohioans a minority interest in a newly formed subsidiary called Grumman American Aviation Corp. The subsidiary's most promising asset was the Gulfstream II program and the plant in Savannah. Grumman Aerospace owned 80 percent of the new entity. Contributing $4.8 million of American Aviation assets, the Cleveland group received 20 percent of the new company's equity, plus warrants allowing it to buy another 23 percent of the stock three years after closing the deal. Leading the minority shareholder group was Art Modell. Described as "tough and demanding" by one observer, Modell was the multi-millionaire owner of the Cleveland Browns professional football team.

Based on the Iron Work's longstanding reputation of delivering on its promises, and with all parties in agreement, the acquisition closed escrow on January 2, 1973. But not long after the papers were signed, Modell and two of the minority shareholders protested some of the policies of Grumman

Aerospace. They claimed the company was making self-serving decisions that were not in the best interests of all shareholders.

The Grumman American plant, originally constructed to manufacture nothing but kits, sat a few miles from the shore of Lake Erie on the outskirts of downtown Cleveland. Because the kits were no longer produced, workers spent their days cranking out about 500 of the factory-built airplanes a year. Newly formed Grumman American competed in the small aircraft market but most of its dollar volume came from selling GIIs and AgCats. Its status boosted by the sales of pricy Gulfstreams, the Savannah company emerged as the fourth largest general aviation manufacturer in the world, behind Cessna, Beech, and Piper. Russ Meyer received much of the credit for this success.

Meyer's newfound stature helped get him elected to the presidency of the General Aviation Manufacturers Association in 1973. The appointment attracted the attention of Dwane Wallace, board chairman at Cessna Aircraft Co. In an unexpected move, Meyer left Grumman American during the summer of 1974 to join Cessna as its executive vice president. The Cleveland operation didn't lack a president for long. Corwin "Corky" Meyer, a senior vice president in Bethpage and board member of the Grumman American subsidiary, assumed the vacant post. Unrelated to Russ Meyer, Corky had spent years in Bethpage testing Grumman's airplanes. From the chief test pilot's job he moved to the front office and then on to Cleveland—but wasn't impressed with what he saw. He felt that the climate and smokestack image of the region was the wrong place to locate a progressive aircraft manufacturer. "Cleveland was not an ideal place for an aviation company," said Skurla in referring to the harsh winters interrupting flight testing operations there.[5] Because vacant land was available at the Gulfstream site in Savannah, another building was erected. All general aviation management, manufacturing, and marketing functions were relocated from Cleveland, but only a small contingent of employees decided to transfer. The move severed the few ties that Grumman maintained with the former Cleveland operation, those relationships seemingly unimportant to Corky Meyer. Skurla noted that the Ohio transplants "seemed to get along very well with Corky at the Savannah operation."[6] By Christmas 1976, the Savannah facility jumped in size by 60 percent.

Deliveries of the moneymaking GIIs continued. Meanwhile, Grumman American's engineers began to research another opportunity. It was a remake of the venerable GI to transform the turboprop into a turbofan-powered transport. For commuter airlines and military customers, a smaller size airplane than the GII, but one considerably larger than a Lear Jet, would fill a neglected gap in the marketplace. Designated the G-159A, the aircraft would retain the basic airframe and systems of the GI, but incorporate a stretched fuselage to seat up to thirty passengers. Two 6,500-pound-thrust Avco Lycoming ALF-502D turbofans would replace the 2,190-shaft-horsepower Rolls-Royce Dart turboprops.[7] Detailed studies of the airplane's sales potential were developed to assist the Grumman board of directors make a decision whether to proceed or not. Consumed with more pressing issues, they said *no* and the project died.

Three years after the acquisition, the Grumman board learned that the light plane manufacturing business was just about in the black. The only issue that nobody wanted to discuss was how the AA-1 Yankee flew—and *why* a number of them had crashed and killed people. The airplane could surprise a pilot while trying to recover from a spin. "We were not told how serious the Yankee's spin problem was," Skurla said of the time when Grumman bought American Aviation.[8] Litigation arising from the fatal crashes was increasingly haunting the company.

Unbridled enthusiasm on the part of customers welcomed the GII during its introduction in 1965. A little over a decade later that euphoria continued when a concept for the next generation of the jet was unveiled—the Gulfstream III. Grumman American marketers briefed the press about the jet's superlatives in November 1976. The need for a longer-range version of the GII had become evident as more corporations were flying international as well as transcontinental trips. The GIII would handle those trips easily with its range of more than 4,000 nautical miles. To prevent pilot fatigue and not exceed crew duty time limits in the cockpit, the GIII was expected to reach its destinations in no more than 8 hours at a cruising speed exceeding Mach 0.8. To attain such performance, Grumman developed an all-new wing, featuring winglets at the tips, to take advantage of the latest "supercritical" aerodynamic technology. Technically, it was a wing designed to delay the onset of drag in the transonic speed range. The goals were greater speed, range, and improved fuel economy, the latter a requirement because a prolonged energy crisis was keeping fuel costs high. The price of a barrel of oil showed no sign of returning to what it was in the 1960s. Gas-guzzling business jets were fast becoming passé.

The GIII suffered an aborted birth. Its complex supercritical wing proved too expensive to build, resulting in the entire program being cancelled in June 1977. Grumman spent more than $120 million to design the GIII before reaching the planned prototype stage. When the company unveiled the airplane's concept a half-year earlier, its selling price was estimated at $6.4 million, not including avionics or cabin interior. Immediately prior to the program's cancellation, the estimate rose to $12 million. Forecasting sales of 300 airplanes, Grumman already received forty orders, each one accompanied by a $100,000 deposit. All deposits were refunded with interest.

The failed program angered the senior executives in Bethpage. The company had wasted money that was needed for other operations. It also upset the most vocal of the minority shareholders in Cleveland: David Ingalls, Duane Stranahan, and Art Modell. But the GIII fiasco wasn't the only thing upsetting them. They were disgusted with Corky Meyer's management style. And even more upset when the Securities and Exchange Commission was planning to probe Grumman's alleged illegal payments to foreign buyers of its F-14s and Gulfstreams. The rift between Cleveland and Savannah was widening by the day. Meyer was removed from running the subsidiary to lessen the tension, but Jack Bierwirth, Grumman Aerospace chairman, didn't like the minority shareholders telling him what to do. The prevailing sentiment in the Grumman boardroom was that its subsidiary was an annoying venture that didn't contribute enough income to prop up the parent company's bottom line. If someone had shown up with oodles of cash it would have changed hands in a flash.

It would be another year before a revised design of the GIII came off the company's drawing board. The expensive wing disappeared, replaced by a modified wing from the proven GII. The "new" GIII would come to represent a new beginning for Grumman American—with an unlikely new owner at its helm.

~ ~ ~

In the mid-twentieth century the city of Bethany offered a case of culture shock for aircraft engineers relocating from more liberal Los Angeles. Most prominent was the Oklahoma city's tepid pace. Longtime residents appeared to stick together with remarkably similar work, moral, and religious beliefs. Founded in 1909, Bethany evolved into a community where members of the Church of the Nazarene openly expressed their religious beliefs. The city hadn't forgotten its humble roots seventy years later. Located 10 miles across the prairie from Oklahoma City, part of U.S. Route 66 ran directly through Bethany's downtown area.

Dominated by an agriculture-based economy, it surprised outsiders that the small city was home to a manufacturer of airplanes designed for business travel. The company was a division of Rockwell International—the latest name for a corporation renamed North American-Rockwell in 1967 following its merger with North American Aviation. Beyond producing aircraft, Rockwell companies manufactured everything from power tools and parking meters to truck axles and ball bearings.

In 1958, Willard Rockwell and his son spearheaded their company's purchase of what was originally called Aero Design & Engineering Co. As licensed pilots, they took special interest in the company's operations. By 1978, the father retired and his son was about to join him. Rockwell's new leaders decided that its general aviation business had run its course. Soured by depressed sales and increased manufacturing costs, they wanted out of the aviation industry. The word on the street was that the aircraft division in Bethany was about to go on sale to the highest bidder.

The Bethany plant had its beginning in 1951 when iconic light airplane designer Ted Smith began manufacturing Aero Commander executive transports there. A major investor living in Oklahoma had caused him to relocate the fledgling operation from Los Angeles to Bethany. Compared to competing airplanes, owners of twin-engine Aero Commanders considered them to be Cadillacs of the business aircraft fleet. President Dwight Eisenhower was a regular passenger aboard the planes. The company's products were popular but Rockwell couldn't sell enough of them to make the effort worthwhile.

More than 1,200 workers in the plant waited to hear their fate. They built both twin-engine, high-wing, turboprop-powered Aero Commanders, along with single-engine four-seaters called Commander 112s and 114s. In its haste to strengthen the company's positioning in the general aviation marketplace, Rockwell had developed still another twin-engine, piston-powered executive transport. Unlike the existing Aero Commanders, it had a low wing configuration. Featuring a pressurized cabin to keep occupants comfortable at higher altitudes, the plane carried four passengers compared to the seven-seat Commanders. Fuji Heavy Industries and Rockwell signed an agreement to develop the aircraft as a joint venture. Design work began in Japan during 1971. In June 1974, Rockwell named the plane the Commander 700 for the North American market. The first of five prototypes flew on November 13, 1975, followed by FAA certification on October 31, 1977.

There was little or no interest from major aircraft manufacturers such as Beech, Cessna, or Piper to buy the Rockwell division. A long shot was Paulson, whose Hustler 500 required more production space than available in his overcrowded American Jet Industries hangars. "Word had gotten out that I was in the market to buy a company," Paulson said.[9] He spread the word about what he sought. Familiar with the spacious factory in Bethany, its skilled workforce, and satisfied with the quality of Aero Commander products, Paulson considered the Oklahoma facility a logical place to manufacture the Hustler. Following a meeting with Rockwell executives, he prepared to visit Bethany and considered making an offer.

A tour of the plant satisfied him, but his pitch for the company didn't resonate with executives sitting on the opposite side of a conference table. The negotiations collapsed shortly after talks began. The deal died because the Rockwell team felt that the Hustler 500 and Commander 700 would compete with each other, even though one was turbine-powered and two piston engines powered the other. Rockwell had delivered a total of twenty-five Commander 700s at the time of the negotiations. Paulson refused to pay a premium price for the company because Rockwell included the value of the

700 program as a part of the deal—and he expected the Hustler to render the 700 obsolete. Holding steady, Rockwell wouldn't drop the price. Abandoning what appeared to be a futile exercise, Paulson explored whether Rockwell might consider selling its Sabreliner business jet program. A dated, twin-engine, mid-size business jet first flown in 1958, the plane could carry as many as twelve passengers. North American Aviation owned the program when that company was acquired by Rockwell-Standard in 1967. Preliminary discussions bogged down, leaving Paulson stymied in his quest to find a suitable factory for building the Hustler.

While Paulson searched for a company to acquire, the word was spreading around the corporate office at Grumman Aerospace in Bethpage that the Grumman American subsidiary might be sold. John Carr, Grumman's vice chairman, became privy to a flurry of bad news that favored selling it. More negativity contributed to the scenario, as a lackluster economy made Gulfstream IIs about as difficult to sell as used Edsels. Grumman's vice president of development, Peter Viemeister, was told to work up a list of possible buyers for the subsidiary.

The 1970s were rife with investigations of the nation's major aircraft manufacturers. Some of the companies were orchestrating under-the-table payoffs to overseas agents for enticing foreign countries to buy American-made aircraft. Members of Congress took a dim view of the illicit deal making. In 1976, the senior executives of Lockheed Corp. caused $20 million in bribes to be slipped to such agents for selling L-1011 TriStar jetliners.

The following year, the world community condemned Uganda's Idi Amin for his disregard of the sanctity of human life. He ordered the deaths of 300,000 political opponents. The ruthless dictator had seized power and installed himself as president of the beleaguered country. The bad publicity for Grumman was that Amin was flying around in a Gulfstream II. Making matters worse, there was a rumor that he received a new Cadillac from Grumman's sales agent as a gift for buying the jet. Under pressure from Congress, federal investigators visited Bethpage to determine if Grumman had violated the Foreign Corrupt Practices Act. Passed by Congress in 1977, the law banned American companies from bribing foreign customers either directly or through their agents. In addition to the sale of Gulfstreams, the SEC and Justice Department began to probe whether Grumman officials had made illegal payments to promote sales of F-14 jet fighters to Iran.

"The cloud has extended over the Grumman American subsidiary, whose leading sales agent, Page Airways, has been accused by the SEC of paying off government officials in Africa and elsewhere to foster sales of the Gulfstream II," reported an article in the *Washington Post*.[10] Although the agent at Page insisted that his actions were lawful, the SEC continued probing the work of anyone associated with foreign sales of the jets. The investigation was intense: personal bank accounts, money transfers, travel documents, and sale contracts.

Facing the threat of investigations coming at Grumman from all sides, fifty-four-year-old chairman John Bierwirth told his executives: "I think [the] best thing in the world would be if somebody would buy the Gulfstream business from us."[11] The overseas payment investigation appeared to be the impetus for unloading Grumman American, but slow sales of *all* business jets intensified the pressure to move in that direction. For another take on why Grumman decided to sell, Viemeister surmised, "I suspect that one factor was a desire to avoid a risk of tarnishing the parent corporation's reputation for integrity."[12] Anticipating a disastrous outcome for the company, possibly bankruptcy, Bierwirth and his fellow board members seldom got a good night's sleep.

In 1977, as a corporate vice president at Grumman, Viemeister tried to sell the aircraft subsidiary. His assignment was to quietly discuss the possibilities with a potential buyer until a deal looked like a sure thing. A leak to the press would signal the appearance of a desperation sale and cause Grumman's stock to plummet. "I went on a merry chase, following leads from members of the Grumman board," he said. "I would visit the prospect, usually alone, to brief him and answer any questions."[13]

The good news was that weeks passed with no rumors finding their way into print about selling the company. The bad news was that there were no viable leads. As fate had it, Carr, Viemeister's boss, spotted a small news item in an aviation magazine. It turned into the only serious lead. The article reported that Paulson was considering buying the Sabreliner program from Rockwell. Carr reasoned: "Why would he buy the Sabreliner if he had a chance to buy the Gulfstream?"[14] He called Viemeister to his office. "Carr told me that Mario Borini, a managing partner of Grumman's auditors, knew of a man who was looking for an aircraft manufacturing facility," Viemeister said.[15] Viemeister immediately picked up the phone to call Paulson in Van Nuys. An hour-long conversation paved the way for a person-to-person meeting in New York.

"Al had earlier gone to Oklahoma and tried to make a deal to buy the Oklahoma plant," longtime Grumman executive Goldie Glenn remarked. "[Borini] was the same accountant who worked for Grumman. He told Al to not waste time trying to buy the Rockwell plant, as it was old, while Grumman on Long Island was trying to sell its [newer] plant in Savannah."[16]

Clay Lacy watched the drama from the sidelines in Van Nuys. "[Viemeister] called Al out of the blue and asked him if he'd like to buy Gulfstream. Al said it would be great, but he could never raise enough money. He was told not to be so sure. Al needed to go to New York."[17] For Paulson, it took on the feeling of a dream too good to be true. "I couldn't believe it," he said of the opportunity presented to him.[18] More than anything, he wanted a modern, well-equipped plant such as the Grumman facility in Savannah. He assumed that it would be the perfect site to begin production of the Hustler 500.

Lacy recalled how fast the deal making progressed. "Al called me right away and said he'd take the Lear to fly back to New York on Friday." At least that was the plan, but in fact, Paulson moved even faster. "I got in my Learjet and flew there immediately," he said. "I never dreamed Gulfstream would be put up for sale. I was like a kid in a candy store. I was afraid I was going to blow it because I was so eager to buy it."[19] He pointed the Learjet's nose eastward from Van Nuys and clicked off the miles to Long Island.

"Paulson came to Bethpage, and we had lunch together at the Maine Maid," Viemeister said. The historic Maine Maid Inn, in nearby Jericho on Long Island, was an almost 200-year-old landmark. Describing Paulson, Viemeister described him as "Tall, in his mid-fifties, slightly balding, with alert eyes and aristocratic bearing."[20] He discovered Paulson's intense sensitivity about two judgments people made about him: his lack of a college degree and being labeled an aviation junk man.

Munching on a club sandwich, the man from California wanted details. In spite of his many trips to Georgia, Paulson had never paid much attention to Gulfstream's facilities on the Savannah airport. Following the lengthy luncheon, the two men drove to Bethpage to tour a few of Grumman's buildings and ramp areas. Viemeister stressed how similar the facility was to the Savannah plant. Upon completing the brief tour, they adjourned to a conference room to peruse financial statements for the Grumman American subsidiary. Because the company had manufactured different model Gulfstreams for twenty years, and those airplanes were packed with complex systems, Viemeister assured him that assembling the Hustler wouldn't present a technical challenge. Throughout the discussions, Paulson remained optimistic they could make a deal—although he didn't know exactly *how*. "He explained that he had a backer, a wealthy investor who was a part-owner of American Jet," Viemeister said. It was his old benefactor, Jerry Henderson. The Grumman man asked Paulson, "Can he really supply the cash you would need?"[21] Paulson nodded in the affirmative.

A few days after the meeting, a report arrived in Bethpage disclosing financial details about a foundation controlled by Henderson. The entity was a major shareholder in billion-dollar Avon Products. There were investments in a large seafood producer and a boat manufacturer. It owned a 36,000-acre sheep ranch in New Zealand, as well as millions of dollars of gold coins and a trust company in Switzerland. The report revealed that Henderson controlled almost $100 million in assets. The man's finances were rock-solid.

"Henderson had quite a lot of cash," Lacy said. "He inherited most of it. It was a pretty big number. The Citibank of Chicago and the Bank of New

York would come up with the rest of the money. The banks would loan Al the money, but they said he had to raise another $20 million for operating capital."[22] The banking community considered Paulson to be a businessman with unblemished integrity. His reputation in this regard was solidified by way of an incident that took place long before the Gulfstream opportunity emerged. "Al had sold some Connies to a company in Lima, Peru," Lacy recalled. "They had an accident with a 749 Connie that was the biggest crash in Peruvian aviation." Lineas Aereas Nacionales (LANSA) Flight 501 was a scheduled domestic flight that departed Lima for Cusco on April 27, 1966. The Lockheed L-749A Constellation smashed into 12,000-foot Mount Talaula, killing all forty-nine people on board. Paulson had sold the Connie to the airline. Finding no evidence that mechanical failure contributed to the crash, investigators concluded that the crew simply miscalculated the airliner's climb performance and flew into the mountain. "The government grounded all its airplanes," Lacy continued. "Al made a deal to help the Peruvian company. Although there was about $500,000 that Al was owed, Citibank was out a couple million. After the crash, Al made a couple of payments to reduce the bank's loss and the word got out. He wasn't obligated to do this. I always figured that making those payments for the airline, that he didn't have to make, helped him when it came time to borrow money to buy Gulfstream. By paying off a little money to help the bank, the favor later came back to help him."[23]

Within weeks after lunching at the Maine Maid, "Paulson returned to Bethpage in a Learjet," Viemeister said.[24] The Grumman facility was shut down for the day, but the control tower on its private airport remained staffed for his arrival. Huddled in a conference room with Viemeister and senior Grumman officers, two days of negotiations began. Tightening the terms of a proposed deal, Grumman wanted a high dividend rate on the American Jet Industries preferred stock Paulson offered; he and Henderson were the sole owners of that corporation. Paulson wanted it lower. The officers felt that Grumman should be paid royalties for the first 200 Gulfstream IIIs sold, the future variant still in the planning stage. He wanted to make it 100, but lost on that position. By the end of the second day, the two sides compromised, partly due to exhaustion, and agreed on tentative terms.

Grumman was growing increasingly anxious to sell, but Paulson was even more anxious to buy. "We came up with a figure of about fifty-two million," he said. The parameters of the deal finally agreed to, Bierwirth got rubber stamp approval from his board and that of the minority shareholders in Cleveland. To smooth over any ill feelings, Paulson agreed to meet with the Cleveland shareholders. He would give them cash in return for the 20 percent of Grumman American stock they owned. Art Modell and 200 other minority shareholders, some owning only a few shares, would be more than happy to cash out following the stormy relationship with Grumman.

"When it came to buying the plant from Grumman, Al didn't have enough money," Glenn remarked. "He borrowed from some of his friends and Henderson." One of those friends was hotel and movie studio magnate Kirk Kerkorian. He maintained a friendship with Paulson, whom he'd known since the early days of California Airmotive when he bought airplanes and parts from him. During later years they enjoyed spending time together at the Del Mar racetrack watching Paulson's horses run. Leisure hours found them playing tennis. Kerkorian ended up buying a $1.6 million vacation home on the ninth fairway of the Del Mar Country Club that Paulson came to own.

"Al got enough money to offer a downpayment," Glenn said. "Jack Bierwirth was so anxious to sell the program that he agreed to give Al [what was] in effect a loan for the first 200 Gulfstream IIIs that were to be built and sold."[25]

Paulson made the offer to buy the company, with contingencies, but still hadn't seen the Savannah plant. Viemeister prepared the company for his visit. "I called Al Lemlein, the general manager at Savannah: 'Al, there's a guy in a Learjet who'll be flying into Savannah just after lunch.'" He made it clear that Paulson might buy the company, closing the conversation by saying, "He may end up being your boss."[26]

Spending much of the afternoon inspecting the Savannah plant, Paulson telephoned Viemeister in the early evening to report that the facility looked fine to him. He concluded the conversation with "We've got a deal."[27] After telling Mary Lou the news, his next call was to Lacy. Paulson's friends and close associates were impressed with his adroit dealmaking. "He worked out a deal that was way cheaper than what the company was worth," Lacy remarked.[28] Glenn said, "He thought it would be a great place to build the Hustler."[29] Bruce McCaw offered an interesting perspective: "I've always said that the Hustler was the most successful business airplane ever built—because *without it*, Al would have never ended up with Gulfstream."[30]

On July 19, 1978, Paulson told reporters that the two sides had reached "agreement in principle" to transfer ownership of the Grumman subsidiary to American Jet Industries. Grumman Aerospace issued its own news release announcing the deal. The next step required buyer and seller to work out dozens of details. Meetings in Van Nuys and Las Vegas followed—the latter location chosen to meet with Henderson, whose money was vital in closing the deal. The trip to Nevada revealed nothing negative about his integrity or financial strength. "Henderson had his underground life, but had no part in the underworld," Viemeister said.[31] The Grumman staffers breathed a sigh of relief, although they did think it was strange that Henderson and his wife lived in an underground home in the middle of the desert.

Questioning the accuracy of Grumman's accounting practices, Paulson called in McCaw, relying on his broad knowledge of insurance matters. Shock set in. "When Al sealed the deal with Grumman, I went to Bethpage to find out where the bones were buried on the insurance program," he said, continuing,

> I found out how badly they were cooking the books of the subsidiary. Grumman was pushing all its costs into the subsidiary trying to screw the shareholders. They'd take an engineer who had worked thirty-five years and transferred him to Georgia for his last year, charging his retirement costs to Savannah. It also carried 80 or 90 percent of the insurance cost for Grumman Aerospace. They thought they were being clever.[32]

Although annoying, the purchase price was seen as such a bargain that it didn't make sense to revisit the deal.

Three weeks after the public announcement, Viemeister found himself seated in a stuffy conference room of American Jet Industries in Van Nuys. "Eighteen well-dressed men, many with attaché cases, sat down at a big table to wrap up the final details," he said. The team from American Jet Industries included Paulson, Henderson, Farrow Smith, and Mario Borini. The Grumman team included Bierwirth, Carr, Lemlein, and Nat Bust. "One of the first to speak was Jerry Henderson," Viemeister said. "His raspy voice spoke with confidence: 'How many of you here are lawyers? Raise your hands.'" Five hands went up, and Henderson told them to leave the room. The lawyers headed for the door.[33]

Ownership of Grumman American Aviation Corp. transferred to American Jet Industries, Inc. on September 1, 1978. Thirteen weeks had elapsed since Paulson and Viemeister first met at the Maine Maid Inn. American Jet's new board of directors consisted of Paulson, Henderson, and the latter's close associates: Smith, Borini, and Oswald Gutsche. Throughout the negotiations, Henderson had relied on these advisers—personal friends who functioned as trustees for his foundation. Smith began his career at Blue Channel Foods shucking crabmeat; he then studied accounting and moved up the corporate ladder to become president. Gutsche was appointed the executive vice president of Gulfstream. Paulson was appointed president and chairman of the board with Borini as vice chairman. Borini, the man who tipped off Carr about Paulson's interest in Gulfstream, was Henderson's tax expert. It was a tightknit bunch, with Paulson the only outsider.

The acquisition involved executing two agreements: one with Grumman, it owning 80 percent of Grumman American's common shares. The second involved the minority shareholder group, it owning the remaining 20 percent and holding warrants for a further 23 percent stake of Grumman's 80 percent share. For its 80 percent holding, Paulson paid Grumman $15 million in cash plus $10 million of existing American Jet Industries preferred stock. An additional $10.5 million worth of Grumman American preferred stock, then held by Grumman, was exchanged for a new issue of American Jet Industries preferred stock. The minority shareholder's stock and warrants were purchased outright for $17 million. Leaders of the vocal minority group, controlling 70 percent of the minority shares, quickly accepted the offer.

The transaction bought Paulson all the company's commercial aircraft product lines and facilities on the Savannah airport. It also required Grumman to design, develop, and FAA-certify a GIII version of the Gulfstream— $35 million worth of work to be paid for by Grumman. In return, Paulson would pay Grumman a 2 percent commission on the first 200 GIIIs sold; the commission expected to approximate $40 million.

"We're not buying assets; we're buying a corporation, lock, stock, and barrel," Paulson told the press. "It is operating well and we don't intend to do anything to disrupt that."[34] A critical part of the deal stipulated that Paulson bought the right to use the Gulfstream trade name, it having immense value as a recognizable brand.

"Mr. Paulson got the money together by the grace of God—and that's no kidding," remarked Kathy O'Sako, soon to be his secretary at Gulfstream. A transplant from the Grumman American plant in Cleveland, she worked part-time in Savannah. "I filed, answered the phones, and kept my mouth shut. They called me at home and said, 'the new man's coming into town. Will you come in to take his shorthand and answer his phones for a couple of weeks?' I went in, met him, and knew right away he was the kind of man I wanted to work for."

One of the first things O'Sako learned about her new boss was that "he was always wide-awake between three and four in the morning."[35] Granddaughter Crystal Christensen agreed about his sleep cycle: "He slept only four hours a night. When he would say we're taking off at seven in the morning, you'd better be on the tarmac ready to rock and roll. I had a hard time keeping up with him."[36] The clock meant nothing to Paulson; some employees probably thought that he never slept.

In short order, Paulson renamed the company Gulfstream American Corporation and moved to the Savannah area with Mary Lou. He planned to split his time between Van Nuys and Savannah.

"The first time I went to Van Nuys, Al left his bag in the airplane," Glenn recalled:

> He was getting ready to enter his car. I picked up the bag. He said to me, "Why are you carrying my bag?" I said that presidents of companies don't carry their own bags. He kind of chuckled and said, "Give me that bag." It was my first experience with him. On trips from Savannah to Van Nuys, he would give somebody twenty dollars to buy buckets of country-fried chicken. But we had a galley and flight attendant on the airplane to do the cooking. It was a different lifestyle for him. He was an ordinary guy. It was the first time he was seeing how the other half lived.[37]

Journalist Murray Smith also experienced Paulson's simpler side. "I wondered why he carried his laundry in the back seat of his car. He told me that
the guy who delivered the laundry smoked, and the smell permeated the bags
carrying the clothes. 'So now I pick up the laundry myself so I don't have that
smoke smell,' he said."[38] Paulson didn't want to address the situation with the
owner of the laundry.

Not everyone at Grumman agreed with Bierwirth's insistence to sell
Gulfstream. A loud exchange with a group of irate shareholders occurred
during the 1979 annual meeting of Grumman Aerospace at the Waldorf-
Astoria Hotel in Manhattan. The chairman explained how the company
needed the cash from the sale to survive. "At a time when Grumman was not
financially very well off, the fact that it was going to get paid for developing
the Gulfstream III, and get some cash out of the deal to boot, didn't sound
that bad," said George Skurla, destined to become president and chairman
of Grumman Aerospace.[39] To other executives in the aviation industry, the
expensive business jet was the corporation's crown jewel. Skurla said, "I
remember Frank Hedrick [president of Beech Aircraft] asking me, 'Why did
you sell Gulfstream? Are you crazy?'"[40] Lacy noted, "Al was lucky to get Gulfstream. Grumman was worried about getting in trouble because of [overseas
sale] of two of their GIIs. Grumman was also scared because they were also
selling F-14s to Iran and getting nervous about that deal, too. The problems
overseas were the reason why they sold it so cheaply."[41]

Depressed sales, looming scandals, and Grumman's lack of interest in
the program helped drop Gulfstream into Paulson's lap for a bargain price.
He was, as Lacy said, a lucky man. The lack of foresight on the part of Grumman turned into a nightmarish dream for Bierwirth when Gulfstream grew
into a billion-dollar golden goose for the man from California.

"Paulson recognized the potential that Grumman's top leadership did
not," Skurla concluded.[42]

9

Peregrine

Paulson booked seventy-six fully refundable deposits for the Hustler 500 by the time he signed the papers to buy Grumman American. His top priority was to find a company capable of building the airplane. "I'm convinced this is going to sell a lot of them," he proclaimed in referring to Gulfstream's manufacturing capabilities. "I wanted a company that would build it properly."[1]

Goldie Glenn saw things differently. "I spent a couple of weeks in Van Nuys," said the executive destined to become Paulson's right-hand man. "He called me into his office and asked what I thought of the Hustler. I looked at him and said, 'Mr. Paulson, I don't think much of the airplane.'" Glenn was told to go back to Savannah.

> Two weeks later, he told me to visit again. I told him that I knew what it takes to sell Gulfstreams and he'd been selling Learjets. This was a bigger airplane. It takes a lot of attention to work with customers, which he was not used to doing. Customers said, "This guy doesn't really have a feel for us." We were dealing with billionaires. He was in the big time now, but wasn't used to selling to presidents of big companies. I stayed with the company to help him out.[2]

By 1986, Glenn would rise to the presidency of what became Gulfstream Aerospace.

Overnight, the relatively small American Jet Industries operation in Van Nuys grew into a $200 million empire by acquiring the assets of Gulfstream American. Examining the negative side of the picture, the Savannah operation lost $2 million during the year that Paulson bought the company. It was plagued with a dispirited workforce and salesmen who expected the airplane to sell itself. Paulson concentrated on planning to manufacture the Hustler and sell more Gulfstreams; the latter, he believed, was never marketed aggressively. Asked what he intended to do with the unprofitable light airplane product lines that came with the deal, he responded with three words: "Make them profitable."

Gulfstream American employed 2,000 workers when he took control, occupying 600,000 square feet of space in Savannah. Although the immensity of the company dwarfed that of American Jet, Gulfstream wasn't profitable. "[American Jet Industries] got up to about $40 million gross sales and I was making about $5 million a year," Paulson said. "After I bought Gulfstream, people were wondering how a little company like mine could buy it. Here, I had a company doing $40 million, making $5 million a year, and then you had a company doing over a hundred million losing money."[3] In the form of an analogy, he described making the deal as being similar to "a mouse taking on an elephant."

Glenn recalled the early days in Savannah. "Al wanted to put a sign on the building. He showed me a photo of the sign they made in Van Nuys." The sign looked homemade. "I said, 'we can't do that. If you want to put a sign on the building saying Gulfstream American, let's do it right.'"[4] Acknowledging Glenn's suggestion, professionally designed signage was erected. In Van Nuys, the drab paint covering the two hangars was adorned with new signage: *Gulfstream American Corporation.*

"A big difference existed between the staff Al had in Van Nuys and what we had in Savannah," Glenn continued. "He stepped into an organization with an engineering staff, a sales staff, a medical staff—we had everything in Savannah."[5] It was a different world and not an easy one for him to grasp. He carried over at least two obsessions from his workdays in California. Spending time in his office, an unusual occurrence, he preferred to sit behind a heavy wooden executive desk—the desktop staying uncluttered. Most of the time, nothing could be seen on it except a telephone and coffee cup. He took to Gulfstream another habit acquired early in his career—using the phone and not wasting time writing memos. When he did write one, it was as abbreviated as his conversations about business.

A few months after Paulson settled into his new digs in Savannah, Jack Bierwirth in Bethpage got an earful from him. Aware of disparaging remarks being made behind his back, Paulson perceived that Grumman executives thought of him as little more than a junk dealer. He thought they considered him a "caretaker" for the Gulfstream program; Grumman would buy him out at some point in the future and take over the jet's production. Fed up with the gossip, he demanded that Bierwirth instruct his executives to behave themselves and shut up, which they did.[6] Thoughts about not having a college degree and being labeled a junk man continued to haunt him.

Hallway gossip was annoying, but there were pressing customer relation issues as well. "A few people buying Gulfstreams wanted their money back," Glenn recalled. "They were critical of Al. They called him Sanford and Son." The characterization referred to a television sitcom of the 1970s called *Sanford and Son.* The show starred Redd Foxx playing Fred Sanford, a junk dealer living in the impoverished Watts neighborhood of Los Angeles. "Customers felt that Al was a junk man in aviation. I made six or seven trips with him to convince them that he knew the business. Al told them, 'Give me a year and you'll see what I can do.' When we delivered their airplanes on schedule all this faded away."[7]

Whether it was colleagues or customers, the junk man moniker dragged on for years. So did Paulson's shyness. "Al bought the program just before the NBAA convention in 1978," Glenn continued. "People there started calling him 'Mr. who ... who's this guy named Paulson.' We set up a meeting at the convention for Al to make a speech before a bunch of aviation writers. He was shy and said to me, 'I've never spoke to so many people in one room in my life.'"[8] To most people in the aviation community, and the public for sure, he was an unknown figure. "When Jimmy Carter was running for president, the wags were saying, 'Jimmy who?' Recently, at the announcement of the sale of Grumman American Aviation Corp. to American Jet Industries, the question 'AJI and Allen Who?' was making the rounds," reported *Aviation International News*.[9] No longer an obscure aircraft parts dealer, he was now in the spotlight.

Jerry Henderson stepped up to the plate when Paulson needed money to help develop the Hustler. He continued to provide cash to close the deal for Grumman American. A fellow member of the "greatest generation," Henderson believed that capitalism represented the best economic system in the world by offering opportunities to anyone who was willing to work hard. He and Paulson stuck to their concept of the American dream—champions of a laissez faire business environment. But in spite of their mutual beliefs, as time went by, their once solid business relationship began to erode. The men quarreled about the path Gulfstream was taking and what projects it should pursue. "After a year or so Jerry was very difficult to do business with," Paulson said. "I tried to get him to sell his interest to me but he wouldn't do it."[10] Henderson remained hardheaded and felt that he didn't have to justify his actions, or lack of them, to anyone.

"Henderson's accountant [Borini] didn't know a lot about the business, but Henderson convinced Al that the man needed to be on site as his representative," Glenn said. "It was an everyday kind of itchy thing that didn't work out."[11] More than a "representative," as vice chairman of the board at Gulfstream, Borini monitored Henderson's investment like a hawk. To rid himself of the annoying interference, Paulson spread the word that he was seeking an investor to buy Henderson's stake. In the midst of doing so, a phone call came in from Texas.

The caller was an officer at Tesoro Petroleum Corp. in San Antonio. Tesoro's roots dated back to 1964, when entrepreneur Robert West, Jr., bought a handful of oil-producing properties to put together a petroleum company.

"Tesoro became a hodgepodge of business interests," reported *Business Week*. "Gasoline marketing in California, a refinery in Alaska, oil equipment rental and manufacturing, contract drilling, oil transportation and production, even coal mining."[12] Seeking an even broader cross-section of businesses, West acquired companies having little or no connection to the petroleum industry. Gulfstream American was now under his magnifying glass. Tesoro's intent involved nothing more than to buy into Gulfstream at a reasonable price, even though the aircraft manufacturer had no ties to the oil business. Tesoro was interested because the sale of business jets threw off plenty of profit. When the cash register rang up a sale at Gulfstream, it wasn't the same as selling a hamburger at McDonalds. It meant at least a $20 million sale, many of those all-cash transactions.

"I talked to them and told Henderson that Tesoro would buy his interest, but they needed a price," Paulson said. "Jerry came up with a price of $52 million for his interest in the company."[13] The oil company agreed in principle to buy Henderson's shares in a stock swap, contingent on the Gulfstream III receiving FAA certification. Paulson's only goal was to force Henderson and his cohorts out of the company.

A month after announcing the proposed deal, Paulson nixed it. He wasn't happy about making Tesoro a partner, it an oil company with a cursory understanding of the aircraft industry. Aware from the beginning that Tesoro's officers weren't "aviation men," it didn't bother him at first. But on closer examination it did. Henderson happened to be a skilled aviator but underlings like Borini were not. It was a scenario he didn't want to repeat with future investors. In San Antonio, Tesoro wasn't happy because Paulson wanted to change some terms in the agreement they felt were non-negotiable. Adding to the turmoil, Tesoro was becoming a victim of cheap oil after the price of a barrel took a plunge, followed by a corresponding decline in the company's cash reserves. Both parties wanted out.

"The deal with Tesoro fell through but at least I had a price from Jerry to buy his interest out, without putting one dollar up," Paulson said.[14] He didn't need to use his own money to buy Henderson's stake; there were investors anxious to step in. Gulfstream was fast growing into a golden goose.

Paulson thumbed through his Rolodex to contact the moneymen he trusted, being unusually selective in the process. Successful in the effort, Henderson's stake was bought, freeing Paulson from the eccentric industrialist. "I own 80 percent of the stock," he said upon completing the transaction. "EF Hutton owns 10 percent, and there's a consortium of European bankers that own the other 10 percent."[15] Henderson's interference was no more. "He was out and Al was on his own," Glenn said.[16]

Adding the $52 million from the buyout to his portfolio, Henderson and his wife went on to live in his 6,000-square-foot bombproof home situated below the desert sands on the outskirts of Las Vegas. Henderson died on November 16, 1983, at the age of seventy-eight.

Free of his relationship with Borini, Paulson revisited his earlier effort to buy the Rockwell General Aviation Division. He discovered that its executives were more eager than ever to unload the manufacturer. Restarting talks, he hoped to strike a better deal than when he last tried. It had been a couple of years since he and Rockwell negotiators became deadlocked attempting to close a deal. The existence of the Commander 700 program is what killed it. This time, the price was more favorable. In October 1980, Paulson signed a letter of intent to buy the company, although the one item still not to his liking—the Commander 700 program—was still a part of the deal. In January 1981, Rockwell shifted the terms of the deal more in his favor after Fuji and Rockwell terminated their agreement to manufacture the plane. It paved the way for him to renegotiate the final price. He did so without delay. In February, Gulfstream American bought the company. Renamed the Commander Business Aircraft Division, Paulson showed no interest in building the single-engine airplanes, but continued to manufacture turboprop Aero Commanders. They were renamed Gulfstream Commander Jetprop 840s and Commander Jetprop 980s. He also inherited the ultimate embodiment of the popular twin-engine airplane—the ten-passenger Commander Jetprop 1000. He kept the Commander 112 and 114 programs on ice, seeking a buyer for the product line. The single-engine Commanders faced the same fate as the Yankee and other Cleveland-era aircraft, those programs awaiting buyers as well. He viewed any of the single engine aircraft as being more trouble to manufacture and market than it was worth.

"We need the company's facilities and people for the production of the Gulfstream III and the Hustler," Paulson said of the Oklahoma plant. "Besides, it does not make sense to have the large gap in aircraft size and performance between the twin-engine Cougar and the Hustler and Gulfstream III. The Cheetah, Tiger, and Cougar are well-built aircraft and will outperform anything in their weight and power category, but they do not fit in with our goals. We plan to sell the whole program," he concluded.[17] "The Cleveland operation was a mistake from the start," Glenn remarked. "What you had was a Woolworth five-and-ten on one end and a Tiffany on the other end. It was a disaster. Al recognized this at the very beginning."[18]

The combined Bethany and Savannah plants totaled 3,500 people on the payroll working in 1.7 million square feet of factory and office space. It was a far cry from Paulson's days selling aircraft parts from a 10,000-square-foot concrete block building on Vineland Avenue in California.

Less than a year after buying Grumman American, Paulson attempted to sell the AgCat agricultural aircraft product line. Manufactured under license from Gulfstream by Schweizer Aircraft Corp., he wanted to sell all rights to the program to the New York manufacturer or another buyer. Sales of the specialized aircraft had turned sluggish with some of the extra tooling and raw material stored in Savannah. When initial negotiations with Schweizer failed, he ordered that the remainder of the tooling be moved from New York to Savannah. The action caused talks to resume with an agreement reached to sell the entire program to Schweizer.

The economic news during much of 1979 was anything but positive. In common with earlier years of the decade, an energy crisis gripped the world. The Iranian Revolution was the spark igniting it. The Shah of Iran fled his country in early 1979, enabling the Ayatollah Khomeini to seize control. The new regime continued to export oil, but the shipments were smaller, pushing up the price of a barrel. Saudi Arabia and other OPEC nations increased production to offset the decline, resulting in a loss in overall production amounting to only 4 percent. But consumer panic in the United States drove prices higher than expected, creating long lines at service stations with motorists paying up to $8 a gallon. On the heels of Iraq's invasion of Iran in 1980, oil production almost came to a halt. Jet fuel prices shot up while inflation and unemployment soared. Adding stress to an already tenuous scenario, the Federal Reserve boosted the prime rate by a full percentage point. Looking ahead, 1982 would become the worst year of the recession.

"I was Al's key to the back door of Grumman," Glenn said about the level of coordination the engineers in Savannah needed with their counterparts in Bethpage during the GIII's development. "We encountered some problems with the airplane that we couldn't fix. The engineering folks involved in its early design worked at Grumman. I'd call them up and get their engineers to solve the problems."[19] The activity continued for a year after Paulson's arrival, while Grumman functioned as the subcontractor to Gulfstream American for the GIII.

Although the engineering for the GIII was accomplished in Bethpage, the first airplane was built in Savannah. It consisted of a standard GII airframe pulled from the assembly line converted to GIII specifications. Compared to the GII, the wingspan was increased 6 feet, with 5-foot-high winglets added at the tips. A 2-foot fuselage stretch completed the more significant changes. It was decided to retain the Spey 511 engines, well known for reliability and high altitude performance. But doing so brought a shortcoming: extreme noise and high fuel consumption. In addition to the reworked wing and winglets, an aerodynamically efficient fuselage nose was developed. The changes meant that the latest embodiment of the GIII would provide at least 80 percent of the performance that would have resulted from using the supercritical wings planned for Grumman's earlier GIII project. Under Paulson's direction, the first GIII was completed for less than *half* of the former project's research and development costs.

Builder of the wings for the GII, Nashville-based Avco Aerostructures machined the wings for the GIII as a subcontractor to Grumman. It was a challenge to shape any of the Gulfstream upper wing skins: each aluminum alloy "plank" was 45 feet long and 12 feet wide. Shaping the huge slab of metal into a wing took proprietary tooling capabilities and much finesse. "Avco was all screwed up on the GIII wing," Bruce McCaw remarked. "And Grumman was charging Savannah four times more than what the work was worth. Allen started sniffing around and renegotiated this stuff."[20] In addition to the wing, Paulson saved money and shortened the delivery time for many of the aircraft's parts by performing more of the work in the Savannah plant. Rather than contract with Avco to build the wing's flaps, ailerons, and associated control systems, Gulfstream Aerospace fabricated and assembled those components in-house. In the end, 80 percent of the airframe parts were produced in Savannah.

The Hustler project was the reason why Paulson bought Gulfstream, but the GIII now received most of his attention. "It was a short time after he arrived in Savannah when Al realized that the Hustler program was not what he expected to be," Glenn recalled, "so he concentrated on the Gulfstream III."[21]

The GIII's maiden flight took place on December 2, 1979. At the controls were Bob Smyth, who'd flown the GII on its first flight thirteen years earlier, and Morgan Cobb, a test pilot at American Jet Industries. No technical show-stoppers being encountered during its test phase, the FAA certified the latest Gulfstream on September 22, 1980. Not waiting for official approval, Paulson jumped the gun and shattered several world records with the third airplane off the production line. Two of the records were set in April 1980, when he joined Smyth to fly nonstop from Savannah to Hannover, West Germany. They covered 4,569 miles in 8 hours, 58 minutes. Upon arrival, the airplane went on display at the Hannover International Air Show. Making these flights was dear to Paulson's heart—particularly when grabbing a record might bring in an order.

"He was a natural born pilot," Glenn remarked about his boss. "The rule at Grumman was once you were above the supervisory level you didn't pilot an airplane. Of course, Al didn't abide by that rule. He flew all the time."[22] The old timers in the company continued to be upset about his piloting activities, worried there could be an accident. "His flight operations department couldn't stand him flying airplanes," McCaw said.[23] Owning the company offered plenty of perks. Flying its airplanes whenever he wanted was one of them.

It came as a relief to Paulson when he watched the GIII take off from Savannah following its protracted birth under the Grumman regime. The jet met all customer guarantees and was soon chalked up as another winner for

The second generation of Gulfstream business jets: the GIII. First flown December 2, 1979 (©Gulfstream Aerospace Corporation, reproduced with permission).

the company. Paulson became its biggest fan: "We still have a Learjet, but I sure miss the Gulfstream III class of flying when I get in the smaller jet."[24]

For all his efforts, Paulson had yet to manufacture any kind of aircraft for the U.S. government. The opportunity presented itself when the Air Force solicited the airframe industry to supply a new generation of jets to transport government VIPs. Assigned to the 89th Military Airlift Wing outside the nation's capital, the airplanes would be used to fly the president, vice president, cabinet members, and senior government officials. They were designated C-SAM aircraft, short for special air mission, and destined to replace venerable C-140Bs, the military variant of the commercial JetStar. Built by rival Lockheed, the C-140Bs were proving difficult to support due to a scarcity of spare parts. Proposing the Gulfstream III, later designated a C-20A, Paulson ran into a roadblock. The length of runway the airplane required for takeoff was greater than the maximum distance the Air Force specified in its proposal request. On an expedited basis, Charles Coppi, Paulson's top engineering executive, reevaluated the runway data for the GIII. He proved to the Air Force that the jet was safe to operate from shorter runways.

In June 1983, Coppi and Paulson visited the Pentagon to attend a procurement conference. They expected to answer questions about their proposal with the hope of walking away with a contract. Surprised upon arrival, they noticed that executives from more than thirty competitors were in attendance. Gulfstream found itself competing against far larger companies: Boeing with its 737, along with the team of Fokker and Lockheed Air Service pitching the Fokker F-28–3000.

The C-20A's biggest advantage was that it could fly both long and medium range missions efficiently. Eventually beating the competition, Gulfstream's initial contract for C-20As totaled $3.2 million, the Air Force leasing three airplanes through 1984. Following the initial lease period, the service would buy these airplanes along with eight more. Eventually, the value of the aircraft and their logistical support totaled $300 million. The deal was a breakthrough for Gulfstream as a government supplier. Algeria, Egypt, and Saudi Arabia also ordered the militarized aircraft. The Air Force order meant more than money to Paulson; it proved to the world that a Gulfstream jet was safe enough to transport the president of the United States.

The employees in Savannah cheered when Paulson came aboard to run the company. The corporate culture began to change, freed of needless bureaucracy, turning into more of an informal organization. There had been morale problems before his arrival, related to the real or perceived remoteness of workers from managers and executives. An ivory tower mentality existed. He brought about a welcome change, the kind of guy who'd connect with people at any level, whether on the assembly line or in the White House. It was like the old days in Van Nuys with him prowling around the hangar, poking his nose into small problems before they festered into major issues. He kept the future in mind, while making sure that daily business activities stayed on track. Employees relished his down-to-earth simplicity, frankness, and accessibility. Based on a soft-spoken demeanor, some employees thought he might be too easy-going—until they watched him in action. It became clear that he got things done.

Paulson believed fervently in the adage that a camel is a horse designed by a committee. He sought advice and suggestions from others—but never decisions. It became his modus operandi from the start of California Airmotive to the day he would finally leave Gulfstream. His aversion to committee meetings, written memos, and filing useless papers was well known. He disliked staff meetings unless they were essential. He preferred talking with people on a one-on-one basis.

Inheriting a dispirited workforce, he felt that his presence in the plant might quell dissent among the rank-and-file and improve communication. "Allen and Goldie walked around all the time," Kathy O'Sako remarked. "Goldie would walk first thing in the morning, arriving around six, have breakfast, then go into the factory and talk with the people there. He was the one who had his thumb on the relationships."[25] Whatever Paulson missed

Glenn caught, and his strolls on the factory floor kept the CEO knowledgeable of what was happening from a human relations standpoint.

"Allen Paulson was exactly what the Gulfstream program needed to endure," offered Jack Olcott, former president of the National Business Aircraft Association. "His understanding of aviation as a businessman, his strong commitment to business aviation, and his love of flying breathed new life into a design Grumman mistakenly thought of as a dinosaur," referring to the GII.[26]

~ ~ ~

While the backlog of Gulfstream work in Savannah showed no sign of letting up, Paulson juggled an increasing mix of business in Van Nuys. He planned to turn the California operation into a service center where business jets could be fitted with interiors to please the discerning tastes of entertainers, corporate moguls, and heads of state. The Hustler 500 was still planned for production and a stream of orders were received for cargo conversions of passenger airliners. There was more than enough work to keep his employees busy.

Adding another possible project in March 1979, he initiated talks with the executives at VFW-Fokker in West Germany about starting up production of its twin-engine VFW 614 regional jetliner in the United States. An unsuccessful program that resulted in selling only ten aircraft, production in Europe was shut down in 1977. Paulson proposed modifying the airplanes by increasing their seating from forty-four to sixty passengers and upgrading the engines. "There is a large gap between the less than 100-seat transports and the smaller transports that is not being filled," he rationalized.[27]

The VFW 614, to be renamed the GAC 616 by Gulfstream, would be a 50,000-pound gross weight airplane having two 40-inch extensions to lengthen the fuselage. Power would be supplied by two General Electric CF34 turbofans, each developing 8,650 pounds of thrust. Unusual for a jet transport, the engines were mounted atop the wings, not unlike the far smaller Honda Jet executive transport of today. "The wing mounting gives a better center-of-gravity envelope and better noise characteristics," Paulson said, "and it enables maintenance personnel to stand on the wing to work on the engines." An abbreviated development time for the project was envisioned because the VFW 614 was already FAA-certified, production tooling was available, and enough components were in stock to assemble fifteen aircraft. "I have people all over the world conducting the market survey for the 616," he continued. "If the market is there, we will build it; if it is not there, we will not build it."[28] Apparently, the market wasn't as robust as he hoped. Optimism for the project faded three months after completing the survey. He withdrew from further negotiations with VFW-Fokker.

Switching gears, he concentrated on developing a stretched version of the turboprop-powered Gulfstream I for the regional airline market. "Overall we are bullish about the market for the aircraft, but we are approaching it cautiously," he commented.[29] The Grumman American acquisition included the inactive GI program that Grumman had little interest in reviving. Because the plane's assembly line had been shut down in February 1969, Paulson decided to convert whatever GIs were already manufactured into stretched, high-density passenger airliners. The boost in capacity would seat thirty-seven passengers. Prospective customers were regional airlines, multiplying in number due to air carrier route changes brought about by the Airline Deregulation Act of 1978. The major airlines were serving fewer smaller airports because the government no longer subsidized their operating into communities where few passengers boarded. Regional airlines picked up the slack.

Paulson began by purchasing five GIs out of the 190 airplanes in service. The first one served as a prototype. Nowhere near new, it had a manufacture date of 1963, already sixteen years old. The newest plane was ten years old. All of them required complete overhaul to "zero-time" status, making the planes comparable to brand-new condition. Working with his engineers to design the needed modifications during the summer of 1979, Paulson designated the upgraded aircraft as the GI-C. By splicing a 9.5-foot barrel section into the GI's fuselage, the airplane morphed into a GI-C. The project was a no-brainer for him as much of his earlier work in California involved modifying the airframes of far larger airplanes. The total cost to a customer for a converted GI was projected to be $3 million. It was at least a half-million dollars *less* than the price of a newly built competitive airliner.

"We have three airplanes finished," he reported about the GI-C program in November 1980. "Air North has one already and they have a second one coming. The third one's going to Air US."[30] Judging by the order book, the concept looked promising. But in comparison with more efficient airliners built specifically for regional carriers, the GI-C was plagued with a heavier empty weight, requiring increased fuel capacity to supply its uneconomical Rolls-Royce Dart engines. To remedy the latter issue, Paulson planned to retrofit more fuel-efficient engines. Other than these shortcomings, the GI-C made sense. But many regional airlines, much like non-scheduled carriers in the early 1950s, lacked enough cash or credit to buy the planes. However, pilots loved them. "I found the 'stretch' was easier to fly than the standard GI," Scott Morris said, a 10,000-hour GI pilot. "It didn't porpoise and float as much in the landing flare."[31]

It made sense for Paulson to introduce the airplane when he did, as a readymade market existed. "It's a great airplane," he explained, but alluded to the difficulties in selling it. "The commuters have a rough time with high interest rates and everything, but they all want airplanes. We could sell hundreds of them tomorrow."[32] Only five G1-Cs rolled off the assembly line before the program died an unceremonious death in 1984. Paulson's concept of stretching a proven business transport into an airliner for two-thirds the cost of a new aircraft had proven itself. It was the lack of working capital and bank credit at cash-strapped airlines that killed the program.

In Savannah during 1981, the Gulfstream product line grew with a new GIIB sharing the stage with the GII and GIII. Not an "all-new" airplane, the GIIB consisted of a GII fuselage mated to the wings of a GIII—essentially a hybrid Gulfstream. Upon acquiring the company, Paulson told the 258 owners of existing GIIs that he wouldn't render the capabilities of their airplanes obsolete. Following through, he offered a conversion of their jets to bring

Paulson relaxing in his office at Gulfstream Aerospace discussing the unique features of the Peregrine business jet (Kathy O'Sako).

them up to GIII standards. The changes involved strengthening the fuselage center section to accommodate the GIII wing, together with upgrades such as carbon brakes, engine hush kits, and drag-reducing winglets. Compared to the GII, the changes gave the GIIB about a 900 nautical mile increase in range. Forty-two GIIBs were sold during its short appearance on the market. There was concern on the part of Gulfstream salesmen that it was impacting sales of GIIIs.

Paulson re-branded Gulfstream American with his own personality and business philosophy. Above all, he continued to focus on getting the Hustler 500 into production. He reminded the press that the airplane's FAA certification was expected to take place in California; the airplane would be manufactured in either the Georgia or Oklahoma plant. Going in different directions with several projects at the same time, there was some doubt in the minds of journalists that the program would ever see the light of day.

An oft-repeated maxim says to never put all your eggs in one basket. In business, it means that a single customer shouldn't account for the majority of sales. Paulson's conservative leaning caused him to respect that philosophy. Successful in marketing airplanes to the civil aviation sector for decades, he decided to try winning a military contract to build a jet trainer. It was something new for him. The Super Pinto had been a *conversion*, not an all-new aircraft, and it never entered production.

Paulson began developing the Peregrine 600 trainer in response to a request for proposals from the Air Force that described requirements for the Next Generation Trainer (NGT) program. The aircraft would replace the military's inventory of aging Cessna T-37 trainers. Most appealing to him was that the procurement called for an eventual production run of 700 airplanes.

The Peregrine program got special attention from Paulson. His enthusiasm for the airplane was apparent whenever he spoke about it, but he continued to direct any discussion away from himself. The only way to get him to sit still for an interview was to tell him that a resulting story might promote the Peregrine or other Gulfstream products. When a reporter at one of those interviews asked him why he felt competent designing airplanes without a degree in aeronautical engineering, he replied: "I've watched more airplanes being designed and built ... you learn by watching. There are a lot of engineers in this world who haven't gone through engineering school."[33] It was not the kind of question he liked to answer.

Talking up the project at the Paris Air Show, he sensed interest in the Peregrine from the military forces of other countries. A realist, he knew that Gulfstream American would need to compete against other well-established airframe manufacturers to win a contract from *any* country.

Assembly work on a prototype began in earnest during August 1979. Unlike the earlier Super Pinto work in Van Nuys, Paulson made full use of the administrative, engineering, and production resources of Gulfstream American in Savannah. A single tail-mounted turbofan engine powered the Peregrine 600 prototype. It shared the same wings and rear fuselage of the Hustler, but sported an all-new forward fuselage to accommodate either side-by-side or tandem seating for an instructor and student pilot. At the option of the military, a single Pratt & Whitney JT15D turbofan, or a pair of Williams International WJ44 turbofans, could power the plane.

The prototype Peregrine 600 was scheduled to fly during the final months of 1979, but the timing proved to be optimistic. In spite of the delay, Paulson remained confident that he'd trump the competition. When a reporter asked how Gulfstream American could afford to build a military jet trainer without government funding, he replied: "We are a very solvent company."[34] He forecasted that the Peregrine would enter production during the first quarter of 1983.

Following final assembly of the prototype at the former Rockwell plant in Bethany, the Peregrine took to the air from Wiley Post Airport on May 22, 1981. Paulson and Mary Lou were close by, living in Bethany on a part-time basis after acquisition of the Rockwell division. Witnessing the first flight was a bittersweet moment for him; he suspected that Gulfstream would

The sole Peregrine 600 jet trainer, later destroyed in a non-fatal accident during flight testing (©Gulfstream Aerospace Corporation, reproduced with permission).

likely lose the competition. He was correct. The Air Force rejected both the Peregrine and the competitive entries—except the T-46 Eaglet trainer proposed by Fairchild Republic Corp. On July 2, the New York–based manufacturer won the NGT contract. The military funded Fairchild to build two prototypes of its trainer and handed it an option to build fifty-four production airplanes. The first T-46 flew on October 15, 1985.

The Air Force cancelled the Fairchild contract in 1986 with little warning. The T-46 was rumored to have "undesirable" handling characteristics. Prior to its cancellation, military officials considered forcing Fairchild to modify the aircraft before uncovering a more insidious issue. There were allegations that the company had mismanaged the program, its projected cost climbing from $3.2 billion to $3.4 billion. The T-46 was the last aircraft built by Fairchild, one of the nation's pioneering aircraft manufacturers. A year later, Fairchild closed its sprawling plant in Farmingdale, New York, the facility having operated continuously for sixty years.

Watching the debacle unfold at Fairchild, Paulson made another attempt to market the Peregrine to the Air Force, without success. He displayed the airplane at the Paris Air Show, transporting it to France in the belly of the borrowed Mini Guppy he sold to Aero Union. Trying to interest the air forces of Australia, New Zealand, Japan, and China, the efforts produced no result.

The sole Peregrine 600 met a sad fate. On November 23, 1983, a few minutes into a mid-afternoon flight from Wiley Post Airport, the jet was destroyed in an accident. Gulfstream pilot Bill Lawton ejected from the out-of-control aircraft, suffering minor cuts and bruises. An NTSB accident investigation report described its demise:

> At about 215 knots the pilot rolled the aircraft in order to evaluate newly installed ailerons ... an immediate and rapid aileron roll reversal resulted and any action that the pilot took would not affect the rate of roll or descent. The pilot ejected below 3,000 feet MSL while in inverted flight.[35]

The report stated that the Peregrine's aileron control was "inadequate." Losing an airplane to pilot error might be excusable to Paulson, but the accident pointed to a flaw in the jet's design. It was embarrassing for him. Rather than fight the investigator's findings as Bill Lear might have done, he accepted the conclusions at face value without dispute and moved on to other projects.

Rockwell engineers developed the line of single-engine Commander airplanes in the late 1960s. The prototype Commander 112 first flew on December 4, 1970, with customer deliveries beginning in late 1972. The improved Commander 114 arrived on the scene in 1976, featuring a more powerful engine, the plane manufactured until 1979. After Gulfstream Aerospace bought Rockwell, it continued to support the existing fleet with parts, but didn't build additional airplanes.

It was perplexing for Paulson to decide what to do with the Commander 112 and 114. The light planes from the Bede era didn't fit his plans, either. "I think the most beautiful light airplanes around are the Tiger, the Cheetah, and the Cougar," he said, "but they are not compatible with our plans and manufacturing facilities. A lot of people talk about a family of airplanes. I think that was one of Grumman's big mistakes—trying to go from the bottom of the line to the top of the line. Too late and too big a spread."[36] He faced the same dilemma with the single-engine Commanders.

In November 1982, Paulson agreed in principle to sell the Commander 112 and 114 product lines to Evans-Auch Aircraft Ltd. in Wyoming. The agreement was contingent on the successful sale of $10 million worth of Park County tax-exempt revenue bonds, the jurisdiction where the airplanes would be built. The transaction failed to materialize because the venture's promoters didn't raise enough seed money to proceed. The county backed out of the deal. It wasn't until 1990 when he finally sold the program. An enterprise incorporated as Commander Aircraft Corp. proposed buying the entire package. Luck being on Paulson's side, the deal closed. Production of the airplanes resumed until 2002, when the company filed for bankruptcy. The Commander line of single-engine light planes died a slow death through the decades after burning out three corporate owners.

Grown accustomed to turning cynics into customers, Paulson boasted about the paid deposits to substantiate the perceived value of the Hustler 500. The program continued to drag on. An intense interest in competitive turboprop aircraft, thousands of them already in service, caused some confirmed buyers to drift away. They withdrew their refundable deposits, causing Paulson to push the program onto the back burner. He insisted that the program wasn't cancelled, but it appeared that way. As for the Peregrine 600, finding spotty enthusiasm, and facing bad press resulting from the accident, he stopped marketing it. However, he did concoct a "civilianized" version of the airplane for business users. Taking a long look at the civil aircraft market, he decided to replace the largely abandoned Hustler 500 with the newly conceived civil Peregrine.

"Ryan built an airplane that was really the forerunner of the Hustler, a combination turboprop and jet, and it went nowhere," publisher Murray Smith remarked. "And the Hustler went nowhere. Turboprops and jets both have qualities. But combined together they don't work well."[37] Completing its testing, the Hustler was parked and began gathering dust in the back of a hangar. Its drawings were relegated to a file cabinet. Wanting to move ahead and not dwell on the project's questionable future, Paulson lent a hand to friend Ed Swearingen in Texas who was developing a new business jet. "The size of the Hustler fuselage was the same as the SJ-30 [business jet] that Ed designed," Clay Lacy said. "Al gave Swearingen his mockup of the Hustler. The fuselage diameter stayed the same."[38]

The Hustler faded away, a victim of a seemingly endless road leading to production. "The Peregrine appears to be a better airplane than the Hustler from the standpoint of performance and economy, and that's the name of the game today," Paulson told a reporter from *Aviation Week & Space Technology*.[39]

For the civilian variant, to boost the performance from the former Peregrine 600, the plane's turbofan engine was switched from a 2,900-pound thrust Pratt & Whitney JT15D-5 to a Garrett TFE731–2. The Garrett developed 3,500 pounds of thrust, turning the jet into a veritable hot rod. The compact cabin contained seating for a pilot and five passengers. The wings, tail, and several of its airframe systems came directly from the trainer version, cutting development time and cost. Initially dubbed the Commander Fanjet 1500, its name reverted to Peregrine once the military version was abandoned.

The Peregrine business jet made a maiden flight from Wiley Post Airport on January 14, 1983, with Lawton at the controls. At the time, it was the world's only operational single-engine business jet. Paulson's plan called for Gulfstream to FAA-certify the airplane for single-pilot operation, marketing it to

Evolved from the Peregrine 600 trainer, a business jet variant becomes the world's first single-engine business jet (©Gulfstream Aerospace Corporation, reproduced with permission).

businessmen-pilots who preferred to fly without a copilot. He expected to sell between 500 and 600 Peregrines by the end of the decade. Relying primarily on word-of-mouth marketing, he racked up twenty-seven orders for the $1.6 million machine. Its projected performance is what sold customers: a takeoff weight of 9,400 pounds and a cruise speed of 436 miles per hour—while carrying six people and their baggage. These were the kind of numbers that impressed seasoned pilots.

Introduced at the National Business Aircraft Association convention in Dallas, full-color magazine advertisements picturing the Peregrine caused a stir with some of the older attendees. They disliked the playboy image the ads conveyed. A handsome fellow in a cowboy hat and dark glasses was depicted banking the jet over San Francisco Bay. Sitting beside him was a young blonde woman dressed in a black evening gown. Ignoring the sprinkling of critics, the response to the ads was exactly what Paulson wanted. The ads appeared in the *Wall Street Journal* only two times, but ended up generating 1,400 inquiries.[40]

Richard Collins, in an article for *Flying* magazine, wrote: "The prospects aren't among the lemmings costumed in identical pin-striped Brooks Brothers suits, waiting for the 7:34 to New York." Paulson remained confident. "We believe there are a large number of people out there who have flown single-engine aircraft either in the military or in general aviation that the Peregrine concept does not bother," he said. "With the number of single-engine turboprop aircraft entering the market, there is more acceptance of one engine."[41]

Paulson studied the kind of people likely to buy airplanes such as the Hustler and Peregrine. He figured they either wanted to get somewhere fast or own the airplane as a recreational status symbol. He concluded it was the latter. "Today, there are a lot of pilots who don't want a copilot with them," Smith said. "It's what Allen found out when he designed the Hustler. It was for self-centered, egotist kinds of guys who didn't want anyone telling them what to do."[42]

Long hours at work and a rigorous travel schedule visiting far-flung customers continued to take a toll at home. After eighteen years of marriage, Allen and Mary Lou agreed to a divorce in 1982. "My divorce is sealed," she remarked. "There were all kinds of stories. It was something that misfired for him."[43] The marriage ended amicably, both of them remaining friends as they pursued different paths. O'Sako added: "I'm convinced Allen loved Mary Lou right through it all and regretted the divorce. There's no doubt in my mind. He let her divorce him."[44]

Jasper Dorsey, a columnist with the *Rockmart Journal*, offered his opinion concerning Paulson's achievements in a 1990 column: "Allen Paulson is incredible, possessing a rare and overwhelming combination of a super salesman who has a sixth sense of what customers want, plus design and production skills to create it profitably," he wrote. "He also has a keen sense of timing, can do any job in aviation from mechanic, to designer, to engineer, to test pilot, to production, and can do it at the summit of the art, yet still maintain an informal low key style."[45]

10

Top of His Game

The money directed toward development of the Hustler and Peregrine programs put a dent in Gulfstream American's cash reserves, but remarkably, overall sales doubled from $217 million in 1980 to $442 million in 1981. Sales of GIIIs were a principal reason for the uptick, representing tremendous growth during the final throes of a recession. The sour economy resulted from a significant change in monetary policy intended to curb runaway inflation gripping the nation. Exacerbating the situation, a dry spell of oil supplies lingered long after the energy crisis of 1973. This combination of factors contributed to an 11.3 percent inflation rate in 1979. It soared to 13.5 percent in 1980. During a single year, the price of gasoline at a neighborhood service station zoomed from 63 to 86 cents a gallon. It rose to $1.19 in 1981. Sales of houses, automobiles, and aircraft went into a tailspin. Bank failures reached a post–Depression high, savings and loan failures a monthly occurrence. Gulfstream American was lucky to escape most of the debacle because many of its sales were consummated for cash from overseas customers.

Much of the nation's population was hurting, but Paulson enjoyed the greatest success of his aviation career. During the coming year he expected to sell thirty-four GIIIs, valuing the order backlog at an amazing $850 million. Some industry observers attributed the sales recovery to his moves as a leader. "It's a benevolent dictatorship," he said. "When you have controlling interest … it's a lot easier to get the board to go along with you."[1]

Paulson's mainstay interest continued in aviation, but he found time to dabble in unrelated ventures. One of them turned into a colossal headache for him—oil well drilling.

Marvin Davis was an American industrialist who made a fortune in the petroleum business. He owned properties such as 20th Century–Fox studios, the Pebble Beach resort, and the Beverly Hills Hotel. Joining his father in the oil exploration business, Davis acquired the nickname "Mr. Wildcatter" early in his career. He pioneered oil well deals known as "third for a quarter," where he isolated himself from risk by selling one-quarter of a well for one-third of what the entire well was actually worth. Burned by the transactions, investors filed lawsuits alleging that he inflated the actual profit from the wells, enticing them to invest more money. Davis moved on to become a major real estate developer in Denver, acquiring a shopping center and office complex there.

"I proved that Davis was taking Allen for money on some of the oil wells," said Kathy O'Sako, in telling the story of a previously undetected swindle. She prepared a spreadsheet documenting the expenses of every oil well that Paulson owned.

I had each bill laid out so I could show Mr. Paulson that what he was paying for was baloney. One day, he came in and showed me a photo of an oil well on fire, saying to me, "this is oil well number four." And I said, "Oh really? Let me show you number four." I got the spreadsheet out, put it on his desk, and said, "look, this is number four, and on this day they billed this much to us. It couldn't have been burning all that time [and not pumping oil] or I wouldn't be getting a bill for it." I said, "I'm right" and he said, "yes you are."

Paulson and O'Sako flew to Denver to meet with Davis. "I sat with his accountant and showed him everything. In the end we got a huge credit." She had gotten her boss worked up enough to be confrontational, unusual for him. "It was huge for him, having to confront Davis. He got out of oil wells pretty quickly after that."[2]

In 1981, Davis sold most of his oil holdings for $600 million.

"He was spending a fortune on oil," Christensen said of her grandfather. "And losing a lot. It was sad to see people take advantage of him when he worked so hard."[3] It's ironic that in aviation, a field Paulson knew best, that he could spot a cheat in a second. But with a smorgasbord of non-aviation ventures on his plate, detailed oversight didn't always happen. It was fortunate that O'Sako kept a close eye on his investments.

As winter of 1982 approached, Gulfstream American became Gulfstream Aerospace Corp. "The new name will broaden the scope of Gulfstream's dealings with the entire world since over 60 percent of our sales are currently worldwide compared to past overseas sales of 40 percent," he told employees. "We are proud of our American heritage."[4]

To George Skurla, selling Gulfstream was a stupid move. Witnessing the company's star-studded growth, he felt that Grumman should have never sold it. He admired what the "junk man" from California had accomplished, saying: "Paulson began to swan around the National Business Aircraft Association annual gathering, the Paris Air Show of business flying, with a second trophy wife, bought a race horse stud farm in Kentucky and bought out his backer."[5]

Paulson digested both good and bad news in 1983. His civilianized rendition of the Peregrine took to the air with great hopes in January. Jerry Henderson, the man who anteed up the money in 1978 to buy Grumman American, passed away in November. The best news was that the recession of 1981 and 1982 had tailed off, GIII sales continued to rise, an advanced version of the jet called the GIV was coming off the drawing board—and Gulfstream Aerospace made an initial public offering (IPO) of its stock.

EF Hutton & Co., a minority investor in Gulfstream, tried to pressure Paulson to take the company public in 1982 to "enhance their investment," it was reported. He refused, anticipating that 1983 would be an even better sales year. He felt it would make sense to wait a year before rolling out the public offering. Annoyed at Hutton's short-term thinking, he bought out its 10 percent stake at $8.50 a share. "I went to Citibank's offices in New York and said, 'I want to borrow $50 million personally.' They gave me the money and I paid EF Hutton off."[6]

The IPO was floated in April 1983. To analysts on Wall Street, the move was questionable because the recession had ended only four months earlier. It still exerted a drag on earnings at the nation's corporations. But unlike other aircraft manufacturers, Gulfstream the contrarian, continued to deliver healthy profits.

"I took the company public with Shearson and sold 19 percent of a company with a net worth of $650 million," he told the financial press as the New York Stock Exchange closed for the day.[7] He made history by selling 8.8 million shares to the public. It was the largest stock offering since 1955, when the Ford Foundation floated 10.2 million shares of Ford Motor Co. to raise $640 million. Gulfstream stock began trading at $19 a share in the morning, the entire issue selling out by the end of the day. It was a good day for both Gulfstream and Paulson. Prior to the IPO he owned 96 percent of the outstanding stock, his ownership dropping to 77 percent at day's end. The shares he continued owning were worth roughly half a billion dollars.

Gulfstream needed the money for not only the GIV's development, but to make a large tax payment to the Internal Revenue Service—a result of the firm's newfound prosperity. The IPO enabled the company to borrow additional working capital from commercial banks under a $150 million unsecured revolving credit agreement. "I have the best of both worlds," he told the *New York Times*. "I still have control of the company." Impressed with newfound wealth, the recently minted multimillionaire remarked, "The only way you get personal wealth is to go public."[8] Few entrepreneurs would disagree with that statement.

At a time when other general aviation manufacturers were posting losses, Gulfstream Aerospace reported healthy earnings for the first nine months of 1983. In the third quarter, it delivered ten GIIIs and ten turboprop Aero Commanders, compared with nine deliveries of each type airplane during the same period in 1982. Via a carefully crafted message, Paulson told the press: "We are extremely pleased with the results during such a difficult period in the general aviation industry."[9] Gulfstream jets dominated the world's business jet fleet. The best the competition could do was to play catch-up.

Aside from enjoying unprecedented sales success, there were flight records to set. Paulson believed that setting records was the best publicity tool for causing potential buyers to take note of the Gulfstream's globetrotting capabilities. In February 1983, forty-three-year-old Brooke Knapp set a record for the fastest around the world flight in a business jet. She flew a Learjet 35A, the airplane nicknamed American Dream I. In November, Knapp flew a GIII named American Dream II around the world in an attempt to set a speed record in a heavier weight category. Sponsored by Gulfstream, with Knapp assisted in the cockpit by company pilots Paul Broyles, Bob Smyth, and Curt Olds, she flew over the north and south poles. It took a little over 85 hours to cover 28,470 miles. A landing gear malfunction at Tenerife in the Canary Islands ended an attempt to set a speed record. However, she did set two other records: the first business jet on an around-the-world flight to land at McMurdo Sound in Antarctica, and the first to fly over both the north and south poles.

Continuing to write up orders for the GIII, Paulson faced uncertainty about the future size of the market for such luxury-class products. The strength of the dollar had begun to hurt export sales. Some purchasers were oil barons in the Middle East where the odds of closing a deal were tied to the price of a barrel of oil. Making its presence known, competition was encroaching from Montreal-based Canadair Ltd., it producing the Challenger 600 business jet. In France, Dassault Aviation manufactured the three-engine Falcon 50. Irritating to him, as a conservative, self-made industrialist, many foreign plane makers were affiliated with the governments of their countries. They enjoyed the benefit of either government subsidies or access to greater financial resources than Gulfstream. It was nowhere near a fair playing field to him.

It wasn't long after the IPO that Paulson shared some of his wealth with Gulfstream's 3,500 employees. He gave each of them fifty shares of stock—worth approximately $1,000 at the time. "This is a token of my sincere thanks to all of you," he wrote in a company newsletter. "You are now part owners of the greatest aviation company in the world." His employees were mostly a contented bunch. Managers enjoyed working for him. One longtime executive said: "We would have to make a big presentation in New York and then wait months for an answer [from Grumman]. With Mr. Paulson, he liked it or he didn't like it."[10] His goal was to keep the lines of communication from the front office to the factory floor as short as possible. "He was always shy, even in the shop," Goldie Glenn said. Bashful in his youth, Paulson carried the trait over into his adult life. "We'd walk around together every afternoon about three o'clock. Employees would meet him and shake his hand."[11] He never forgot his roots as a young mechanic at TWA by taking time to appreciate the contributions of the blue-collar workers in his own plant.

Paulson extended his generosity beyond his employees by donating $1 million to Georgia Southern College (now Georgia Southern University) toward construction of a $4.7 million, 18,000-seat football stadium. Following the initial gift, he donated an additional $350,000 to match what a community fundraising campaign raised. On the same day that the stadium was dedicated, September 29, 1984, with Paulson in attendance, the school won a game against Liberty Baptist with a rout of 48–11. "He was a grass-roots type of guy," said Georgia Southern coach Erik Russell. "Despite his millions, he acted just like an ordinary guy."[12]

The sizable gifts earned him a naming opportunity, the facility becoming the Allen E. Paulson Stadium. As the football program matured and garnered national championships, enrollment at the school skyrocketed. Later donations from his living trust helped fund the Allen E. Paulson College of Engineering and Information Technology. The university would recognize him

President Dale Lick of Georgia State College about to introduce Paulson before the first game is played at the new Allen E. Paulson Stadium on September 29, 1984 (Georgia Southern University).

with an honorary doctorate degree in science on June 14, 1997. "Al was always sorry that he didn't go to school to become an engineer," Glenn remarked. "He told me that a hundred times."[13]

Paulson's newfound wealth wasn't a secret around the Savannah area. He was leading a corporation that produced the Rolls-Royce of business jets and he contributed to many charitable causes. It was reported that one out of ten employees in Savannah worked for his company—the area's second-largest employer. When news of his million-dollar contribution to Georgia Southern College found its way into print in the *Savannah Morning News*, it sparked an unwanted result. Like it or not, Paulson was now a public figure, bringing on risks stemming from that notoriety.

On December 12, 1983, two lumber mill workers decided to kidnap him and demand a $1.2 million ransom. The young men, having no prior criminal records, conceived the plot that "just started out as shop talk," according to detective Robert Scott of the Savannah Police Department. "They got to kidding and carrying on about doing a kidnapping, and then they just talked themselves into taking it seriously."[14] The duo had read about the gift to Georgia Southern in the paper and followed up with the kidnap scheme. But instead of kidnapping Paulson, they encountered his son Michael.

Twenty-eight-year-old Michael swung open the door of the pickup truck he'd parked in the driveway of his home. It was a half-hour before midnight. Emerging from behind a row of bushes, the men rushed him. One of them brandished what appeared to be a handgun and demanded the keys to his truck. The plot backfired when Michael reached in his breast pocket for the keys—but *instead* pulled out a .22-caliber Derringer. At close range, he fired two rounds into the chest of Timothy Curtis, killing him. On his body, investigators found a $2.87 cap gun that closely resembled a "Saturday Night Special," according to Scott. The other culprit carried another toy gun but fled the area on foot, uninjured. By morning, the police arrested Michael Newsome, who worked with Curtis at the mill. On Paulson's front porch police found a cassette tape containing "a ransom demand in excess of $1 million," Scott reported.[15]

They didn't care who they kidnapped, either father or son," Mary Lou remarked. "This was in the middle of the night. Mike had been bowling and was going on a camping trip the next morning. He was going out to get gas."[16] For years following the botched kidnapping, John Salamankas, a veteran pilot at Gulfstream having a law enforcement background, positioned himself a few feet from the CEO as his bodyguard. They traveled millions of miles together. As additional insurance against an attack, Paulson carried a concealed pistol. Anyone following him got undivided attention.

Under Paulson's direction in 1982, the managers in Bethany were forced to furlough workers and curtail production of all the plant's product lines for forty-four days. There were no orders. More optimism prevailed in 1983 when ten turboprop Aero Commanders were sold. But by 1985, too many negative factors were working against the sale of Commanders—and the planned marketing of Peregrines in the near future. High interest rates were one reason. There were also rashes of product liability lawsuits resulting from fatal accidents of other aircraft that increased insurance premiums for all owners. The crux of the problem for both the Commander and Peregrine products was that the Beech Model 90 King Air had commandeered the market for twin-engine turboprops. First introduced in August 1963, the airplane was upgraded continuously for over twenty years. It represented dominant competition. Costing about half of what a Peregrine would need to sell for, the King Air was expected to grab the lion's share of customers when Paulson's newest airplane would hit the market.

By January 1985, Paulson had endured enough of the lackluster performance in Bethany. The entire facility was shut down, an historic decision as Aero Commanders had been manufactured there on a continuous basis for more than thirty-five years. "We could not justify the continuance of the Commander line with twenty-seven aircraft in inventory after delivering twenty-one aircraft last year," Paulson told a reporter. "The problem is that the Commander is competing with seven other aircraft in its same class."[17] Seeking a buyer for the company, he indicated there were "four good prospects," including the Chinese government, the Mexican government, and a European organization.

Two months after idling the Commander program, Paulson announced that all work on the Peregrine was suspended. The prototype had accumulated fewer than 100 hours in the air. He'd run into a series of snags with FAA officials in an attempt to certify the plane. The regulators required a maximum stall speed of 70 miles per hour when the plane was configured for landing; it needed 81. Other FAA guidelines were difficult to satisfy. One involved a cabin pressurization system capable of operating at 38,400 feet. Expensive structural redesign work would be required. Combined with a dwindling number of prospective buyers, a result of the Peregrine's $1.6 million price tag being almost double that of a King Air, he decided to scuttle the program. Another factor driving the decision was that the cost of developing the aircraft had contributed to a reduction in Gulfstream's overall income—$48.4 million in 1984 versus $58.8 million a year earlier.

Putting a positive spin on the announcement, Paulson made it clear that the program was suspended but not canceled. Receptive to entertaining bids, he was willing to listen to offers for the Peregrine or Aero Commander product lines—or both of them as a package deal. There were no takers. He took the Bethany plant off the market and redeveloped the site into an automated airframe fabrication center. A new subsidiary, Gulfstream Aerospace Technologies, made use of the 50,000-square-foot facility to handle engineering and fabrication services as a subcontractor to defense contractors. The Aero Commanders and their tooling sat dormant.

None of the proposals to buy the product lines materialized until Paulson hit pay dirt in 1989. Precision Aerospace Corp. acquired the turboprop line, but decided to not build any more of the airplanes. Instead, it sold parts and service to support the fleet of existing aircraft. The same year, the once popular Tiger light plane line was sold to American General Aircraft Corp. in Greenville, Mississippi. When it came to the piston-powered, single-engine airplanes, both Rockwell and Gulfstream discovered that manufacturing them, and trying to make a profit, was a chancy proposition. Before Paulson's acquisition of Aero Commander, Rockwell had shut down the single-engine line. Gulfstream followed suit by not restarting production. Paulson reiterated: "They do not fit in with our goals."[18] It was a relief to unload the money losers.

Many GII sales developed because the owners of GI turboprops decided to upgrade to a jet. In January 1980, at the end of the GII's production run, 256 of the jets had been sold. The milestone came a month after the GIII's first flight. While the latest version of the Gulfstream was moving along in its flight test phase, Paulson mapped future plans for his company. He kept abreast of advances in propulsion, aerodynamics, and avionics—expecting to integrate those technologies into a future Gulfstream. What emerged would be the GIV, far more of a step up from the GIII than that jet was from the GII.

In March 1983, design work began on the fourth derivative of the original Gulfstream. Although the basic airframe was derived from the GII and GIII, the jet would feature a roomier passenger cabin and more efficient engines. Four criteria were kept in mind during preliminary design discussions: compatibility with the environment, fuel efficiency, higher performance, and future growth possibilities. Satisfying all four criteria would turn out to be a tough order.

Airports on every continent were demanding lower noise levels for arriving and departing aircraft, meaning that Gulfstream Aerospace had no choice but to produce a quieter jet than the ear-shattering GIII. And to satisfy customers flying to far-flung locales, the GIV would need a long range.

"Range always sells," said Charles Coppi, senior vice president of engineering and technology at Gulfstream and the prime mover behind the GIV's development. As a child during World War II, he watched Grumman fighters take off and land from the airport in Bethpage. Graduating from New York University in 1952, Coppi joined Grumman to help design Navy aircraft, followed by working on the initial design of the GI. Later as the engineering manager for the GII and GIII, his stature grew within the aviation industry.

Important to the Gulfstream legacy, he nurtured a lasting relationship with Rolls-Royce engineers and executives. To memorialize that association, Rolls-Royce Ltd. created the Charles N. Coppi Award, presented annually to outstanding students serving engineering apprenticeships at Rolls. "Allen spent a lot of time with Charlie Coppi," O'Sako recalled. "He'd tell Allen, 'No, that's not a good idea.' Then Charlie would look at Goldie to sell Allen on the fact it wasn't a good idea."[19] Paulson's response was predictable. "I get my nose into a lot," he admitted. "I spend a lot of time working with the engineers. I want to be in the middle because I believe I can be helpful."[20]

Paulson was pragmatic, yet often revealed a spontaneous, wry sense of humor. Tough at times, he possessed a thick vein of tolerance—but had a willingness to discuss important issues. Developing his own views while grappling with a problem that interested him, it was never an annoyance when someone raised alternate opinions. This trait would come into play as he endured twelve-hour workdays preparing to introduce the Gulfstream IV to the world.

~ ~ ~

Today or yesterday, it's a fallacy to think that everyone welcomes a steady stream of business jets flying in and out of their local airport. Plenty of hate mail arrived at the offices of Gulfstream Aerospace and competitive jet manufacturers during the 1980s. They came from people living in houses that bordered airport property—particularly those residing in normally quiet suburbia. Some of the angst had to do with the Rolls-Royce Spey Mark 511 engines powering the Gulfstream II and III. On takeoff, their screeching whine and throaty roar resulted in instant unpopularity.

The turbofan Spey was developed in the late 1950s, operating for the first time in December 1960. In addition to Gulfstreams, the engine went on to power both military and commercial aircraft, the latter including the de Havilland Trident, BAC 111, and Fokker 28 jetliners.

The topic of airport noise spiraled into a blazing issue by the late 1960s. When the earliest generation of business jets first appeared at smaller airports in 1964, community activists spoke up like never before. The roar and whine from the turbojets signaled an exciting new era in aviation—but also brought about political pressure to enact strict noise regulations. The fielding of the GII in 1967 exacerbated the uneasiness. An immediate solution was to establish noise abatement rules to guide pilots of departing jets over sparsely populated areas. Nighttime departure curfews were other stopgap measures. Some airports, such as Santa Monica Municipal in California, banned jet operations altogether. Failing to appease the residents of surrounding neighborhoods, the next approach became more involved: engine makers would be required to build engines producing less noise and smoke. The tall order caused CEOs in the aviation industry to shake in their boots. The task was expected to devour untold millions of dollars for research and development.

Under pressure by the cities to take action, the FAA issued its first noise ruling in 1969—Part 36 of the Federal Air Regulations. It set limits on noise from newly built transport category and turbojet-powered aircraft. Going a step further, and faced with unrelenting pressure from their constituents to limit noise, members of Congress passed the Noise Control Act of 1972. It set strict limits for all sources of noise, whether emanating from aircraft and automobiles or major household appliances. The FAA amended Part 36 in 1977 to differentiate between three noise levels, each with specific limits. It required applicants for aircraft type certificates issued after November 5, 1975, to meet Stage 3 limits, stricter than what the previous regulations mandated. Any new model of the Gulfstream would not be allowed to exceed the Stage 3 decibel limit. Existing planes not meeting Stage 3 specifications were relegated to so-called Stage 2 status. Although the FAA planned to prohibit Stage 2 operations in the short term, it delayed doing so for decades before permanently grounding all Stage 2 aircraft from flying in the United States in December 2015.

Noise wasn't the only roadblock blocking development of new aircraft or keeping older models in the air. The Environmental Protection Agency issued a rule specifying the maximum air pollution that gas turbine engines were permitted to emit. It set a limit on the volume of unburned hydrocarbons exiting engine exhausts during takeoffs and landings. Offering leeway for a limited time, it exempted certain engines from the pollution requirements. Unfortunately for Gulfstream owners, the Spey was considered a "noncompliant" engine. "The Spey Mk. 511 misses the requirement by a wide mark," reported an FAA official in *Aviation Week & Space Technology*. "The limit for the Spey on the Gulfstream 3 is 2.2 lb., and the actual emission is 24.87 lbs."[21]

The EPA rules required that Gulfstream Aerospace deliver its GIIIs to customers with a notice stating that the airplane couldn't be operated in commercial service, but was legal for non-revenue producing flights. That is, the EPA air pollution limits applied to jets in airline operation, scheduled or unscheduled, but not in private use. GIII customers were upset. "These operators were worried about the resale value of their aircraft with a restriction on no commercial use," said a Gulfstream spokesman.[22] The FAA later intervened to soften the restrictions. Rolls-Royce kept busy by modifying the combustor sections of Spey engines to assure more thorough burning of combustion residue, reducing the emissions. It was a stopgap measure.

To assure compliance with Part 36 standards, Paulson developed a "hush kit" for the Spey, but the device proved too expensive for Gulfstream owners to purchase and increased the airplane's empty weight. The project was abandoned. It appeared that the only viable solution was to switch to an engine that already met Part 36 standards, but none was commercially available in the thrust size needed.

In the mid–1950s, Grumman chose the Rolls-Royce Dart turboprop for the Gulfstream I because the engine had proven itself powering Vickers Viscount airliners. At Grumman, reliability of the Gulfstream's engines was a big selling point. Paulson carried that criterion forward for each Gulfstream he developed. Maintaining a close association with Grumman, and now Gulfstream Aerospace, the marketers at Rolls committed to do whatever was necessary to keep Gulfstream's business. A contributing factor had to do with Rolls not being in the best financial condition. Lockheed, its single largest commercial customer, was facing severe competition from McDonnell Douglas and its DC-10, causing sales of Lockheed's L-1011 TriStar to languish. It stopped production of the jetliner in 1983. The TriStar was powered by three Rolls-Royce RB211 turbofans, but the DC-10 was equipped with General Electric engines. By 1985, Rolls held only an 11 percent share of the worldwide commercial aircraft engine market, compared to Pratt & Whitney's 51 percent and General Electric's 32 percent. Rolls needed Gulfstream's business and that of any other airframe maker to survive.

Finding another engine to power the next generation of the Gulfstream would be the key to minimizing the noise and squeezing more range from the airplane. Retaining the GIII's fuel-gulping Spey was out of the question. Although two engines powered all previous Gulfstreams, Paulson began to consider using four smaller engines to power what would become the GIV.

Executives at the Bristol Engine Division of Rolls-Royce decided to develop an efficient small turbofan engine in 1971. The RB401 was targeted to replace the Viper turbojet that powered several business and military aircraft. First running in November 1977, the engine's impressive performance was derived by using some of the technology embodied in the much larger RB211. From an environmental standpoint, the engine showed promise, emitting only one-third the maximum level of unburned hydrocarbons permitted by the EPA. It was almost smokeless.

Seeking a customer to launch the program, Rolls was fortunate when the RB401 got Paulson's full attention. Compared to the 11,400-pound-thrust Spey, the engine was in the 5,500-pound thrust class, a logical choice to power a four-engine business jet. Powering the GIV with RB401s would satisfy the FAR 36 noise limits and the EPA's pollution regulations. Proceeding with preliminary work for the jet and enthused over its possibilities, Paulson also directed that design work begin on a shorter fuselage version of the GIV, tentatively called the GV, to be powered by twin RB401s. The latter would remain a "paper" airplane and never be built.

Work on the nacelle design for the four-engine GIV began in 1981, but was soon discontinued. Querying Rolls engineers about an engine they called the "Tay," engineering vice president Charles Coppi lectured Paulson with a number of reasons why he should stick to a twin-engine configuration using the new RB183 Tay. It wasn't easy winning over his stubborn boss, as Paulson remained fixated on the four-engine concept. Coppi was not in favor of four engines because it would have doubled the complexity of the airplane's systems. In December 1982, a week before Gulfstream's planned official launch of the GIV, Paulson changed his mind. Heavily influenced by Coppi, he ordered that all work stop on the quadruple-engine jet. Coppi told him that FAA certification for a twin-engine variant could be accomplished under an amended GII type certificate—rather than needing to obtain an all-new type certificate for a four-engine airplane. It meant spending far less money, music to Paulson's ears.

Rolls executives predicted that during the decade to come, the RB401 would power more than 3,000 business jets powered by that thrust class engine. Short-lived enthusiasm for the engine died when Roll's plans progressed too slowly for airframe manufacturers, the company failing to deliver production engines.

The Tay retained many service-proven components of the Spey, but its fan was about a foot larger in diameter. Additional compressor stages were required, along with a new low-pressure turbine to drive the fan. Offering almost twice the bypass airflow of the Spey, the 12,400-pound thrust Tay would hopefully placate the complaints of "noisy" airport neighbors.

What expedited the Tay program at Rolls was that the engine had been selected for an ongoing aircraft program at Fokker, the Dutch manufacturer. It was the Fokker 100, a replacement for the company's aging F28 jetliner. Retaining major airframe sections of the F28, the new airplane would have a redesigned wing and be powered by two Tay engines. The most noticeable physical difference between the old and new jetliners was a stretched fuselage to boost the seating capacity from eighty-five to 107 passengers.

Ralph Robins, head of the commercial engine program at Rolls, moved swiftly to get the Tay project underway. Fokker ordered 100 of the engines for its new plane. However, Paulson beat Fokker to the punch with an even earlier decision to buy the Tay—Gulfstream becoming the first airframe manufacturer in the world to specify it. The engine development program was launched in March 1983 with an order from Paulson for 200 engines, accompanied by a sizable cash deposit. Gulfstream expected to buy hundreds of the engines over a ten-year period. If development of the Tay hadn't been chosen for the Fokker—that action assuring a profitable production run for Rolls— it's likely that Paulson would have built the GIV with four engines rather than two. The Tay's development program moved ahead with few hitches, the engine running for the first time in August 1984, attaining easy FAA certification in 1986.

The purchase negotiations between Gulfstream Aerospace and Rolls took place over lunch at the Waldorf Astoria Hotel in New York City shortly before Christmas in 1982. Paulson and Robins sat next to each other tossing numbers back and forth concerning quantity, price, and payment terms. "Neither of us had a piece of paper, so we wrote it all down on a napkin," Robins said. "Another guest at the luncheon, from Chemical Bank, leaned across the table and said, 'If you two guys are trying to do a deal, you'd better have something a bit more substantial to write it on.' He passed a small card. We sorted out the entire deal on the card. We both signed it (and the napkin) and that deal stuck for all our years of doing business. Allen kept the napkin."[23] The deal scrawled on the back of the card called for Paulson to make an initial buy of 200 engines. The total came to $300 million. A month later, he made the initial public offering of Gulfstream Aerospace stock, in part to help pay for the engines.

"Within the first five minutes you talked with Al you knew he was down to earth and not trying to pull the wool over your eyes," Goldie Glenn remarked, recalling the straightforward negotiations with Robins. "Al never tried to cheat anyone that I was aware of. He was fair with everybody."[24]

The Tay emerged as one of Roll's most reliable and profitable engines. In October 2002, shortly before Robins retired as chairman of Rolls, Gulfstream took delivery of the 1,000th Tay engine for the GIV.

The diameter of the Tay's fan section meant that the GIV's nacelles would need to be larger than those of the GIII. Wind tunnel testing of a scale model GIV revealed a dramatic rise in drag occurred due to the bulkier nacelles. To not detract from aircraft performance, the nacelles were relocated 17 inches rearward along the aft fuselage. A fuselage barrel section was added at the point where the trailing edge of the wing joined the fuselage. Another barrel section was inserted near the front of the cabin to counterbalance the weight of the aft extension. Compared to the GIII, the two fuselage plugs stretched the passenger cabin of the GIV, creating two extra windows to provide traveling VIPs a panoramic view of the world below. A new wing structure reduced the empty weight of the airframe, the decrease needed to offset the increased weight of the Tays and their heavier nacelles.

The fiasco involving Grumman's original supercritical GIII wing remained fresh in the minds of Gulfstream aerodynamicists. To cut cost and schedule risk, the GIV wing was nothing more than a major modification of the proven GIII wing and not invented from scratch. The airfoil contour of the wing was changed, but modification of it was limited to the forward 65 percent of the chord (width). This assured that an expensive redesign of the GIII's control surfaces on the wing's trailing edge wouldn't be necessary. Changes to the rest of the airframe included strengthening the fuselage floor structure to accommodate beefed up supports for the new wing. Compared to earlier Gulfstreams, the series of relatively small but important enhancements would enable the GIV to offer a lower stall speed—and a longer range brought about by less drag, fuel-efficient engines, and increased fuel capacity.

Compared to the GII, the GIII's range was increased 37 percent, enabling it to undertake nonstop transatlantic flights. In the case of the GIV, the redesign translated into a further 22 percent increase in range. The Tay burned 15 percent less fuel than the Spey, giving the GIV a reported range of 4,220 nautical miles. This appealed to foreign-based operators wishing to fly lengthy transoceanic routes. Equally important, the jet complied with all noise and air emission standards then in force. On the flight deck, all-digital avionics were standard equipment. Six cathode ray tube displays replaced older electromechanical instruments—a "glass" rather than "steam gauge" cockpit, the former now standard in today's jetliners.

The GIV program was launched at the same time Gulfstream enjoyed a solid order backlog for the GIII. Taking orders for the latest jet over a period of ten days, sixteen letters of commitment were received. Sparked by the rosy response, Paulson predicted sales of 300 GIVs during the coming decade. History reveals that his estimate was conservative: 535 GIVs were delivered from 1987 through 2003.

The Gulfstream IV, final Gulfstream model produced during Paulson's reign at Gulfstream Aerospace, first flown September 19, 1985 (©Gulfstream Aerospace Corporation, reproduced with permission).

"Gulfstream's claim of having 'the most advanced business aircraft in its timeframe' is understandable," noted an article in *Flight International* describing the GIV.[25] Little doubt existed in the minds of aviation industry executives that Gulfstream Aerospace had created a winner.

Paulson pushed ahead to finish the GIV's development, gain FAA certification, and get the jet into production. While he put in twelve-hour workdays in Savannah, at Chrysler Corp. in Detroit, larger-than-life, cigar-chomping Lee Iacocca had already made history in a herculean effort to turn around the beleaguered automaker's operations.

The automotive icon was no stranger in tackling immense challenges or fighting his way out of nasty corporate politics. In 1978, at the age of fifty-three, he was fired from Ford Motor Co. following a prolonged struggle with chairman Henry Ford II. Iacocca's termination came as a shock because his efforts had generated $2 billion in profits for Ford during the preceding year. The biggest feather in his hat at Ford was overseeing development of the legendary Mustang. Reaching dealers in 1964, the car sold out its initial production run, becoming a sought-after classic in later years.

Five months after Ford fired Iacocca he emerged as chairman and chief executive officer of nearly bankrupt Chrysler. The automaker's board of directors had sought a fearless, brash leader to grab the reigns and turn the company's operations around. Iacocca fit the description. "I went from the frying pan into the fire," he recalled of what he faced. "A year after I signed up, Chrysler came within a whisker of bankruptcy." He wondered why he got himself involved with the failing company. "Being fired at Ford was bad enough. But going down with the ship at Chrysler was more than I deserved."[26] His days were exhausting and worrisome, but the challenges were a precise match for his skills. Going back forty years as a teenager in Pennsylvania, he never quit until he got what he wanted.

Iacocca's initial tasks at Chrysler were to slash costs and try to arrange a gigantic loan to develop a new line of automobiles. After finagling a $1.5 billion government loan guarantee from Congress, obtained under difficult circumstances, he initiated a company-wide austerity campaign. He closed assembly plants and convinced Chrysler's labor unions to accept layoffs and wage cuts under the threat of shutting down the automaker's operations. By July 1983, Iacocca succeeded in turning Chrysler around and paid back the loan, including interest, seven years before its payback deadline.

Chrysler's television commercials featured Iacocca shouting, "If you can find a better car, buy it." By the mid–1980s, owing to his widespread exposure on the commercials, the cocky appearing carmaker became somewhat of a folk hero. The *Saturday Evening Post* described him as "the sex symbol of America." *Reader's Digest* wrote that he was "the living embodiment of the American dream." Talk circulated about drafting him to run for president of the United States. A 1985 poll of candidate preferences for the 1988 presidential race showed that he trailed George H. W. Bush by only three percentage points.

Aided by an improved economy, Iacocca turned the "new" Chrysler Corp. into a cash cow. Pleased with the results, he began to look beyond manufacturing cars. He set out to mimic an automotive industry trend that involved buying high-technology companies. Prime examples included Chrysler's main rivals, General Motors and Ford, each bidding for Hughes Aircraft Co. GM ended up buying Hughes after bidding $5 billion for the defense electronics and satellite maker started by Howard Hughes in the 1930s.

Iacocca liked what he saw at Gulfstream Aerospace and placed the company on a short list to research as a possible acquisition. Having access to a Gulfstream jet to expedite his business travels, he appreciated the quality and performance of the airplane. He also counted Paulson as a friend. Congress wouldn't allow Chrysler to own a business jet while the automaker's government loan guarantee was in force. When the loan was paid off, Iacocca considered buying a business jet *manufacturer* and not just an airplane. He had turned around a nearly bankrupt corporation and built its financial strength to a point where it could pursue such a grandiose acquisition.

Iacocca flew to Savannah to spend the day with Paulson. The men had known each other for years, owning homes not far apart in the Palm Springs area. They respected each other's opinions, although their personalities were strikingly different. Their rags-to-riches backgrounds bore similarities, each surviving a difficult, deprived childhood. As a child, Iacocca earned money for his family's neighborhood grocery store by carrying goods in a little red wagon to the homes of customers. Paulson cleaned toilets in a hotel. "He and Iacocca were two of a kind," Bruce McCaw remarked.[27]

Not one to waste words, Iacocca told Paulson that Chrysler had plenty of cash and wanted to buy Gulfstream Aerospace. By selling Gulfstream to Chrysler, Paulson figured he could have his cake and eat it, too. "[There] came a period when I figured it was a good opportunity to sell and still be involved in Gulfstream. So I sold it."[28]

During the afternoon of June 19, 1985, Paulson sold his entire stake in the company to Chrysler. The boards of Gulfstream and Chrysler approved the automaker's acquisition of the aircraft manufacturer's outstanding stock for $19 a share, totaling $637 million. The deal required Chrysler to pay $310 million in cash and issue $327 million worth of promissory notes. The payment hardly dented the $3 billion pile of cash and securities sitting in the automaker's treasury. In the days following the acquisition, Gulfstream Aerospace first appeared on the Fortune 500 list, ranked number 417.

"My deal with Chrysler was that I would continue to run the company for five years and be chairman and chief executive officer," Paulson said,[29] clarifying the terms of the agreement with reporters. Briefing the press, Iacocca said the acquisition represented an "important step in our long-range plan to diversify into high-tech industries like aerospace and electronics, fast-growing industries like financial services and to continue to invest heavily in the automotive industry."[30] Diversification was the automobile industry's current craze. "Chrysler didn't need Gulfstream and Gulfstream didn't need Chrysler," Iacocca said without blinking an eye. "That makes the best sort of marriage."[31]

In 1983, Paulson said, "yes" to a blind date. Divorced from Mary Lou, he had met and dated a number of women, but especially looked forward to a date with Madeleine Farris, also divorced. Delayed at the airport until early evening, he was late for their rendezvous. Switching gears, Paulson asked her to play tennis the next day, but it rained. They ended up spending the day shooting pool and talking. Although having vastly different backgrounds and personalities, they found common ground to gradually form a relationship.

Madeleine was born in Kirkuk, Iraq, to an English father and Lebanese mother. Her father, Bill Baker, a businessman in the oil industry after World War II, was also a golf course architect who built his first course in Kirkuk. He went on to develop golf courses throughout Europe. Loving the game, he cut down a set of clubs to suit five-year-old Madeleine's physique and taught the child how to play.

Twenty-six-year-old Madeleine Baker came to the United States and married Glen Farris in Fort Bend, Texas, in June 1973. It was reported that she left Iraq shortly before the country's takeover by Saddam Hussein's Ba'ath Party. Following their divorce in January 1975, she settled in the Los Angeles area, domiciled as a flight attendant with Pan American World Airways. Her life away from flying consisted of part-time modeling gigs, such as McDonald's restaurant commercials and "infomercial" television shows for modeling the latest hair fashions. She then quit modeling completely. "It just wasn't satisfying to me. Modeling seemed so empty," she said in an interview for *Black Belt Magazine* in 1976. "The work is boring and tiring. You have to do too many empty smiles."[32] The holder of a black belt in the martial art of tai kwon do, she was profiled in a lengthy article for the magazine. Home was a waterside condo overlooking the Marina Del Rey yacht harbor, convenient to Los Angeles International Airport. She went on to marry Robert Richter, an orthopedic surgeon. In 1980, daughter Dominique was born to the couple.

Madeleine incorporated a business called Nikki Jet Services, Inc. on December 5, 1979. The company provided flight attendants for upper-crust clientele chartering business jets, including Gulfstreams. Much of her business came from the Mideast where she trained cabin attendants for the Saudi Arabian Oil Co. (Aramco), a steady, good paying client.

Following a multi-year courtship, Allen and Madeleine tied the knot on December 21, 1988, at a church in Savannah. He was sixty-six, she forty-two. Lacy and Iacocca were at the groom's side during the ceremony.

Crystal Christensen asked her grandfather why he wanted to marry for a third time. His response: "She plays tennis, is beautiful, and speaks several languages."[33]

11

Flying Fast

The money that Paulson received from Chrysler catapulted him into becoming perhaps the wealthiest citizen in Savannah. He began to indulge in a first-class lifestyle, building an architecturally significant home on exclusive Dutch Island. Constructed on the ruins of a Confederate fort, the estate was named for Francis Grimball, a contractor who owned several hundred acres in the area during the 1850s. At 35 Waite Drive, "Grimball" was nestled on six lushly landscaped acres along the Herb River within a gated community covering 500 acres.

Paulson's architect, Paul Hansen, described working with the industrialist as, "always wanting things to be first-class and he didn't mind paying for it. He was considerate of other people's opinions and would get impatient with you if he thought you were agreeing with him because of who he was."[1] Noting the immense scale of the property, Paulson said, "It's not a castle. I've built two or three homes and get a lot of enjoyment from working on the details. It's like the airplane I use at Gulfstream. I got involved in picking the interior design, the fabrics, and everything else for it."[2]

Construction of the 12,254-square-foot home consumed three years. Built for lavish entertaining, it featured six bedrooms, ten bathrooms, a mahogany paneled lounge with a full-size bar, paneled library, movie screening room, billiard room, elevator—even a wine cellar capable of storing thousands of bottles at just the right temperature. The lounge had an elliptical coved ceiling covered with fourteen-karat gold leaf. There was a full-size ballroom on the second floor. Silk material covered the walls of the master bedroom suite on the first floor. The bath fixtures were gold plated. The floors in several rooms had handcrafted marble. On the grounds could be found a ten-hole golf course, a huge swimming pool, and a concrete dock to accommodate vessels as long as 125 feet. The guesthouse and garage alone totaled 3,500 square feet.

Paulson could be thought of as a man who never flew anything smaller than a Learjet. But he did enjoy flying another kind of aircraft: the helicopter. It didn't take long for him to appreciate its usefulness for traveling short distances. Having flown most everything with fixed wings, he added a helicopter endorsement to his pilot license. Perhaps benefactor Jerry Henderson influenced the decision—his former business partner beginning to fly helicopters at the age of seventy-two.

After leaving California, and years before Paulson built Grimball, he and Mary Lou spent two years living in a home on Hilton Head Island in South Carolina. It's a resort town situated on an island of the same name some 20 miles northeast of Savannah. Paulson used a single-engine Bell JetRanger helicopter to commute to his plant on the Savannah airport. It was a short, enjoyable trip on a clear day. But on a stormy day it could be dangerous, causing him to take a car. "He was going to fly his helicopter to work but the weather was such that he wasn't always able to fly," Mary Lou said. "So we bought a condominium in Savannah."[3] The two-bedroom condo at 519 Howard Street was located in the historic district of Savannah. Seeking more room for guests and entertaining, they later moved into a four-bedroom, 3,733-square-foot home at 405 Stuart Street, still under construction when it was purchased. Seeking to replicate a Southern California style of outdoor living, Paulson built a casita, pool, and tennis court on an adjacent lot he bought from a neighbor.

Moving to Dutch Island, Paulson was adamant to use a helicopter for commuting the shorter distance between there and the Gulfstream plant. Replacing the smaller JetRanger, he bought a twin-engine Sikorsky S-76 to make the abbreviated jaunt. He acquired the Cadillac of helicopters after making a deal with Sikorsky to promote their rotary wing products in advertisements. The five-ton craft could fly 178 miles per hour and cover a range of 400 miles without refueling. He made regular use of the machine while in Georgia, and later during his years in Southern California. "For short trips, the S-76 can get me where I'm going faster than the Gulfstream III, because it flies point to point, not airport to airport," he was quoted in a Sikorsky advertisement that appeared in magazines.[4] Next to his home on Dutch Island sat a concrete helipad for parking the helicopter.

The engineers and mechanics in the Savannah plant devoted three months of round-the-clock effort to assemble the first GIV. Two twelve-hour shifts, seven days a week became the norm. Under the direction of Glenn, the task consumed tens of thousands of man-hours to prepare the jet for its promised September 1985 rollout. It became a herculean undertaking to assemble the one and only GIV for the year's biggest aviation exposition in New Orleans, scheduled for October. There was barely enough time to piece the airframe together. The engines arrived weeks late, adding to the anxiety. Its wings showed up on August 15 from subcontractor Avco. Growing impatient, workers began to paint the airframe while mechanics were still assembling the jet's mechanical parts.

Weeks after the GIV's maiden flight on September 19, Paulson flew it from Savannah to New Orleans for the trade show. There were no technical problems, not so much as a burned-out light bulb. The jet had logged a total of only 8 hours. Because the Tay engines weren't yet flight proven, the FAA required that a minimum of 5 hours of restricted flight be logged before it permitted the plane to fly outside the Savannah area.

The GIV arrived at New Orleans Lakefront Airport a day before the annual National Business Aircraft Association convention opened. It would have a starring role. The night before the convention hall doors swung open, two eager customers signed purchase contracts upon seeing the jet. The deals brought the order backlog to eighty-three airplanes.

Introducing the GIV to attendees and members of the media on the first day of the show, Paulson stood alongside the aircraft for photo opportunities

Lee Iacocca with Paulson alongside the first Gulfstream IV at the National Business Aircraft Association convention at New Orleans in October 1985 (©Gulfstream Aerospace Corporation, reproduced with permission).

with Iacocca, his admiring new boss. Paulson emphasized that the GIV was an all-new aircraft and not a warmed over GIII. Pointing out its features, he stressed how the wing weighed 900 pounds less than the wing of the GIII. There were new landing gear assemblies featuring brake-by-wire and steering-by-wire controls. Asked about the Tay engines, he told the attendees that he experienced a "fantastic response" from them during the flight from Savannah, describing their functioning as "super quiet and performing five percent better than the Rolls-Royce figures."

Iacocca was more than impressed, beaming during every photo opportunity while standing next to the glistening jet in the static display area. "When I took over Chrysler, I was renting parking lots to put unsold cars in," he said. "An order backlog of this magnitude is unheard of in the motor industry."[5] Years later, Paulson reflected about his lengthy association with the automaker: "Chrysler did well with us. We made money every year. They didn't have to put any investment in it."[6]

Certification testing of the GIV consumed the remainder of 1986. There were few hiccups. The biggest change was to modify the wing to improve its slow-speed and stall characteristics. Paulson was especially thrilled with the

Paulson prepares himself for a flight in his Gulfstream IV (©Gulfstream Aerospace Corporation, reproduced with permission).

GIV's computerized flight management system. "The whole flight plan can be entered into the system," he said. "I flew here the other night by putting it on auto approach and flying right on down to fifty feet off the runway. The Gulfstream IV has to be the most advanced aircraft in the world flying with this type of technology."[7]

Adding more workload for his engineers, as did the cancelled GI-C regional airliner program earlier, Paulson decided to develop an airline version of the GIV. Although it would never leave the drawing board, the proposed airplane had a 12.3-foot fuselage extension inserted forward of the wing and a 6.1-foot section inserted behind it. He labeled the jet the Gulfstream 4B. "[Airlines} are looking for a low-cost alternative to provide first-class travel on some routes because of the demand," he said. "A stretched Gulfstream IV could hold twenty-four or twenty-six seats, and with two pilots and two cabin attendants, first-class travel could be provided. By using a different aircraft for first class, the aircraft could leave at a different time to avoid lines and retain a first-class atmosphere."[8] The Chrysler board members told him to "wait" before going any further. Lacking a budget approved by corporate, the project went nowhere.

Experiencing much of his early business success in the San Fernando Valley, Paulson continued to maintain a residence at 3806 Alonzo Avenue in Encino, built in 1976. Occupying the top of a steep hill a thousand feet over the valley floor, the seven-bedroom, eight-bath home was located in the most affluent part of the trendy Los Angeles suburb. After moving to Savannah, the Paulsons were lucky to live there one weekend a month. When Paulson was in town, Lacy would drop by the Alonzo house. "I visited Al on weekends," he remarked about their time together. "I had my perfectly restored 1955 Chevrolet. Al would hop in and we'd head over to my place. Walking along the sidewalk was a man and his son. They stopped and watched a Gulfstream take off from Van Nuys. I said to Al, 'you know what he's saying to his son, don't you? There goes another one of those Learjets.'"[9]

To the average guy, planes with two jet engines in the back all looked alike.

～　～　～

Swooping low over the ground while twisting around the pylons in a DC-7 during the California 1000 Air Race, Paulson relished his time in the cockpit with Lacy. The industrialist's DC-8 made hair-raising flights carrying "The Human Fly." For years he sponsored Lacy in the P-51D Mustang at a string of races. His Lear Jet demonstrator flew Jack Conroy and Lacy across the country in a record-setting dawn-to-dusk dash. These were the do-anything years in civil aviation for the maverick plane maker. At the age of sixty-five, long after participating in such performances, he was eager as ever to topple existing flight records. He hoped that setting them in the Gulfstream IV would garner publicity as the earlier adventures did. Proving that his $22 million machines could fly faster and farther than competitive jets was a matter of pride for him.

He climbed into the cockpit of a company-owned GIV on June 12, 1987, to set one of those records. His flight plan called for flying *westbound* around the world, departing and ending in Paris. Flight in this direction is subject to stiff headwinds, presenting a battle to rack up speed. A Learjet 35A flown by Brooke Knapp had set an around-the-world speed record for business jets on February 16, 1983. However, her flight was in an *eastbound* direction. Knapp flew with the wind but Paulson would fly against it. His attempt to fly such a long distance would demonstrate how fast the Gulfstream could fly against headwinds. To assure the most publicity, it helped that the Paris Air Show was in full bloom during the time of the flight.

Paulson occupied the captain's seat for much of the journey, receiving credit in the record books as pilot-in-command. Bob Smyth, longtime Gulfstream Aerospace pilot and vice president, accompanied him. Company pilots John Salamankas, Keith Edgecomb, Jeff Bailey, and Colin Allen rounded out the pilot crew. To handle unforeseen mechanical issues, a flight engineer was aboard. Monitoring the jet's progress, an official from the National Aeronautic Association stationed himself in the cabin to confirm they passed geographic checkpoints and checked the flight's elapsed time on behalf of the Federation Aeronautique Internationale (FAI).

After leaving Paris in N440GA, they touched down at Edmonton in Alberta, Canada; Midway Island in the Pacific Ocean; Kota Kinabalu in Malaysia; and Dubai in the United Arab Emirates. The turnaround times at each of the four stops averaged 15 minutes, a credit to military-like preparedness on the part of Gulfstream ground crews. A minor annoyance was a half-hour delay waiting for a landing slot at Le Bourget Airport in Paris. The GIV touched down shortly after noon on June 14. "We flew it at red line all the way," Paulson said of the airplane's performance.

The jet had circled the earth in 45 hours, 25 minutes, 10 seconds. Two world records and twenty-two city-to-city records were set in a new FAI category dedicated to westward around-the-world flights. "We did it to prove that an aircraft with a high Mach cruise number can go against a 100-knot headwind from Paris to New York," an elated Paulson told reporters. "We are the only transport aircraft to go for this [globe-circling] record, and we challenge anyone else to break it."[10] In 1987, a total of forty-four GIVs were sold with forty-two more scheduled for delivery in 1988. The volume of business had never experienced such an upswing. The publicity from setting this and other records may have helped close some of the deals.

Paulson participated in the records game again in February 1988. It turned into a friendly case of rivalry with Clay Lacy and a Boeing 747SP dubbed the *Friendship One*. At the time of the 1987 Paris Air Show, Lacy, Joe Clark and Bruce McCaw met to plan an around-the-world flight to beat the record set in an easterly direction in a GIII by Knapp on February 15 1984. She took 45 hours, 32 minutes, and 53 seconds to complete the flight. Lacy and his team wanted to fly a larger airplane. Doing so would require generous sponsors to foot the costs. Paulson had set his records in business jets, this causing Lacy to use something different—a jumbo jet. Enter United Airlines. The carrier had bought Pan American World Airway's overseas routes in 1986. Pan Am's fleet of 747SPs came with the deal. Coincidentally, United wanted to publicize introduction of the long range Boeings on its routes. Lacy talked with Ed Carlson, United's CEO, who was willing to lend one of the fuel-efficient Boeings for a weekend. Fifty-six-year-old Lacy, nearing the top of the pilot seniority list at United, would command the flight. Managing the flight attendant duties would become the responsibility of his wife Lois, a former flight attendant at the airline. A team of volunteer pilots, flight engineers, cabin attendants, and ground personnel joined them. Although United provided the airplane gratis, Boeing, Pratt & Whitney, and Volkswagen of America helped with its maintenance support and fuel.

The purpose of the flight involved more than setting a record and gaining publicity for the sponsors. It was to raise money to fund charitable organizations to help disadvantaged children. The Friendship Foundation was formed for this purpose, Lacy, McCaw, and Clark joining together as founders. Organizations destined to benefit from the donations included the City of Hope Children's Cancer Fund, the Children's Hospital of Seattle, and UNICEF. To raise an anticipated $500,000 for charity, each of 100 passengers donated a minimum of $5,000 to the foundation. The paying guests included Apollo 11 astronaut Neil Armstrong, test pilot Bob Hoover, and Moya Lear. Alex Kvassay and his two sons were also aboard. Seventy-seven of the passengers and crewmembers were licensed pilots.

Departing Seattle at 7:14 p.m. on January 28, 1988, the 699,000-pound *Friendship One* flew 8,350 nonstop miles to Athens for refueling. Along the route, Lacy was fortunate to encounter tail winds over the Atlantic reaching 180 miles per hour. Next was Taipei for refueling, the only other stop. The time spent on the ground wasn't more than 45 minutes, although the passengers didn't deplane. There was no lack of luxury aboard. Filet mignon, abalone, smoked salmon, and lobster were on the menu—accompanied by an endless flow of champagne and other libations. The guests remained on board enjoying cocktails, cuisine, and endless socializing. Many were long-time friends. "The flight quickly formed into a 6-mile-high house party," reported the *Los Angeles Times*. "Books went unread. Tapes remained unheard. It was scrambled nights and days of talk (tales of combat, test flying and space travel) and laughter; gourmet food and toasts and one monumental, fraternal gathering."[11]

Friendship One arrived back in Seattle at 8:45 a.m. on January 30. A brass band and 1,000 people cheering their arrival, the flight had set a record of 36 hours, 54 minutes, 15 seconds elapsed time. "They had not touched foot to earth in almost two days, having had neither time nor permission to deplane at two refueling stops," the *Times* reported.[12] A win-win for aviation history and charity, the Friendship Foundation raised $525,000.

Paulson never expected a non-military jet to beat the records set by Gulfstreams, particularly his westbound flight from Paris. At the Paris Air Show following that flight, he told visitors that he could knock hours off the eastbound record then held by Knapp. He didn't have a clue what Lacy and his friends were thinking. "[Knapp's] record attempt simmered on the back burner until *Friendship One* turned in its remarkable performance," reported an article in *Flying*.[13]

Hearing the news, Paulson's desire to beat *Friendship One's* record intensified. The decision to try for it came about after a short conversation at a Chrysler board meeting in Detroit. Fellow board member, Malcolm Stamper, vice chairman of Boeing, whispered into Paulson's ear asking how he felt about Goliath beating David, referring to the 747SP flight—Paulson obviously thought of as David. The comment was enough to spur him into action. Lacy, unbeknownst of Paulson's plan to compete, remained confident that the 747SP's record would stand the test of time.

"The Boeing record made us knuckle down and do everything possible," Paulson said of his detailed planning for another record-setting flight. He knew the GIV could fly faster than the Boeing and Gulfstream Aerospace was equipped to minimize the jet's refueling time on the ground. "We wanted to challenge them without being cocky," he said. "Once you hold these records you hate to see them go."[14] It annoyed him that Lacy had broken a record set by a business jet.

N400GA, another Gulfstream demonstrator, departed Houston's William P. Hobby Airport on February 26, 1988, Paulson again at the controls. Company pilots Bob Smyth, John Salamankas, and Jeff Bailey joined him. Ahead was Shannon, Ireland. Other planned stops were Hong Kong, Honolulu, and back to Houston.

Ground preparations were rehearsed down to the minutest detail. To refuel the jet, two mechanics and a pilot were flown to each airport well in advance of Paulson's arrival. The crews made sure that four fuel tanker trucks were positioned in place on the ramp. When the GIV taxied into place, a hose was quickly connected to the jet's single-point refueling port. To refuel the plane even faster, two hoses were fitted to the filler ports on each wing to pump in more fuel. A fourth hose was hooked up to fill a tank installed in the cabin especially for the flight. All went well at each stop.

Landing in Houston, the good news for Gulfstream was that Paulson's eastbound record eclipsed the 747SP flown by Lacy. The GIV traversed a similar route as the United airplane, but took only 36 hours, 8 minutes. It beat the big Boeing by 45 minutes, 41 seconds. "The winds were cooperative," Paulson said of the 23,002-mile journey. The FAI rules required that a record had to beat an existing one by at least 1 percent. Paulson beat the 747SP record by more than 2 percent.

What Lacy wasn't counting on was his friend's tenaciousness in wanting to topple the 747SP's record less than a month after it was set. "He did kind of upset me," Lacy admitted.

> Al went out and beat us. It was my fault, as I should have leaned on the airplane a little harder. I was going fast, cruising about point nine [Mach number], but I didn't fly as direct a course as I could have. I thought there was no way anyone was ever going to beat us. The thing is, I don't think he beat us. One of his pilots told me they cut some corners during the flight. On my 747, I had to take a guy along who was the head of the contest committee. At every place we turned, he'd come up with a camera and take pictures of the INS [inertial navigation system] to be sure we were actually there. I later found out that Al's guy never came into the cockpit.[15]

There was another hitch that affected the 747's progress. "They failed to get an overflight permit from China," Kvassay said. "[It] necessitated diverting south over Vietnam and losing much of the push from the jet stream. Even with these problems, we achieved an average ground speed of 626 miles per hour, bettering the previous world record set by Knapp. But we could not rest long on our laurels."[16]

During the forty-five years that Lacy and Paulson remained close friends, such rivalry didn't hurt their friendship or respect for each other one bit. Said Lacy, "We were ultraconservative and Al's a competitive guy."[17] When it came to setting speed records, or tossing the dice at the crap table in Las Vegas, Paulson would put everything on the line. Joe Clark, a guest aboard the 747SP, said: "Al was so enamored of our record that he went on and beat us. He was very competitive, but also very quiet about it."[18]

Among the workers in Savannah, the world record turned into a big deal. "This had a big impact on the morale of our employees," Paulson said about setting this and other records. "The people who bought our airplane have their decision confirmed that they bought the best." The GIV chosen for the flight was a sales demonstrator. The only expenses incurred were for buying fuel and paying the salaries of the Gulfstream employees involved with the project, "that cost us less than an ad in the *Wall Street Journal*," he said.[19]

"It was a Concorde that took those records away," said Art Greenfield, editor of the *World and United States Aviation and Space Records* at the National Aeronautic Association. It wasn't until October 1992 when an Air

Paulson and Clay Lacy share a lighter moment while discussing racehorses and airplanes in 1994 (Clay Lacy archives).

France Concorde snatched the around-the-world record from Paulson. Its 32 hour, 49 minute time bettered the GIV by 3 hours, 19 minutes—and beat the 747SP record by a remarkable 4 hours, 5 minutes. As a supersonic transport, it surprised no one that it smashed both earlier records. "This was definitely a new world record," Kvassay said. "Considering that the average flying speed was 1,084 miles per hour, the overall ground speed of 765 miles per hour was not all that impressive, at least not for an aircraft flying at twice the speed of sound."[20]

These were good times for Paulson. He collected the 1987 Harmon Trophy as the "world's outstanding aviator." In February of the same year he won the Howard Hughes Memorial Award. In December, the Wright Brothers Memorial Trophy came his way.

The luxury of having a Gulfstream or Learjet at his disposal meant that Paulson could enjoy a bi-coastal lifestyle. Besides owning the mansion on Dutch Island, he bought a 15,000-square-foot estate in the trendy Holmby Hills environs of West Los Angeles. In 1938, actress Joan Bennett built the French provincial style home at 515 South Mapleton Drive. She commissioned noted architect Wallace Neff to conceive its design. Lauded as an American stage and film actress, Bennett appeared in more than seventy movies during the mid-twentieth century. In an area of spacious estates set far back on meticulously manicured grounds, the neighborhood is situated midway between Westwood and Beverly Hills. Eva Gabor lived two blocks away in an estate once occupied by Frank Sinatra and Mia Farrow. An article in *Variety* described the neighborhood: "There is not a more coveted address in all of Los Angeles than one along South Mapleton Drive in the perennially hoity-toity Holmby Hills 'hood."[21]

Paulson lived near a number of other well-known celebrities. Sylvester Stallone was around the corner while Hugh Hefner held court a block away at the Playboy Mansion. When Paulson's home needed roof repairs he hired a contractor. Kathy O'Sako recalled: "Allen asked the contractor, 'How come every time I come over here you've got a different crew on the roof?' He replied, 'Allen, if you want the truth, the Playboy Mansion is over there and if they [the workmen] stand on your roof they can see it."[22] The obvious attraction was to catch a glimpse of bikini-clad young women lying around

the pool working on their tans. Visiting the Paulson estate, there was never a lack of big name visitors. "Al loved to rub shoulders with celebrities," Goldie Glenn said. "For his birthday party on Mapleton, Bob Hope, Lee Iacocca, and Nancy Reagan were there."[23] President Ronald Reagan, another Paulson friend, couldn't attend due to declining health. The star-studded group joined Paulson's close friends Bruce McCaw, Joe Clark and Clay Lacy.

Fortunate to have accrued the money to participate in a bold way during the mid–1980s, Paulson began buying thoroughbreds—*hundreds* of them. It was a lifelong dream now coming true. He spent what-

President Gerald Ford and First Lady Betty Ford attend an event with Paulson (Paulson family archives/Crystal Christensen).

ever money was needed to buy the best horses with the expectation of competing for the biggest purses at the racetrack. When the proceeds from the Gulfstream IPO appeared in his checking account, he traveled to auctions nationwide and made dozens of deals. In late 1983, he dished out $11.8 million to buy yearlings and two-year-olds. He continued the spending spree in 1984, paying $11 million to build his equestrian inventory. The following year he spent nearly $20 million, with $17 million of it to buy still more yearlings. Between 1983 and 1987, he purchased a total of 210 thoroughbreds at auctions along with scores of horses bought through private deals. His strategy was clear: the more thoroughbreds he owned, the better his odds of becoming a big-time winner. But his timing in entering the business was less than ideal. The prices he paid for the horses were hardly a bargain. It was a seller's market at the time with most of the animals commanding exorbitant prices. Focusing on the long rather than short term, spending the extra money didn't faze him one bit. The sprawling breeding farms he built in Kentucky, Florida, and California housed the animals.

After his divorce from Mary Lou, Linda Evans, costar of *The Big Valley* and *Dynasty* television shows, could be seen with him at racetracks. Other actresses in his company drew attention away from the quiet industrialist.

Celebrating Cigar's 16th straight victory on July 13, 1996, at Arlington International Racecourse, Illinois. From left, trainer Bill Mott, jockey Jerry Bailey, and Paulson (Paulson family archives/Crystal Christensen).

"The reaction was unfailingly amusing. 'Oooh, ahhh, look there!' and then, 'Huh? That's Allen Paulson," wrote Jay Hovdey in *Cigar*.[24] His pairing with stars like Evans may seem unlikely. He was a self-made, wealthy industrialist but his low-key Midwestern style of presenting himself was the antithesis of the persona most celebrities in Hollywood coveted. Actresses loved publicity; he abhorred it—unless it involved airplanes or horses. His adventuresome side, as test pilot, racehorse owner, and big-stakes corporate risk-taker, balanced out his subdued demeanor, making the man a sought after bachelor.

Named by Paulson for an aeronautical checkpoint, "Cigar" would evolve into the crème de la crème of racehorses by the mid-nineties. Checkpoint Cigar lies in the Gulf of Mexico about a hundred miles west of Tampa, Florida. It's ironic that Paulson, a nonsmoker at the time (he stopped at age forty-three), decided to name the horse for a tobacco product. Born on April 18, 1990, Paulson raised Cigar with the hope that he'd turn into a legend, although such an outcome didn't seem likely early on. Hundreds of thousands of fans couldn't see enough of him during his sixteen-race winning streak stretching from 1994 to 1996. Cigar was honored as horse of the year in 1995, when he won the Breeder's Cup Classic. Other awards followed: horse of the year again in 1996, followed by Eclipse Awards as champion older male in 1995 and 1996. Paulson won the Eclipse Award as leading owner in 1995 and 1996.

Cigar earned Paulson just short of $10 million at the track. Before the horse was diagnosed as infertile, the Japanese Racing Association offered him $30 million for the horse. He

Taking a well-deserved break from work, Paulson enjoys his time in California's horse country (Kathy O'Sako).

turned down the deal. "I would miss him," he said. His love of the horse meant more than money. "I want to provide a good home for the horse for the rest of his life," he said. "He gave a lot to me and my family and the world."[25]

On October 7, 2014, at the Kentucky Horse Park's Hall of Champions in Lexington, Cigar died from complications following surgery for severe osteoarthritis of the neck. He was twenty-four-years-old. The famous horse outlived Paulson by more than fourteen years.

12

Going Supersonic

The approach of the Christmas season in 1989 wasn't a particularly joyous time around the Iacocca household. Nor was it in the executive suites of Chrysler, where the mood was downright somber. The automaker was reporting a $664 million loss for the fourth quarter, posting its first red ink in seven years. Toyota and Honda had established a strong foothold in the North American car-buying market and pulled a devastating share of sales away from Detroit. A nationwide economic dry spell further exacerbated the weak sales picture.

Chrysler bought Gulfstream with the cash generated by selling its cars to dealers. Shifting gears, the acquisition of large technology-based businesses, unrelated to automobiles, was intended to bolster Chrysler's cash flow when the purchasing loyalties of car buyers temporarily swung to competitive brands. At Chrysler, "temporary" seemed to be turning into permanent. By late 1989, the automaker had shut down assembly plants and furloughed thousands of workers. Japanese carmakers were bagging one sale after another, taking away far more business than expected. Iacocca, who joined the automaker eleven years earlier to nurture it back to health, decided to sell Gulfstream Aerospace, albeit grudgingly. Chrysler needed the cash to prop up its automotive operations. Gulfstream was the automaker's golden goose—the one business unit owned by Chrysler that could be sold for a premium price. It wasn't that Iacocca was unhappy with Paulson or Gulfstream's order backlog of $1.5 billion—the largest business aircraft backlog in history. The move was based on nothing more than Chrysler needing a sizable cash infusion to develop a new line of cars to counter what the Japanese were selling.

"That cash goes in the car and truck business worldwide, and that should make it clear where we intend to focus and where we intend to compete," Iacocca told the press, keeping in mind Toyota and Honda. "We are going after the Japanese head to head. We're ready to play against them...."[1]

In addition to Gulfstream, Chrysler planned to sell other assets of a non-automotive nature, including an immense defense electronics subsidiary, Chrysler Technologies. Four years after Paulson sold his company to the automaker, Gulfstream's ownership was about to change hands again. Chrysler made it clear to the financial community that Gulfstream was on the block and requested bids through First Boston Bank. Not wanting to lose Gulfstream, Paulson had an idea. "I was attending Chrysler board meetings all the time," he said. "I told Lee [Iacocca] that I would be interested in buying the company back." To do so, Paulson would need to relinquish his seat on the Chrysler board, a potential conflict of interest. "When I did, I went out and arranged financing. I was working with Barclays bank and they agreed to come up with the money. My understanding with Iacocca was that Chrysler would be willing to sell the company for book value, which was $650 million, or in that neighborhood."[2]

It didn't take long for Chrysler's board members to nix Paulson's plan. They worried that his former involvement as a corporate insider, especially as a director, would bring suspicion to any deal and cause a potential sale to fall through.

Regrouping, Paulson stepped back and assumed a low profile, staying away from Chrysler's headquarters in Highland Park, Michigan, as well as his office and home in Georgia. His whereabouts were unknown to almost everyone except Kathy O'Sako in Savannah—and she wasn't talking. Paulson wanted to revive the company's entrepreneurial roots after five years of Chrysler ownership. The management style in Detroit didn't mesh with his concept of building and marketing aircraft. Chrysler required reports, meetings, and travel that added $30 million a year to Gulfstream's overhead. "I felt I became less productive than I was capable of being with all the controls," he said. "We were looking for synergism between the two companies, but I don't believe there was a lot of that. Chrysler is a tremendously large corporation and Gulfstream does business differently. We think it's a great opportunity to get the company back, basically becoming a private company and be more productive."[3]

Paulson worried about an expected bidding frenzy for the company. He could be found at his secluded home in the Palm Springs area, enjoying tennis matches and rounds of golf to lessen his anxiety about who might buy the company and end up becoming his boss.

Sitting in his office overlooking Central Park on the forty-fourth floor of the General Motors Building in Manhattan, Ted Forstmann, known in social circles as Teddy, was well aware of Chrysler's interest in selling Gulfstream. As chairman of Forstmann Little & Co., the crafty financier appreciated the intrinsic value of the acknowledged leader in business jet manufacturing. He wanted in on the action. As the owner of a GIV, he knew that an airplane as well built and popular as the Gulfstream meant that the company producing it had to be a rock-solid investment—particularly with Paulson at the helm.

Born February 13, 1940, Teddy began his business career by selling his car and a few meager possessions to buy a small, financially distressed manufacturer. Equipped with an engaging personality, analytical brain, and plenty of persistence, he somehow closed the deal, turning the unhealthy enterprise around and selling it. He went on to produce wealth by buying weakened companies with money borrowed against their assets. Joining forces with younger brother Nick and mutual friend Brian Little, Forstmann Little & Co. came into existence.

The financier's early life could be characterized as having a silver spoon in his mouth. Born in Greenwich, Connecticut, Teddy was an heir to one of the largest textile dynasties in the nation. Raised around yachts, mansions in Manhattan, country estates, and private schools, he went from a life as a rich teenager to near poverty by the time he graduated from Yale University. In spite of the family's earlier affluence, the actions of his alcoholic father, coupled with a series of financial setbacks, dissipated the family's wealth. Not a quitter, Teddy went on to attend law school at Columbia University in 1962, drawing $150 a month from a trust fund set up to pay his expenses. For extra money, he hustled up card games. Graduating from Columbia, he transferred those gamesmanship skills to Wall Street, learning the rough-and-tumble world of finance from the ground up. He relished making ever-bigger deals while competing in sports, as both a participant and a spectator.

In the 1980s, his firm catapulted into a starring role on Wall Street, a pioneer in making leveraged-buyout (LBO) acquisitions. The "L" in LBO is what made the deals so profitable, generating billions in wealth for the dealmakers and investors who pieced together the deals. LBO deals involved borrowing 60 percent of the money from banks, secured by the assets of the company being acquired; 10 percent was financed with unsecured equity and 30 percent came from unsubordinated debt carrying a high interest rate, it not backed by collateral. The latter is where high-risk junk bonds were commonly used to close shaky deals. Soon after, the corporate raiders would pick apart beleaguered companies and sell off their assets on a piecemeal basis. The longevity of the original companies was of no interest to them.

Teddy handled deals in a different way. He refused to use junk bonds to close deals, resorting to a less precarious form of leverage. He used money from funds set up by his own company, the money raised from investors. The nation's largest pension funds contributed much of it. Contrasted with contemporary LBO operations, Forstmann resisted, and often spoke against using junk bond financing.

At an average height with dark eyebrows, silver hair, and eyes penetrating like radar, the financier maintained a personal lifestyle that made newspaper headlines as often as his moves on Wall Street. Tabloids linked him to Elizabeth Hurley and Diana, Princess of Wales. In spite of these and other well-publicized relationships, the eligible bachelor never married. He did spend prodigious amounts of time and money to aid children's causes. Unusual for a top executive, many fixating on the bottom line and little else, the man appeared to have a heart—at least to the public.

Forstmann wanted to seal a deal for Gulfstream by coming in the back door rather than submitting a bid as dozens of other suitors were prepared to do. Due to the forthcoming auction, Iacocca wasn't interested in talking to him. To reach the automaker, Teddy needed to get Paulson's blessing—but he was unavailable and incommunicado at his desert home. "Forstmann tried the damndest to get to me," Paulson said. "I'd say there must have been forty or fifty investment bankers who wanted to partner with me. So I stopped taking calls. Forstmann kept trying. After four or five attempts he went to Drew Lewis and had him call me." Lewis was the former secretary of transportation in the Reagan administration, followed by CEO and chairman posts at Union Pacific Railroad. "Drew told me that I'd better talk to this guy. I called Forstmann up and told him I've already got my financing arranged but he said, 'I can make you a better deal than you've probably got.' I said, 'okay, do you want to come to Palm Springs?'"[4] Forstmann agreed to meet at his home. Lewis vouching for the New Yorker, Paulson familiarized himself with Teddy's approach in pursuing acquisitions and the kinds of deals he'd made. He didn't expect it to be a wasted meeting.

The next morning, the financier left his lofty perch on Fifth Avenue, boarded his GIV, and flew to the desert oasis. Past experience told him that with a deal in the offing, you'd better move faster than other guys. He was well aware there were Wall Street vultures on the sidelines waiting to capture the company via an auction.

Paulson told Forstmann to look for a chauffeur, who would meet him at the executive aircraft terminal at the Palm Springs Airport. Upon landing, he and an associate marched down the jet's air stair and glanced across the ramp in search of a limousine. Parked a hundred feet away wasn't what they expected to see—a vintage Bentley convertible. Paulson loved to collect and restore classic automobiles, but Teddy was quick to see that this car's top was jammed half shut and half open. It wasn't a good way to start the visit. "This story is wacky from the very beginning," Teddy said of the half-hour ride to Paulson's home. "This crazy butler is driving this Bentley with the top half up, all over the road," he said. "I have an associate who's hanging on to the seat for dear life as this thing is careening down the highway."[5] Ruffled up a bit, but still in one piece, they arrived at the industrialist's abode, tucked away in the posh Vintage Club development at Indian Wells.

Located adjacent to the Eldorado Country Club where Paulson played golf with Eisenhower in the 1960s, Vintage Club opened in 1979 with its empty lots starting at $330,000. Locals considered it the most exclusive gated community in the desert. It was the first planned development having not one, but two, eighteen-hole golf courses. Paulson's residence stood in sharp contrast to the surrounding homes, featuring breathtaking eighteenth-century, French-inspired architecture. Located at 47355 Las Cascadas Court, the five-bedroom, eight-bath residence occupied more than an acre, overlooking one of the courses with majestic Mount San Jacinto framing the view. As a part-time resident of Vintage, Paulson hosted the Gulfstream Aerospace Invitational there—a golf tournament on the PGA Champions Tour. Played at Vintage from 1981 to 1992, it attracted golfers who were at least fifty years old. Many of the PGA Tour's most successful players graduated from the tournament to compete in the Champions Tour.

Sitting down for refreshments, Paulson gravitated toward straight talking Forstmann immediately. He wasn't a fan of the New Yorker's silver-spoon upbringing and lifestyle, but understood the merits of his down-to-earth philosophy about acquiring businesses. The financier explained that by acquiring Gulfstream, they would cut costs, pump up sales, improve profits, and sell the company via a public offering in three to five years. It was pretty much the standard LBO formula. Teddy knew that Iacocca, an old friend of Paulson, was the person he needed to talk with to snag the deal. He had to connect with the automotive icon before competitors commenced a bidding war for the company.

The meeting in the desert was a crucial step in eventually making a deal. Teddy didn't want anything to do with an auction. It would cause the price to skyrocket. Starting negotiations with Paulson, he got down to brass tacks rather abruptly. "'I'll give you 40 percent of the company and I want you to stay on and run it. I have all the pension fund money, and we can get that at a low interest rate." Paulson pondered the proposal for a few minutes that "convinced me at my age, it would be a great deal. I figured, so what, and I agreed to go with him on the deal."[6]

Lasting 3 hours, the meeting ended with an agreement about how to proceed. By gaining Paulson's concurrence, Forstmann walked away from Vintage Club with a plan to convince Iacocca to cut a deal before the bidding got underway. As promised during the meeting, Paulson telephoned Iacocca, the conversation paving the way for Teddy to negotiate with the automaker directly. Upon returning to Manhattan, he called Paulson and was glad to hear that no cognitive dissonance existed on his part. The stage was set to meet with Iacocca. During the same conversation, Paulson gave him some advice.

"During the negotiations he [Forstmann] came up with the idea that the company was worth a billion dollars," Paulson said. "I said, 'Teddy, I'll tell you how you can buy it for $650 million.'"

"No, we don't want this to go into a bidding war like an auction," Teddy replied. "The company is worth one billion and we should make him an offer."

"So, he made an offer, even though I kept telling him one billion was too much. I think they started out at $800 million, and at that point, Chrysler knew how eager he was.

"They said, 'We want $850 million.'"

Paulson continued, "We'll, it ended up that they agreed on $825 million plus all the fees we had to pay Forstmann Little. They got a percentage of the purchase price so they made money right from the beginning of the deal."[7]

Forstmann and Iacocca hammered out an agreement to buy Chrysler while investment houses were still calculating what to offer during the formal bidding process. To piece together the $825 million deal, Manufacturers Hanover Trust contributed $425 million in secured senior debt. Forstmann Little provided about $300 million in subordinated, unsecured debt, it coming from pension funds managed for companies such as IBM and United Technologies. Forstmann provided the largest part of a $100 million equity investment. Paulson remained chairman and CEO, and invested $30 million, owning 32 percent of the corporation's equity. Forstmann Little held the other 68 percent. The interest on the borrowed money was projected to amount to as much as $75 million annually, Paulson remarking that one of his goals was to pay down the debt as soon as possible.

Almost three-dozen institutional investors were anxious to work with Paulson to finance the deal. He selected Forstmann Little because Teddy refused to participate in acquisition schemes financed by junk bonds. The financier hadn't done much business in the year preceding the Gulfstream deal because he refused to pattern its deals like those engineered by Drexel Burnham Lambert, the acknowledged junk bond king of the LBO world.

Teddy would have needed to outbid dozens of other suitors to buy Gulfstream if he hadn't short-circuited the process. "There is only one winner," Paulson said of the deal.[8] For the time being, he was happy with the financier's tactics.

The price paid to Chrysler was $188 million higher than the $637 million that Paulson received from the automaker in 1985. Of course, it was now a far larger company as well. "Being integrated with Chrysler, we took some extra expenses," he said. "We can get more efficient without Chrysler." Never comfortable with the automaker's bureaucracy or its political cliques, he concluded, "I took the crown jewels out of Chrysler."[9] He was particularly unhappy with the roadblock that Chrysler put in place when he tried to buy Learjet Corp., it available for a bargain price. Problem-plagued Chrysler balked, citing a lack of profits to buy anything due to declining car sales. Disappointed, he wanted the Learjet as a companion product for the GIV.

On February 13, 1990, Paulson caused a scramble among journalists attending an impromptu press conference. He announced that he and Forstmann Little were buying Gulfstream Aerospace from Chrysler for $825 million—together with Learjet Corp. for another $80 million. He said that a letter of intent to buy Learjet had already been signed.

At the age of sixty-seven, Paulson was happy with the deal and remained eager to keep working, "I'm not the retiring type," he said.[10]

Paulson had kept a close eye on Learjet, the company poised on the verge of bankruptcy for months. Its products possessed the image and track record lacking in his abandoned Hustler and Peregrine projects. The timing was opportune to snatch Bill Lear's legacy from Learjet's weakened parent corporation, it showing no interest in manufacturing airplanes other than trying to make money. The recession was killing sales, leaving nothing but red ink on the company's income and loss statement.

Charles Gates, who bought the company from Bill Lear in 1967, sold his ownership stake to New York–based Integrated Acquisitions in 1987, a subsidiary of Integrated Resources, Inc. The troubled insurance and investment giant changed the aircraft company's name from Gates Learjet to Learjet Corp. Beginning on August 17, 1989, troubled Integrated listed Learjet for sale in an attempt to raise cash to pay off the parent company's mounting debts.

Stephen Weinroth, Integrated Resources chairman, entertained twelve bids for Learjet Corp. before accepting Paulson's bid for $80 million, the deal expected to close within sixty days. Asked if his bid was a bargain, poker-faced Paulson replied, "We hope so."[11] To others in the aviation industry, it appeared to be a winning deal for him.

"The $80 million price is fair value in that we solicited those twelve bids," said Weinroth. "We felt it was the best alternative."[12] He didn't say if the bid was the highest one received. The acquisition looked like a done deal to many observers. "We are very pleased to join forces with Gulfstream," said Learjet spokesman Bill Robinson.[13] His fellow employees looked forward working with Paulson after the tumultuous relationship with Integrated.

Paulson's longstanding reputation for seldom (if ever) paying too much for an airplane or a company was a sure sign that it must have been a steal. "The $80 million strikes me as a bargain," remarked Henry Ogrodzinski, director of communications for the General Aviation Manufacturers Association. He went on to say that the two companies were "very complimentary to each other."[14]

At the time of the bidding, Learjet was competing for an Air Force contract to produce 211 of what were called Tanker Transport Trainer System (TTTS) jets. The contract's value could exceed $1 billion. Employees of New York–based Flight Safety International, Inc. would train military pilots to fly the planes. If Learjet won the contract, it would work with Flight Safety, the

Wichita plane maker providing the airplanes and their maintenance support. It was coincidental that Flight Safety maintained a training facility next to the Gulfstream Aerospace plant in Savannah. In addition to Learjet's potential involvement in the TTTS project, Paulson remarked that the company offered, "A good product and a good customer base."[15]

Optimism prevailed, but a monkey wrench was about to be thrown into the Learjet portion of the deal. Not a surprise to Wall Street analysts, weakened Integrated Resources filed for Chapter 11 bankruptcy during the afternoon of February 13. Hours earlier, Paulson announced that he and Forstmann were set to buy both Gulfstream and Learjet. When word of the bankruptcy filing reached Teddy in New York, he told Paulson *no* to the Learjet acquisition.

Teddy backed out because Integrated's bankruptcy could lead to a bidding war for Learjet and raise the ante. Although the airframe manufacturer wasn't part of the parent company's bankruptcy filing, it was clear that a sale would require bankruptcy court approval. The delays would prolong the sale process, causing the court to open solicitation for the company to a host of bidders. "In the beginning it looked like a great opportunity to advance our product line," Paulson said. "But the bankruptcy meant that Learjet would have to go on the auction block and we weren't in the mood to bid for it. So we decided to not go any farther with Lear."[16] Forstmann wanted nothing to do with an auction.

The decision to drop the bid for Learjet that afternoon may have been influenced, at least in part, by Paulson sensing that Learjet was about to lose the TTTS contract to Beech Aircraft Corp. He knew that Learjet wouldn't get rich by winning the contract, but doing so would have subsidized factory production for a few years until commercial sales recovered from a recession. However, according to spokesmen for Gulfstream and Learjet, the Paulson-Forstmann agreement to buy Learjet lapsed *before* Learjet was dropped from the TTTS competition.

Integrated Resources tried to build a financial services empire propped up with $800 million of junk bond financing. Drexel Burnham Lambert, itself seeking federal bankruptcy court protection a few hours after Integrated Resources filed its own bankruptcy petition, was the investment house that provided Integrated with its capital. It turned into a house of cards. Because Integrated was unable to pay anything toward the extreme amount of debt that it owed, bankruptcy was the only option. It took Drexel Burnham down with it.

After the deal collapsed, when Paulson was asked if he wanted to reconsider a possible buyout of Learjet, he said, "forget it." The response was understandable. "The high-flying business of Paulson has met in mid-air its enemy: the low-flying, crashing world of greedy folks who finance whatever comes their way with junk bonds," wrote columnist Benjamin Hebebrand in the *Savannah News-Press.*[17]

~ ~ ~

A half century before the invention of Skype, Facetime, and a myriad of related Internet-based communication tools, the only way for executives to talk with—*and see*—people in faraway places was to get on an airplane, go there, and negotiate a deal faster than competitors. Jetliners of the late 1950s were a welcome advance over propeller-driven transports, flying twice as fast. But it wasn't long before executives and celebrities wanted to travel faster than the speed of sound. The supersonic transport (SST) held great promise.

The history of the American SST program is about as convoluted as can be. What caused it to gain momentum was the planned development of European and Soviet SSTs. It would be a blow to America's pride, the nation's leadership in aeronautical technology unquestioned in the 1950s. To level the playing field, President John F. Kennedy ordered a go-ahead for an SST program in June 1963 by proclaiming: "It is my judgment that this government should immediately commence a new program in partnership with private industry to develop the earliest practical date the prototype of a commercially successful supersonic transport superior to that being built in any other country of the world."[18] But on Capitol Hill, lobbyists for the aircraft industry made it clear that their clients could not bear the expense of going it alone.

Within two months of Kennedy's go-ahead speech, the FAA sent a request for proposal (RFP) to the airframe industry. In December 1966, Boeing and General Electric, the latter chosen as an engine maker for the SST, were selected for further review, along with a competing team of Lockheed and Pratt & Whitney. Following evaluation of the proposals, the Boeing 2707 entry won—a 350-passenger airliner offering a projected cruise speed of Mach 2.7 and capable of flying 4,000 miles.[19] In May 1967, the FAA issued a contract that funded Boeing to build two SST prototypes and subject them to 100 hours of flight testing.

The competition in Europe wasn't sitting still. An advertisement appearing in the May 29, 1967, issue of *Aviation Week & Space Technology* predicted that a market for 350 Concorde SSTs would develop by 1980. The plane's maker, a consortium of Aerospatiale in France and British Aircraft Corp., gloated about the head start of Concorde compared to the American effort. Also beating the United States to the punch, a Soviet-developed SST, the Tupolev Tu-144, first flew on December 31, 1968, followed by the Concorde, taking to the air two months later on March 2.

On September 23, 1969, President Richard M. Nixon lent more support to the U.S. program—subject to Congress continuing the funding. In a speech, he said, "the decision is that now we do go forward and that the first prototype will be flown in 1972 and that the United States will continue to lead the world in air transport."[20]

It was August 1970 when Boeing announced that its prototype's maiden flight was scheduled for November 1972. The first production SST would be delivered in early 1977. None of this would happen. Aside from encountering unprecedented technical challenges, rumblings about the wisdom of continuing the plane's development spread through Congress during 1970. Taking action, the Senate blocked the project's future funding but authorized the sending of progress payments to Boeing until a new session of Congress could debate the issue. In the midst of relentless concerns over sonic booms, environmental pollution, safety, and cost, the program came to an abrupt halt on March 24, 1971. The Senate voted to slash the project's entire budget after spending about $1 billion of taxpayer money over the preceding years. Seeking funding elsewhere, Boeing talked up the project with its bankers to no avail. America's SST was never built, only a mockup of the Boeing 2707 fuselage surviving at the Museum of Flight in Seattle.

A Tu-144 crashed at the Paris Air Show in 1973, delaying that SST's further development. In November 1977, the Soviet planes finally began carrying passengers, almost two years after Concorde. In May 1978, another Tu-144 crashed during a test flight, causing the entire fleet of passenger-configured airplanes to be grounded permanently. They had flown a total of only fifty-five scheduled flights. The Tu-144s were deemed safe enough to transport cargo, locking the aircraft in that role until 1983 when all of them were retired.

The horrific television footage showing the Tu-144 crash at Paris shocked the world, particularly aspiring Concorde passengers. Thoughts of sonic booms and environmental pollution further damaged a once positive public opinion of all SSTs.

What airline executives didn't foresee was an army of environmentalists making political football of the American SST program. To a lesser degree, the same negativity buffeted the Concorde program. By 1976, only Air France and British Airways kept their orders for the jets. Orders from other airlines were cancelled for environmental and economic reasons. The rationale for most of the cancellations was obvious: supersonic flight was *not allowed* over land, thus restricting the airliner's income potential.

Scheduled flights for Concorde began on January 21, 1976, along London-Bahrain and Paris-Rio de Janeiro routes. Citing environmental concerns, Congress banned any SST from flying over the United States. Far bigger news came years later on April 10, 2003, when Air France and British Airways announced they would ground their Concorde fleets later that year. The carriers blamed a lack of passengers following the fiery crash of an Air France Concorde on July 25, 2000, a general slump in air travel following the September 11, 2001, terrorist attacks, and the spiraling costs needed to maintain the aging aircraft. The once promising SSTs became history. The airlines shifted their emphasis to "busing" as many passengers as possible in a new generation of wide-body jumbo jets, filling seats by offering the cheapest fares possible. To John Q citizen, the SSTs weren't missed, thought of as nothing more than luxury chariots to fly rich folks to and from European vacations.

Paulson cherished technological progress that some people thought belonged in the science fiction category. After delivering what aviation journalists believed was the ultimate subsonic business transport in the form of the Gulfstream IV, he dreamed about a supersonic business jet (SSBJ) to slice through the stratosphere at Mach 1.5. The project would take off where the Boeing SST program left off. He envisioned the plane as a ten- to twelve-passenger, 80,000-pound transport capable of taking off and landing on the runways of existing general aviation airports. Viewed as a pipe dream by scoffers, he was dead serious about developing such an aircraft. He believed that the principal roadblock preventing the operation of noisy SSBJs over the mainland was regulatory and not technical. Longstanding concern over sonic booms caused the FAA to prohibit civilian aircraft from flying over land supersonically. The booms, resulting from aerodynamic overpressure occurring when an airplane exceeds the speed of sound, were challenging scientific phenomena to mitigate. The issue couldn't be ignored, as was standard practice with supersonic military airplanes that produced earth-shaking booms. The FAA had little jurisdiction over military aircraft operations. However, for a civil aircraft to fly supersonically, the booms would have to go.

Under Paulson's direction in 1989, Gulfstream Aerospace embarked on what it called a "concept development program" for an SSBJ. The company planned to invest a reported "several million dollars" each year to fund the study project. Rolls-Royce, the tentative choice of an engine maker for the airplane, would underwrite some of the research cost. Although Gulfstream welcomed the British company's participation for developing the engines, other risk-sharing partners were also sought.

A preliminary analysis revealed that the cost of developing an SSBJ airframe and its engines would exceed $1 billion. To recoup that investment, each jet would need to sell for more than $50 million. "Even though an SST would cost twice as much as a Gulfstream IV, it would be three times more productive," Paulson said. "Most people buy a business jet because they want to buy time."[21] He took the tentative concept for an SSBJ to the Farnborough Air Show in England, prompting some attendees to wonder how serious he was about the project. His reply: "This isn't a publicity stunt ... we're serious."[22]

A world apart from Gulfstream's endeavors in Savannah, Soviet leader

Mikhail Gorbachev's *glasnost* policy of openness, and his country's recent military cutbacks, were changing the focus of its aircraft development programs. By 1990, the country's population was increasingly oriented toward Western values, freedoms, and democratization, bringing on the eventual collapse of the Soviet Union on December 26, 1991.

The country's Sukhoi Design Bureau was best known for developing supersonic jet fighters, such as the Su-25 Grach, fielded during the Soviet intervention in Afghanistan. Founded in 1939 by engineer Pavel Sukhoi, the bureau's resources were repositioned to generate income from outside the country's borders. Its technical expertise was gradually redirected into producing and exporting airplanes for the global commercial aviation market. Relying on the experience gained from designing military jets, the bureau began work on an SSBJ, a scale model of the airplane displayed at the 1989 Paris Air Show.

Paulson gained wind of Sukhoi's plans from reading a news item published in *Aviation Week & Space Technology* during spring 1989. Visiting the Soviet display at the Paris exhibition, he couldn't believe how far the Soviets had progressed with their design. Likewise, Sukhoi was intrigued to learn that Gulfstream was on a parallel course. Their intersecting paths led to informal discussions in Gulfstream Aerospace's chalet at the show. The conversation between Paulson and Mikhail Simonov, Sukhoi's chief designer, was friendly and productive. "They were comrades in less than an hour," said a company staffer who attended the meeting. Sixty-year-old Simonov had served as the first vice minister of the aviation industry in the Soviet Union. In 1987 he became general designer at the Sukhoi Design Bureau, participating in the design of a number of advanced jet aircraft. Paulson told the media that Sukhoi "appears to be years ahead of the rest of the world in the design and development of supersonic aircraft, which can be used for business flying."[23]

The day after the show, Paulson guided his GIV across the Atlantic to a smooth touchdown on the Savannah airport. He got busy, preparing a memorandum of understanding that spelled out the tentative details of a joint venture between Gulfstream and Sukhoi to develop an SSBJ. The MOU detailed how Paulson's engineers would provide the systems and the Soviet group the airframe, Sukhoi basing it on the Su-27 Flanker fighter. The bureau would subsidize the project's research and development work. Rolls-Royce would be tasked to design the aircraft's engines in collaboration with the Lyulka Engine Design Bureau in Moscow. Gulfstream's specific role involved perfecting the flight controls, environmental control system, auxiliary power unit, and avionics, the latter based on the existing "glass" flight deck instrumentation aboard the GIV.

Paulson faxed the MOU to Simonov on June 18, 1989. It was signed by the Soviets without hesitation. The teams, working halfway around the world from each other, began to research the feasibility of collaborating on the design of a Mach 2 aircraft capable of carrying at least ten passengers. Paulson believed that the Soviets wanted the partnership to succeed for two reasons. Sales of SSBJs would generate hard currency for the country; and it would give the Soviets access to coveted U.S. technology, such as the latest digital avionic systems.

"We will have a meeting in the USA, then one in Moscow, or maybe vice versa ... and make a joint team to make the first steps," said Alexei Komarov, head of foreign economic relations at the design bureau.[24] Weeks later, Paulson led a delegation to Moscow to review the work at the Soviet Aviation Ministry, "where I received complete support," he said. In Savannah, he spent a prodigious amount of time planning the venture, cramming the work into late nights and weekends. It became a consuming interest, more intense than any project of his career. Because existing business jets were restricted to cruise speeds of less than Mach 1, he knew that the SSBJ would be the next major step to advance civil aviation. Wherever he journeyed, he talked up the project and committed himself to turning what started as a vague idea into production airplanes.

"I am sure it is workable," Paulson said. "I have found no negative reaction inside or outside Gulfstream [Aerospace] to the idea, and have every intention to put a lot of effort into this to make it work."[25] There were silent doubters in his company, but he believed that the program was unstoppable. He arranged a meeting in Washington, D.C., with Vice President Dan Quayle and Transportation Secretary Samuel Skinner. "In both cases we've been encouraged to proceed with our Gulfstream-Sukhoi business arrangements," he said.[26] The meetings were essential because any work undertaken by the international teams had to comply with U.S. government constraints governing technology exports. Simonov and Paulson then met with Skinner and FAA administrator James Busey to discuss bilateral plans for airworthiness certification of the jet.

Paulson expected that the airframes would be manufactured in the Soviet Union, the assembled airplanes then ferried in a "green" (unpainted) condition to Savannah. Gulfstream crews would "Americanize" them with avionics, plush cabin interiors, and snazzy paint jobs. Gulfstream would market the finished airplanes. "The Soviets can develop the aircraft for a lot less cost than we could in the USA," he said.[27]

Before Sukhoi's involvement, Paulson anticipated that a ten-year program would be required to develop a $50 million SSBJ. "The general designer of Sukhoi has suggested a much shorter program," he said after working with the Soviets a short time. He noted that the Sukhoi design had "a lot of commonality" with Gulfstream's approach. "To me, their design has good possibilities. They have been working on it for two years and could fly a prototype in two years' time."[28]

The preliminary design evolving from the joint effort was an SSBJ promising a range of 4,000 to 5,000 miles while cruising at 55,000 to 65,000 feet. Sukhoi had two propulsion concepts under study: one with four engines and another with two. A later design featured a three-engine configuration.

To determine the expectations that existing aircraft owners might have for an SSBJ, Gulfstream commissioned a series of market studies. During workshops held in Savannah, opinions were solicited from the GIII and GIV operators in attendance. Almost 600 pilots and flight department managers participated. Based on the survey, Paulson confirmed that his prior estimate of an initial market for up to sixty jets, priced at $50 million apiece, was a realistic assumption. When detailed specifications for the SSBJ would finally be frozen, his plan called for soliciting refundable deposits from prospective buyers. He wanted 100 orders on the books before funding the aircraft's full-scale development and production startup.

Although enjoying many supporters, there were skeptics questioning the practicality of developing and operating such a plane. "The whole idea is preposterous," said Richard Perle, a fellow at the American Enterprise Institute in Washington and a former undersecretary of defense. "There would be immense licensing problems."[29] Perle maintained that export controls wouldn't permit a free flow of technology between the countries. Pessimism existed in the Soviet Union as well. Analysts there surmised that Moscow would abandon the project. "I don't think the Soviets are in a position, considering the state of the economy, to stick their neck out on a project that no Western company, even a consortium, would consider doing," said Jan Vanous, research director at a Washington consulting company specializing in the Eastern bloc and Soviet economies.[30]

There was skepticism even in some quarters of Gulfstream. "Its time was not there," remarked Goldie Glenn. "Al even put some of his own money into it. The Russians said the time wasn't right for a supersonic airplane. They said, 'We can't fly it over land, [and] it's going to take a lot of money to develop it.'"[31] The rule prohibiting supersonic flight over land continued to threaten scuttling the program.

The project began to face weak support on both sides of the Atlantic but none of it dampened Paulson's determination to bring the jet to fruition.

The SSBJ was expected to roar and shake the earth on takeoff as no other civilian aircraft did. Paulson kept that undesirable aspect in mind as he studied the airplane's design details. Toward the middle of 1990, he turned his thoughts to the noisy aircraft already in service. He knew that the public's continued acceptance of airline and business jet operations depended on aircraft manufacturers reducing noise and pollution emissions. The owners of older business jets, and the first generation of jet airliners, were facing the costly prospect of replacing the engines on their aircraft unless their environmental impact was reduced in some other way. The GIV's Tay engines met the regulations, but the 11,400-pound-thrust Speys powering the GII and GIII remained problematic. At a Gulfstream operator's workshop in Savannah during June 1990, Paulson introduced an invention he called the "free turbine noise suppressor." He told the attendees that earlier model Gulfstreams fitted with the device would not exceed the latest decibel limits mandated by the FAA. Kits to retrofit the airplanes were expected to be available within two years.

The patented suppressor exemplified Paulson's ingenuity. It consisted of an additional turbine wheel mounted at the rear of the existing engine to absorb much of the energy from the high velocity exhaust gases. Fan blades fitted around the periphery of the wheel pulled extra air through the engine's bypass duct to increase the volume of propulsive airflow. The velocity of the exiting exhaust gases would be cut almost in half, a key to reducing the noise. As a bonus, the suppressor was expected (although not substantiated by testing) to boost the engine's thrust by as much as 25 percent, improving takeoff and climb performance. Paulson compared the device to the power recovery turbines (PRTs) used to boost the horsepower of Wright R-3350 Turbo Compound engines powering DC-7s and Super Constellations.

According to Paulson, some GII and GIII owners "favored the aft fan" over converting their planes to expensive Tay engines. He expected the fan devices to cost $3.8 million per aircraft, while changing to Tays was estimated to cost $10.1 million. It was planned to flight test the device during November 1991.

Because the turbine suppressor had a number of moving parts, it would be more expensive to manufacture than simpler exhaust hush kits then under development by other firms. However, it would be far less expensive than replacing the loud engines with new ones. Although designed for the GII and GIII, the suppressor could be adapted to the 727 and 737, DC-9, F28, and BAC 111. The relationship that Paulson established with the Sukhoi Design Bureau and Lyulka Engine Design Bureau presented a business opportunity beyond building the SSBJ. Working with Gulfstream, Lyulka would develop a prototype turbine suppressor through a company named Aeroconversion U.S.S.R. To market the device, Paulson formed Free Turbine Corporation. Williams International, Inc. was retained to perform testing and FAA certification. Aware of the Soviet's expertise in thermodynamics, it made sense for Gulfstream to join forces with Lyulka. Following the suppressor's certification, the firm would compete with Gulfstream to manufacture the device—the lowest bidder winning a production contract.

Although promising, the aft fan suppressor became obsolete when the cheaper hush kits arrived on the scene. The newer ejector-type suppressor offered "the best opportunity for a Stage 3 device," Paulson admitted because it "has no moving parts." The aft fan program was put on hold. The "upfront research and development costs are too high," he added. The price of the fan would need to be twice what the ejector suppressor cost.[32] It was an honest assessment on his part.

Paulson teamed up with entrepreneur Joe Clark for another unusual project, at least at the time. "I went to see Al in 1991," Clark began, he wanting to install winglets on a GII. "Al said to me, 'Why do you want to do that? It's like putting hub caps on a Cadillac.' I told him that we have a new technology to test that's called a blended winglet. We want to put it on a Gulfstream and certify it. I needed him to sell me the structural data for the wing, which he did." Through Aviation Partners, Inc., Clark proceeded to develop winglets for the business jet, launching him into the successful winglet business. The GII's blended winglets were FAA certified in June 1993. Combined with minor aerodynamic changes to the plane's wings, they reduced the fuel burn by more than 7 percent at cruising speed. "From there, we went on the Boeing airplanes, all because of my association with Al on the GII."[33] All newer jetliners and business jets today have winglets on their wing tips.

13

Moving On

As Teddy Forstmann skimmed the sports section of the *New York Times* in his forty-fourth-floor office overlooking Central Park, he assumed that everything was running according to plan at Gulfstream Aerospace. The leveraged buyout deal had closed on February 13, 1990, putting him at ease. No news was good news. Forstmann delegated the responsibility for overseeing Gulfstream's operations to partner Brian Little. Teddy expected to be pressed for time from spring to well into summer of that year, involved heavily in the $1.75 billion acquisition of General Instrument Corp. When fall arrived, he took a close look at what was going on at Gulfstream—and its order backlog. He was upset. The promising investment was about to lose money. It appeared that Little wasn't watching the store in Savannah.

Not helping things, the United States was headed for another recession. Beginning in July, it would stifle the economy until April 1991. The decline marked the end of the longest peacetime economic expansion in the nation's history. Its cause was pinned on a loss of confidence—both consumer and business. A spike in oil prices was a big contributor. Economic expansion would not return to the level of the 1980s until 1993, when the Internet boom, cheap oil, and a strong housing market fueled the prosperity. Robust growth would last through 2000. But for Gulfstream Aerospace in 1990, the volatile economy dried up the intent of some corporations and individuals to order the company's expensive jets. Some of them deferred the delivery of airplanes they had already ordered.

"When Forstmann first took over, the loss of the investment tax credit really hurt sales," said Goldie Glenn about its lingering effect. The Tax Reform Act of 1986 had repealed the popular tax credit for purchased assets, including business airplanes. Compounding the angst, revenue agents made sure that the expensive aircraft were flown for business travel *only* and not for jaunts to vacation locales. "Every time a customer landed, the IRS had a guy at the door making sure only business people were aboard and not family members."[1] The IRS stuck to a so-called "90-percent use test," meaning that a company was forced to prove that its aircraft was used for business travel at least 90 percent of the time or it would lose a hefty tax deduction.

The recession and the IRS roadblocks weren't the only damning issues. The acquisition that Forstmann had engineered was creating a financial drain—the loans needed to buy Gulfstream requiring interest payments amounting to about $75 million a year. Ignoring Brian Little, Teddy put the pressure squarely on the CEO in Savannah. "I keep telling everyone we need to become slim and mean," Paulson said. "Before we were operating without the big debt burden—today we're a different company and we have to operate differently."[2] In a letter to Gulfstream employees, written by Paulson but demanded by Forstmann, the rank and file was informed that the company would need two years to reduce its debt to an acceptable level. He went on to infer that its "savings account" would need to be dipped into to buy some of the debt and reduce the amount of interest payments. It was clear that the action would involve employee layoffs, something Paulson found distasteful. There were no other options available. "He was very thoughtful toward his employees," Kathy O'Sako remarked. "He would lie awake at night thinking about his responsibility to them and their families. If Gulfstream stumbled, it could be harmful to Savannah. That weighed on him heavily."[3]

In 1986, Bombardier Inc., a Montreal-based manufacturer of trains and buses, acquired Canadair, Ltd., manufacturer of the Challenger 600 business jet. During a buying binge, Bombardier later added aircraft manufacturers de Havilland Aircraft of Canada and Short Brothers plc, a UK manufacturer, to its holdings. Following Paulson's failed attempt to buy Learjet Corp., Bombardier came forward and nailed the deal to buy the company in June 1990. The Canadian firm grew to become a formidable competitor for Gulfstream, as the Challenger featured a similar size cabin as the GIV. An unseen threat was the aggressive team that Bombardier put in place to market the plane.

It appeared to Forstmann that Bombardier's success in capturing ever-increasing market share was going unnoticed by Paulson in Savannah and Brian Little in Manhattan. Pushing Little aside, Forstmann decided to oversee, and eventually take over the reins at Gulfstream.

After buying Gulfstream American, Paulson kept the company on an even financial keel, monopolizing the top end of the market by building Gulfstream's reputation as the Rolls-Royce of business jets. The only direct competition in the late 1970s was the Lockheed JetStar, an excellent airplane but one losing luster, with a basic design dating to 1957. Sticking to a narrow assessment of prevailing market conditions, Paulson didn't consider the business jets of Bombardier and Dassault Aviation in France as major competition. He stuck to the belief that only one Rolls-Royce automobile (his preferred car) existed in the world, and in aviation, the Gulfstream was its equal.

Based on the weak order book, Forstmann began to suspect that Paulson wasn't up to the job of selling enough jets. Now sixty-eight years old, the plane maker had invested millions of his own money in Gulfstream, nurturing the company during its stumbling early days, followed by a meteoric rise to the top of the industry. Before Forstmann's arrival, he ruled the roost without interference from committees, a management style he despised. Many of his executives had spent their entire careers working at Grumman and Gulfstream and weren't much younger than he. In response, Teddy decided to replace many of the aging leaders with younger executives from other companies, whether or not they had aviation experience.

"For the first year under Forstmann Little, it was a strained relationship," Glenn said about the tension existing between Paulson and Forstmann. "Al would tell Teddy, 'You're picking the wrong guys to come down here and run this place; they don't know anything.' After buying a company, Teddy was famous for putting his own people in charge. But most of them were misfits."[4]

Keeping Paulson's age in mind, Forstmann recognized that he was a brilliant innovator in aeronautics and a shrewd dealmaker, but began to think he should step back from active management. Paulson's take was different. He admitted that some inefficiency existed in Savannah, although the company was doing its best to ride over the rough spots of a sick economy. Maintaining morale and keeping his team intact for the long term ranked above all else in importance. He didn't want to strip away the humanity of the organization and risk sacrificing the quality of its products. When asked about retirement, he remarked, "It scares the hell out of me thinking about retiring. I'm just getting rolling now." He and Teddy were clearly not on the same page.

"Everybody was very old," Forstmann observed about the residents of mahogany row. "Allen's people were the nicest guys going, but they were chronologically really old. Nobody ever left."[5] Forstmann started a campaign by asking them if they'd "like" to retire. He considered Gulfstream overloaded with dead wood, from the front office down through its supervisorial ranks. Not only did he want Paulson out, but his entire executive staff as well, perceiving them as slow-moving senior citizens. "Al was ready to go," Glenn remarked. "He was really fed up. Teddy and Al didn't get along at all," he observed. Their relationship was disintegrating. "Forstmann wanted his own person to be president. Al [also] disagreed with loading the board with people like Donald Rumsfeld and others. So he never went to board meetings."[6] By stuffing the board with VIPs, Forstmann hoped their international connections might sell a Gulfstream or two.[7]

"I was ready to retire," Glenn remarked, "but Teddy said, 'No, I don't want you to retire. I want you to stick around and nurture these guys I've been bringing in.' But each one of those guys was a failure. You couldn't talk to them; they were kicked out of other companies."[8] Paulson's executives considered Forstmann an interloper, a corporate raider, a pirate eating away at what Paulson had built during fifteen years at the helm.

On those occasions when Forstmann flew to Savannah in his Gulfstream, he demanded star treatment as if he were Frank Sinatra. "He was egotistical," O'Sako recalled. "It was not that his airplane would arrive at a certain time; it was that his airplane would arrive at a certain time and he wanted this kind of water, this kind of juice, only this kind of food—and *never* the wrong thing."[9] Teddy was impatient, intolerant of mistakes, and could be as abrasive as sandpaper.

Forstmann dropped by to see Paulson during one of those trips. He wasted no time in telling the CEO to think about naming a successor for his job and prepare recommendations. Over the months to come, Paulson stalled in suggesting candidates to replace him, while the company's fortunes continued to decline. Realizing that his departure was inevitable, but shocked by Forstmann's abrupt edict, he was forced to comply. Forstmann Little owned 68 percent of the company's stock compared to his 32 percent. He finally recommended three people for the job, but Teddy and his partners wouldn't vet the selections.

In May 1991, eight months into a formal executive search process, a candidate emerged that everyone thought would be ideal. Everyone but Paulson, that is. It was William C. Lowe, a fifty-year-old marketing executive who held senior executive posts at International Business Machines and Xerox. An expert at marketing computers and office machines, Lowe had no experience in the aviation industry. He passed muster with Teddy by convincing him that the Gulfstream was nothing more than an expensive business machine. Lowe came in as president with the understanding that he'd replace Paulson as CEO in a few months.

Lowe talked a good game with the board of directors by interjecting the right buzzwords at the appropriate time. However, after a few months as president, Forstmann began to suspect that the former computer executive didn't have the leadership skills to make the company profitable. Paulson wanted Lowe thrown out the day he arrived, but Forstmann, not happy with Paulson's performance either and sensing a bit of jealousy, told him to take it easy. "You've got to give him his rope, give him a chance," Forstmann said."[10] Ignoring that appeal, Paulson remained outspoken in wanting Lowe fired. Forstmann recalled: "Paulson was calling me and saying, 'Do you see what that stupid sonuvabitch is doing?'"[11] One of Lowe's actions involved slashing the GIV's price, which incensed Paulson. He argued that Rolls-Royce never put its automobiles on sale and neither should Gulfstream with its jets.

One of the disagreements concerned ongoing development of the supersonic business jet. Luring Forstmann into his corner for concurrence, Lowe stepped behind Paulson's back and killed the program. He planned to use the money allocated for the SSBJ's research to develop a larger, long-range derivative of the Gulfstream called the GV. "Frankly, the supersonic business jet was a figment of Allen's imagination," Lowe said, a derisive comment considering the intense involvement that Paulson devoted to the promising project.[12] Cancelling the SSBJ was an enormous assault on Paulson's pride, as he had spent years in a quest to bring the revolutionary concept to life. He expected that the unique aircraft would represent the crowning achievement of his half-century career in aviation. With the stroke of a pen, the company's new leader killed it. Paulson's communication with Lowe stopped completely, while his relationship with Forstmann headed for the deep freeze. "Allen inherited the Gulfstream and improved it," publisher Murray Smith said, "but he wanted to be remembered for the first supersonic business jet."[13] Loss of the project was emotionally draining for him.

"Al lost total interest in the company," Glenn said. "I was at a meeting with Teddy, Al, and a couple of lawyers. Al got up and walked out [to use a pay phone]. Teddy came down the stairs from the conference room and threw the papers he was carrying all over the floor. He said a lot of words [to Paulson] that weren't nice. Al had a Rolls-Royce convertible parked outside, got in, and drove off. This was the end of it, right then and there."[14] The person on the other end of the pay phone, Paulson's secretary, O'Sako, had a ringside seat that day and was mesmerized by what unfolded. "I overheard Teddy in the background saying to Allen, 'If you're older than seventy, you should be dead.' Mr. Paulson didn't hang up the phone on me; he just left the receiver dangling with me repeating, 'hello?'"[15]

Disgusted with anything that Lowe had to say, Paulson stepped back from active management. It wasn't the best time to do so. The latest financial statement painted a grim picture of Gulfstream's status. It posted a net loss of $49.7 million in 1991, with the company's finance chiefs forecasting a loss of $49.6 million for 1992. Paulson let subordinates carry on with most of his responsibilities. He was a lame duck waiting for Teddy to promote Lowe to CEO. During April 1992, he decided that enough was enough and cleared out of the office he'd occupied for fifteen years. He left without fanfare saying, "I'm the sort of guy who had to own and control it. If I can't I want out."

Finished as CEO and no longer serving as board chairman, Paulson was offered an olive branch by Teddy—the title of chairman emeritus, something he perceived as meaningless. As a major stockholder he would remain a board member, although seldom making an appearance at meetings. Gulfstream was no longer the thriving entrepreneurial enterprise he'd grown to love. He lost all interest in its corporate happenings and began to spend time pursuing long-neglected interests outside of aviation, particularly horse racing.

"It was a terrible time," O'Sako remarked. "I think one reason Allen left was because he couldn't stand watching Bill Lowe taking us into the ditch." But there was another reason. Unknown to the public, a life altering issue had surfaced. "Allen had a physical exam in April 1992," O'Sako recalled about a checkup he underwent the same month he left Gulfstream. "In August he called and said, 'Kathy, do you have the records from my last physical?' I did. 'Would you pull them up and tell me what my PSA score is?' It was zero in April and 4.0 in August. He went back to the doctor who said he had prostate cancer and ended up being sick for many years."[16]

As a parting gift to Georgia Southern University, Paulson set up a $7.5 million endowment for the Allen E. Paulson College of Engineering and Information Technology. To be funded from his estate upon death, the money would provide student scholarships, endow academic chairs, and fund faculty research projects in the college's engineering laboratories. It was time to become a philanthropist for causes that were important to him. He would earn accolades from higher education circles that recognized his achievements—in spite of earning only a high school diploma. Not ignoring his own material wants, he purchased a GIV from Gulfstream for his personal transportation. Of all the airplanes he flew, it was his favorite.

To pay down more of the mounting debt brought on by the LBO, Forstmann Little engineered a public stock offering in April 1992. The debt burden was costing the company $73 million a year in interest. In return for their money, Forstmann Little investors would receive a 17-percent slice of Gulfstream's equity. The timing for the offering was not ideal—it would come on the heels of the plane maker's nearly $50 million loss posted in 1991. The only price the stock would fetch in such a lackluster financial marketplace wouldn't be high enough to make the offering worthwhile. It was cancelled.

The failed offering embarrassed Teddy and his partners. Meanwhile, the cost of doing business at Gulfstream continued to rise, dampening the possibility of making a profit. In September 1992, Forstmann Little invested $250 million of its client funds in the company. The infusion of money reduced the amount of the interest payouts and helped fund development work for the GV. Another $50 million was used to buy Paulson's stake in the company. At this point, Teddy gave up hope of reaping a profit from the LBO, at least in the short term. Making matters worse, he learned that developing the GV would require at least four years and a capital investment far higher than estimated.

By November 1993, with Paulson out of the picture and Forstmann disgusted with Lowe's performance, the CEO was ousted. Teddy installed himself as chairman and de facto chief executive of Gulfstream Aerospace. When the latest financial statements showed up on Forstmann's desk, the damage was clear. "At the end of Lowe's tenure, we were selling fewer planes and had increased costs by $40 million a year," he exclaimed. "That's a recipe for disaster."[17] Grabbing the reins to the company seemed like the only move making sense. He had run out of options to stabilize what was essentially a sinking ship.

"I don't have a talent for running companies; I have a talent for Gulfstream," Teddy told the press. After a few months of overseeing the operation, he added, "running Gulfstream has been the best experience of my business life."[18] Rather than relocating to Savannah, he managed the company's direction via phone and memos from his Manhattan office. He was not interested in walking through the factory and greeting workers. The team-building afternoon strolls of Paulson and Glenn belonged in the past, just like them.

In early 1994, Gulfstream took a $204 million charge against its 1993 earnings, contributing to a whopping $275 million loss for the year. Half of it was attributable to costs associated with developing the GV. Orders for future deliveries of GIVs had further declined, with seven of the finished but unsold jets sitting on the ramp outside the plant. Disgusted, Forstmann considered selling his firm's stake in the company. His friends in the banking business told him that he might fetch $200 million or even $300 million— but the move would leave him $600 million in the red.

In California, Paulson sat on the sidelines toying with the idea that he might buy Gulfstream on the cheap. He called Teddy and proposed a deal. The Wall Streeter snapped back: "I've got two words for you, Allen, and the first one begins with F."[19] It was the last time they spoke.

By the end of 1994, Gulfstream Aerospace finally climbed back onto the road to enjoy profitability after suffering three consecutive years of losses. It posted a $24 million net profit. GIV sales were looking up again and forty-one GV orders were confirmed, each requiring a nonrefundable $2 million deposit.

The newfound prosperity caused Forstmann to market one-third of the company via another stock offering in October 1996, selling 43 million shares to raise $1 billion. The offering was one of the largest of the year, but only about $100 million of the proceeds ended up as working capital. Forstmann Little and Teddy's handpicked operatives at Gulfstream pocketed the rest. At the same time, Gulfstream Aerospace borrowed $450 million to redeem the preferred stock held by Forstmann Little investors. The financial firm now owned 42 percent of the plane maker, a stake worth $720 million.

Twenty-six GIVs were delivered in 1995, the sales valued at $660 million. Revenues were expected to increase by almost 60 percent in 1997, when both the GIV and GV were scheduled for full production. The order backlog and letters of intent for the jets exceeded $3 billion, including sixty-three firm orders for the GV. Careers for the executives in Savannah, most of them transplants chosen by Teddy, were looking up.

Gulfstream Aerospace sold a GV to Paulson in June 1997. It was a former flight test aircraft based in Savannah. A portion of its discounted $12 million purchase price was to be paid over a four-year period. In August, the company bought back his GIV. Paulson also negotiated an agreement with Gulfstream calling for him to be paid a commission on the sale of a GV that resulted from his efforts. He couldn't let go of the Gulfstream legacy. Clay Lacy managed the jet's maintenance for his friend at his sprawling Clay Lacy Aviation fixed base operation in Van Nuys.

Eight years after Paulson left Gulfstream, General Dynamics acquired the company for $5.3 billion—an enterprise that Forstmann and Paulson bought from Chrysler for $825 million in 1990. At the end of 2015, the manufacturer employed 16,500 people, a far cry from the 2,000 working there in 1978. If Paulson were alive, none of this would interest him; he would refuse to look back at what might have been. Ironically, facing a similar economic downturn that Paulson experienced in 1990, Gulfstream sales slowed substantially in 2016. Thousands of employees were furloughed. True to form, prosperity in the aviation industry runs in cycles.

Intrigued with gambling from an early age, Paulson was a longtime regular at the crap tables in Las Vegas. In the 1990s he ramped up that interest by investing in Nevada casino and hotel properties. A hundred miles southwest of the glitzy Las Vegas Strip sat the Gold River Hotel & Casino in Laughlin. Going broke was nothing new for the property. Its latest owners had filed for Chapter 11 bankruptcy protection in 1996. A year later, Paulson paid $28 million for the property that was $75 million in debt—but he visualized a successful future for it. The resort consisted of a 71,000-square-foot casino, 1,300 feet of prime Colorado River frontage, more than 1,000 slot machines, about thirty table games, and 1,003 rooms—most of them stacked into a twenty-five-story tower.

Howard Hughes slipped into Las Vegas in November 1966, holing up behind black drapes on the top floor of the Desert Inn. Under Hughes' orders, during the months that followed, his minions bought hotel and casino properties up and down the Strip. In September 1997, Paulson, albeit a far smaller player than the reclusive billionaire, set his sights on acquiring the massive Riviera Hotel & Casino at the eastern edge of the Strip. On the verge of sealing the deal, Paulson pulled out abruptly, alleging that he was misled about the property's condition. Facing serious health issues, he turned away from future investments in Nevada gaming.

Paulson longed to move back to California on a full-time basis, a state where he achieved early success and raised a family. He systematically cut all ties to Savannah, handing his real estate holdings to grateful commissioned brokers to sell. In Southern California, he settled into his Holmby Hills mansion but later relocated to 14497 Emerald Lane, within the gates of the Del Mar Country Club, outside the city of Rancho Santa Fe. Built in 1995, the

7,300-square-foot residence occupied several acres, containing five bedrooms and six baths. He purchased the country club itself in September 1993, as it suffered financial woes and was in need of capable management. Paulson loved the area's mild Mediterranean climate, situated a few miles from the Del Mar Racetrack. He maintained an office at the club to oversee his business interests, a life interrupted by an occasional tennis match or round of golf— and spending time with his thoroughbreds at the tracks.

A Paulson poodle shares a snack with the boss (Paulson family archives/Crystal Christensen).

14

California Bound

Little known to people outside of his family and a close circle of friends, Paulson's health took a dramatic turn for the worse at the beginning of July 2000.

"When Allen was really sick, I'd talk to Mike all the time," Kathy O'Sako said of her conversations with the industrialist's youngest son. "He'd been with his dad day and night." They agreed that a visit by her would give Michael a break and provide an opportunity for her to cheer up her former boss. "I stayed there for six days during the week of the Fourth of July, sitting at his bedside with my bare feet resting on the bed. He sat up, we watched Fox News together, and just chatted away the time." The weeklong stay turned bittersweet when it was time to leave. "I kissed him and said goodbye."[1] Strong in mind and spirit, his weakened body continued to fade by the day.

On July 19, 2000, at the age of seventy-eight, Allen Eugene Paulson passed away at Scripps Memorial Hospital in La Jolla, California. O'Sako's visit took place two weeks before his death. The outcome wasn't unexpected, but still a shock, as always. It remains conjecture, but perhaps his lifespan could have been lengthened. "In March 2000, we found out he had a cancerous tumor on a kidney," O'Sako said. "He told me, 'I don't want to die one organ at a time.' He refused surgery to remove the kidney. I begged him but he wouldn't do it."[2]

Interred at Forest Lawn Memorial Park in the Los Angeles area suburb of Glendale, he left behind wife Madeleine, sons Michael, Jim and Richard, stepdaughter Dominique, four grandchildren, brother Art, along with former wives Irene and Mary Lou.

Paulson's parents and three of his brothers predeceased him. His father died of heart disease on March 7, 1966, at the date farm he owned and operated on the outskirts of Phoenix, Arizona. His mother died in 1974 in the San Fernando Valley. Brother Marvin died of prostate cancer. Brothers Vern and Carl, blue-collar workers their entire lives, died with alcoholism suspected as a contributing factor. Both were house painters. "Vern died walking across

Paulson's longtime secretary, Kathy O'Sako, poses with the industrialist (Kathy O'Sako).

the street," Mary Lou said, recalling the circumstances of his death in Arizona. "He stopped in the middle of the street, drunk, to take his shoe off to see how much money he hid there—and a car hit him."[3] Carl died in the San Fernando Valley during February 1979, following frequent stays at a Veteran's Administration hospital. He suffered from cirrhosis of the liver.

At the Church of the Nativity in Rancho Santa Fe, friend and NBC-TV sportscaster Dick Enberg eulogized the industrialist, describing him as "a champion of life" who uttered few words. "Allen was a champion of brevity," he said. "With all of his success, he didn't applaud himself."[4]

Lee Iacocca offered further remembrances: "Allen liked everything he did in aviation to be fast," he told the packed church.

I can picture him, during breaks from business meetings, poring over maps and navigation charts, planning his next Gulfstream speed record flight. He'd be planning how to get around the world, if possible without wasting any time landing to get some fuel. Knowing how Allen always carefully planned his flights, I'm convinced that he studied the charts and planned the trip to be sure he'd get from here to heaven fast with no unnecessary stops.

Iacocca concluded his remarks: "Allen was such a good salesman, instead of selling me an airplane, he sold me the company."[5] O'Sako understood the depth of the bond between the men. "Iacocca understood Allen and where he came from. He got the fact that Allen came from nothing. I think he respected that a lot."[6]

During a private reception at the Del Mar Country Club, his Gulfstream V and Sikorsky S-76 roared low over the gathering as a final tribute. Inside the clubhouse, following a toast to his life, guests viewed a film highlighting his racing career, capped by depicting the exploits of Cigar.

Paulson's lawyers had formed the Allen E. Paulson Living Trust on December 23, 1986, to hold title to most of the industrialist's assets. Four months before his passing, he made three amendments to the trust. Six weeks before dying, he also executed a codicil to his last will and testament. The trust document appointed him as beneficial owner of all assets owned by the trust while he was alive. As its sole trustee, the trust was revocable by him only. Upon his death, it was irrevocable, with control passing to the successor trustees he had specified.

Georgia Southern University received a $2.5 million check from the executor of the trust. It represented the first installment of a $7.5 million pledge that Paulson made almost twelve years earlier. "This $2.5 million cash distribution from Mr. Paulson's living trust further enhances his legacy of being the most generous supporter, individual or corporate, in the history of philanthropy at Georgia Southern," said James Britt, the university's vice president of advancement.[7] It was an unexpected gift, considering that many wealthy donors to universities restrict giving to their alma maters. As a high school graduate, Paulson understood the importance of a formal college education, especially engineering. Under his direction in 1988, Gulfstream Aerospace contributed $1.25 million to the university; the money to fund scholarships for students majoring in engineering technology and to provide equipment upgrades in the school's laboratories.

When a young person discovers the world of aviation, it can become addictive. It's logical that he or she might enter a career that involves airplanes. Paulson followed that path and never strayed from it. On April 28, 1999, he filed a patent application for a helium-filled airship designed to operate at high altitudes to replace expensive communication satellites. Launching conventional satellites to provide global communication links was an expensive and risky undertaking. Thinking *way* outside traditional engineering practice, he invented an alternative to replace satellite launch systems. The airship would carry the same equipment as a satellite and perform most of its tasks, such as surveillance and communication. He explained in the patent's description that the operational costs would be close to zero. The patent was issued in January 2000. Without Paulson alive to commercialize the invention, United States Patent 6,010,093 gathers dust in the files of the U.S. Patent and Trademark Office. During his final year, he worried that the airship might suffer the same outcome as his supersonic business jet project did. Turning innovative concepts into marketable products takes inventors with vision, tenacity, and drive—or fragile ideas die when their prime movers do. At a time when people approaching death might relegate such mental exercise to an earlier period of their lives, he continued to pursue new ideas.

If Paulson left this world with one unfulfilled wish, it would be the supersonic business jet. To make sure that the aircraft would take to the sky after his passing, he engineered the project's financial continuance through careful wording in his living trust. Nine years before his death, William Lowe, the man who displaced him at Gulfstream, canceled the project abruptly by proclaiming, "The supersonic business jet was a figment of Allen's imagination."[8] From the time of Paulson's departure from Savannah to the year prior to his passing, he immersed himself in real estate ventures and racing activities, those projects sandwiched between tennis matches. But he never forgot the half-born SSBJ project he initiated at Gulfstream that was dismissed by Lowe and Forstmann.

In September 1998, more than six years after Paulson left Gulfstream, the Savannah manufacturer announced at England's Farnborough Air Show that it had contracted with Lockheed Martin's fabled Skunk Works[9] to conduct an eighteen-month feasibility study for an SSBJ. The decision to continue the research was viewed by some observers as a tribute to Paulson's earlier work with Sukhoi, although it seemed unlikely. Although privy to corporate events within the Gulfstream hierarchy, Paulson remained incensed that Forstmann ditched the original project. If the financier had allowed him to follow through, he believed that Gulfstream would have reigned as the world's first manufacturer of an SSBJ.

"We signed an agreement with Gulfstream to investigate the feasibility of an SSBJ," said Paul Martin, a vice president at Lockheed.[10] The defense contractor's executives cautioned the Gulfstream leadership that development of the airplane, assuming the company would fund the project beyond a research phase, might take eight to ten years before delivery of an SSBJ to a customer. Completing the study, Lockheed bowed out, with future development work transferred to the engineers at Gulfstream in Savannah. "Lockheed Martin is doing strictly government work and didn't want to go ahead with the supersonic," Murray Smith said of the company's decision to bow out.[11]

The following year ushered in a new era in Savannah. General Dynamics Corp. bought Gulfstream Aerospace Corp. on July 30, 1999.

Paulson as CEO of Gulfstream Aerospace Corporation (©Gulfstream Aerospace Corporation, reproduced with permission).

Tom Hartmann, the program manager at the Skunk Works responsible for handling the contract with Gulfstream, recalled the first time he spoke with Paulson about the industrialist's ideas for an SSBJ. Meeting with Hartmann in 1999, Paulson asked him if Lockheed could design a supersonic business jet quiet enough to fly over land. The engineer gave him what he felt was an honest answer: "Allen, I don't know." Both men knew, as Gulfstream did, that overland flight capability, minus the sonic booms, was the key to achieving commercial acceptance of such a plane. Following several meetings at the Skunk Works, Paulson and son Michael formed an ongoing business relationship with the nation's largest defense contractor. The contract with Gulfstream was limited to a feasibility study. However, Paulson wanted to move full speed ahead and develop the airplane for production. His competitive spirit hadn't dulled.

The assumed retirement of Concorde, following three decades of supersonic service, meant that for the first time in history the trend toward ever-faster modes of transportation would shift into reverse. The SSBJ would counter that trend. The jury is undecided at this time about what supersonic business jet, *if any*, will eventually prevail in the marketplace.

Epilogue

By any measure, Paulson led an unusual life. He pursued opportunities other entrepreneurs didn't appreciate or lacked the gumption to tackle. The Super Pinto, Hustler, and Peregrine jets emerged from his drawing board, but none succeeded in the marketplace. Undeterred, he bought Grumman American and shaped the Rolls-Royce of business jets into an enduring legend.

"The greatest accomplishment Al made was that he came from being a junk dealer to become president of a company that's the best there is," Goldie Glenn offered.

A horse lover in his youth, Paulson accumulated the financial wherewithal to pursue a dream of raising thoroughbreds and entered the world of professional horse racing. His wins at the track mirrored his ascent in aviation at Gulfstream. Many of his business ventures didn't pan out as hoped but did give the inveterate risk-taker one hell of a ride, never dulling his entrepreneurial spirit.

He wasn't so egotistical as to believe that Gulfstream could achieve greatness solely from his own abilities. He succeeded because the people working with him became infused with his enthusiasm. He sought innovators, not imitators. He epitomized the self-educated man, with much of his education absorbed from the knowledge and skills of others.

Equipped with a gambler's instincts, he took chances more cautious executives avoided. Some of the ventures failed, but his overall batting average was impressive. Firm in opinion, but far from autocratic, "Allen was the most unassuming and humble rich man I had ever met," wrote Bruce McNall in his book, *Fun While It Lasted.*

As a young man, Paulson possessed something his peers didn't: a laser-like vision to target opportunities, take risks, and reap rewards. He conveyed a quiet, shy persona in public, but used that poker-faced demeanor to the greatest advantage in business dealings. When asked a question, especially something personal, the chances were good that he'd provide a one-word answer. Any verbiage beyond five words was considered an oration for him. "He was a self-effacing man, not at all comfortable being in front," Kathy O'Sako remembered. "He knew he had to be, but didn't like it."

Accolades came with the National Aeronautic Association Harmon Trophy, the Howard Hughes Memorial Award, the James H. Doolittle Award, the Wright Brothers Memorial Trophy, the Georgia Aviation Hall of Fame, and others. Paulson won the Eclipse Award several times for outstanding thoroughbred ownership. There were honorary doctorates from Winthrop University, Georgia Southern University, Bethany College, Lynchburg College, University of Charleston, and Embry-Riddle Aeronautical University.

In common with the people Tom Brokaw wrote about in *The Greatest Generation*, Paulson's loyalty, integrity, determination, and grit overshadowed any doubts he may have had.

The epitaph at his gravesite in California reads: *He became a symbol of the American dream. An inspiration to all. He was a person [who] loved life and proved that a strong work ethic with unwavering determination, commitment, and positive thinking can make dreams reality.*

Cheryl Nicholson, daughter of his brother Art, said, "Both Allen and Dad had true grit and turned struggles into steppingstones." Bill Mott, Cigar's trainer, described the industrialist in an article appearing in the *Ocala Star-Banner*: "Cigar and Mr. Paulson were alike. Both were tough, durable, dependable, and genuine to the very end."

Eighteen years after his death, a supersonic business jet has yet to be produced. One view is that if the industrialist were alive today, the planes would be flying. Son Michael spent more than $28 million of his father's estate trying to develop such a jet—$8.5 million more than his father's trust authorized. The expenditure created a firefight among family members because only minimal distributions were made to beneficiaries from an almost $200 million estate. Paulson's widow, sons, and grandchildren interpreted his trust in conflicting ways. Lengthy legal fights ensued to divvy up the money, with the lawyers appearing to be the only clear winners. At the time of this writing the outcome remains unsettled, approaching two decades after the passing of Allen E. Paulson.

Chapter Notes

Chapter 1

1. Powered by two 1,050-horsepower Pratt & Whitney R-1830 Twin Wasp engines, the DC-3's wing spanned 95 feet with a fuselage length of 65 feet. The Douglas Aircraft Co. factory in Santa Monica, California, couldn't keep up with the demand for the airliner in the late 1930s, with an order backlog of $2 million from U.S. airlines and $5 million from foreign carriers.

2. Air Safety Board Report, *Accident involving aircraft NC-16066 of United Air Lines, off Port Reyes, California, on November 29, 1938* (Civil Aeronautics Authority), 6.

3. *Ibid.*, 10.

4. Air Safety Board Report, Exhibit B, 13.

5. Air Safety Board Report, 12.

6. Air Safety Board Report, Exhibit B, 13.

7. *Ibid.*, 16.

8. *Ibid.*, 17.

9. *Ibid.*, 18.

10. "Five Dead in Freak S.F. Plane Disaster," *The Stanford Daily*, Stanford (CA) University (November 30, 1938), 1.

11. "Radio Log Tells Tragic Story of Plane Disaster," *Chicago Daily Tribune* (November 30, 1938), 1.

12. *Ibid.*

13. "Plane Drifts To Rocky Shore At Foot Of Light," *San Rafael* (CA) *Independent* (November 30, 1938).

14. Allen Paulson, transcript of dictated personal history, July 23, 1995.

15. The narrow beach below the cliffs is believed to be where England's Sir Francis Drake came ashore to repair his ship's dam-

aged hull while circumnavigating the globe during the summer of 1579.

16. Paulson transcript.

17. *Ibid.*

18. *Ibid.*

19. *Ibid.*

20. *Ibid.*

21. *Ibid.*

22. Air Safety Board Report, 15.

23. Peddicord, Ross, "Pilot/inventor Paulson knows meaning of speed," *Baltimore Sun* (April 28, 1992).

24. Mary Lou Paulson, author interview, August 2, 2015.

25. Kathy O'Sako, author interview, May 15, 2015.

26. Email, Cheryl Nicholson to author, August 10, 2015.

27. Paulson transcript.

28. *Ibid.*

29. *Ibid.*

30. Allen Paulson, Pinnacle television interview on *Cable News Network* (January 26, 1985).

31. Jay Hovdey, *Cigar: America's Horse* (Lexington, Kentucky: Blood-Horse Publications, 2003), 48.

Chapter 2

1. Hovdey, 41.

2. Paulson transcript.

3. *Ibid.*

4. *Ibid.*

5. Paulson CNN interview.

6. Two years after the Oakland air races, Rankin organized the Rankin School of Flying in Van Nuys, training thousands of pilots for the military.

7. Paulson transcript.

8. *Ibid.*

9. During 1925, DuPont began construction of the factory in the eastern Kanawha County town of Belle. The chemical giant's research was hailed as a breakthrough, resulting in the first ammonia produced in North America by a high-pressure process.

10. Paulson transcript.

11. Packed into Lockheed's buildings during the wartime years, three shifts totaling up to 90,000 workers assembled thousands of airplanes for assignment to the war front. Situated at the southern edge of the field stood an ornate passenger terminal where TWA flights landed and departed. Until December 1946, Lockheed Air Terminal served as the principal terminus for TWA flights to and from the west coast.

12. Paulson transcript.

13. Paulson CNN interview.

14. Crystal Christensen, author interview, June 1, 2015.

15. Paulson transcript.

16. *Ibid.*

17. Clay Lacy, author interview, January 6, 2015.

18. Paulson transcript.

19. Mary Lou Paulson interview.

20. Lacy interview.

21. Paulson transcript.

22. "Winners Get $200, Atlantic Passes," TWA *Starliner* newsletter (April 12, 1951), 1.

23. Located 9 miles west of Burbank airport, Metropolitan was a gathering place for pioneering pilots. In 1942, the U.S. government purchased the airport, stationing troops and airplanes there to protect the west coast. It reverted to municipal ownership after the war.

24. Paulson transcript.

25. *Ibid.*

26. Robert W. Rummel, *Howard Hughes and TWA* (Washington, D.C.: Smithsonian Institution Press, 1991), 106.

27. Allen Paulson, excerpted from speech accepting the Horatio Alger Award, New York, 1985.

28. Lacy interview.

29. *Ibid.*

Chapter 3

1. Paulson transcript.

2. *Ibid.*

3. Jeffrey L. Rodengen, *The Legend of Gulfstream* (Fort Lauderdale: Write Stuff Enterprises, 2000), 80–81.

4. Paulson transcript.

5. *Ibid.*

6. Mary Lou Paulson interview.

7. Paulson transcript.

8. Lacy interview.

9. Mary Lou Paulson interview.

10. Paulson transcript.

11. Lacy interview.

12. "Allen Paulson: Pursuing Aviation Fame and Fortune," *Flying* (July 1981), 36.

13. Paulson transcript.

14. Lacy interview.

15. Bill Christine, "Longtime Owner Paulson Loses Battle With Cancer," *Los Angeles Times* (July 21, 2000).

16. Lacy interview.

17. Jasper Dorsey, "Allen Paulson an incredible man," *Rockmart (GA) Journal* (March 28, 1990), 3.

18. O'Sako interview.

19. Lacy interview.

20. Wright took the postwar R-3350 engine and fit three turbine wheels around the crankcase. Exhaust gas piped from the cylinders impinged against the wheels before exiting the exhaust stacks. The wheels fed power back to the engine's crankshaft.

21. L. L. Doty, "Airlines, Curtiss-Wright Tackle Problems of Turbo-Compound," *Aviation Week* (April 21, 1958), 38.

22. Lacy interview.

23. *Ibid.*

24. "Allen Paulson: Pursuing…," 36.

25. Unlike aircraft dealers and brokers, Paulson had a competitive advantage by supplying the parts required to maintain the airplanes he sold. New airlines didn't have to stock in-depth inventories of parts. California Airmotive stocked most of what they needed. The parts inventory multiplied in size, as did his "fleet" of purchased aircraft.

26. Lacy interview.

27. The 40,000-square-foot structure sheltered the airplanes of Howard Hughes and Hollywood celebrities in the late 1930s.

28. Lacy interview.

29. *Ibid.*

30. *Ibid.*

31. Bruce McCaw, author interview, July 10, 2015.

32. Glenn Garrison, "Used Plane Market

Soft, but Not Glutted," *Aviation Week* (March 21, 1960), 38.

33. David H. Hoffman, "Hearings Threaten Supplementals' Status," *Aviation Week & Space Technology* (January 15, 1962), 40.

34. "California Airmotive Acquires Firm," *New York Times* (July 17, 1962).

35. Christensen interview.

Chapter 4

1. "Clay Lacy," *Wikipedia*, accessed online October 2016.

2. Stacy T. Geere, *Lucky Me: The Life and Flights of Veteran Aviator Clay Lacy* (Virginia Beach, Virginia: The Donning Company Publishers, 2010), 16.

3. *Ibid.*

4. "Plane Crash Brings Death to Bill Stead," *Spokesman-Review*, Spokane, WA (April 28, 1966), 46.

5. Evert Clark, "Czechoslovakian Refugee Seeks U.S. Air Crown," *New York Times* (September 11, 1964).

6. Lacy interview.

7. Frances Cerra, "Plane Racing: Its Revival Is Still Up in the Air," *New York Times* (March 18, 1978).

8. Lacy interview.

9. Eric Malnic, "Aging Planes Bring Profit," *Spokesman-Review*, Spokane, WA (December 14, 1968), 35.

10. Lacy interview.

11. Howie Keefe, *Galloping on Wings with the P-51 Mustang "Miss America"* (Newcastle, Washington: Aviation Supplies & Academics, Inc., 2013).

12. *Ibid.*

13. Lacy interview.

14. Geere, 104.

15. McCaw interview.

16. William P. Lear, Jr., *Fly Fast ... Sin Boldly* (Lenexa, Kansas: Addax Publishing Group, Inc., 2000), 318.

17. Lacy interview.

18. Keefe.

19. *Ibid.*

20. Lacy interview.

21. Jeffrey R., Werner "What Can a Passenger Do If the Flight is Booked Solid? The Human Fly Has One Solution." *PEOPLE* magazine (July 19, 1976).

22. Geere, 60.

Chapter 5

1. Moya Olson Lear, *An Unforgettable Flight* (Reno, Nevada: Jack Bacon and Company, 1996), 148.

2. *Ibid.*

3. Ronald D. Neal, "Development of the Lear Jet Model 23," *American Aviation Historical Society Journal* (Fall 1989), 169.

4. "The E.F. MacDonald Company," Harvard Business School Baker Library: Lehman Brothers Collection—Twentieth-Century Business Archives, accessed online May 2014.

5. Geere, 63.

6. Lacy interview.

7. *Ibid.*

8. *Ibid.*

9. *Ibid.*

10. *Ibid.*

11. *Ibid.*

12. Mary Lou Paulson interview.

13. *Ibid.*

14. *Ibid.*

15. Lacy interview.

16. *Ibid.*

17. "Sinatra Has Now Become Aircraft Tycoon," *Sarasota Herald-Tribune* (August 29, 1965).

18. *Aviation/Space Writers Association 1938–1988* (Columbus, Ohio: Aviation/Space Writers Association, 1988), 40.

19. Lacy interview.

20. *Ibid.*

21. *Ibid.*

22. Mary Lou Paulson interview.

23. Christensen interview.

24. *Ibid.*

25. McCaw interview.

26. Mary Lou Paulson interview.

Chapter 6

1. Dennis McLellan, "Bill Murphy, 92; Southland Car Dealer, Top California Sports Car Racer in '50s," *Los Angeles Times* (July 21, 2005).

2. Lacy interview.

3. McLellan.

4. McCaw interview.

5. Joe Clark, author interview, June 15, 2016.

6. McCaw interview.

7. *Ibid.*

8. *Ward's Auto World* (February 1, 1992).
9. Hovdey, 47.
10. Clark interview.
11. Lacy interview.
12. "Kaye an Official For Lear Jet," *Lawrence* (KS) *Journal-World* (March 1, 1966), 2.
13. "If I Can Learn to Fly, You Can Learn to Fly," *Popular Science* (January 1967), 199.
14. Lacy interview.
15. Sandor (Alex) Kvassay, *Alex in Wonderland* (Tucson, Arizona: Westernlore Press, 1995), 150.
16. Lacy interview.
17. Mary Lou Paulson interview.
18. Lacy interview.
19. William P. Lear, Jr., 370.
20. Max Gunther, *The Very, Very Rich and How They Got That Way* (London: Harriman House Ltd., 1972), 169.
21. William P. Lear, Jr., 371.
22. On March 17, 1966, the FAA certified the Lear Jet 24 to meet the same FAR Part 25 requirements that apply to commercial jets.
23. Accident report, *Cessna A150K, registration N8321M; Eagle, Idaho, October 10, 1970* (Washington, D.C.: National Transportation Safety Board, NTSB Identification: SEA71AS022).
24. A whipstall is a condition where an airplane enters a nearly vertical climb, pauses, slips backward momentarily, and drops suddenly in a nose down attitude.
25. Mary Lou Paulson interview.
26. Christensen interview.
27. Paulson CNN interview.
28. Mary Lou Paulson interview.
29. Alex Kvassay, author interview, January 12, 2017.
30. "The Used Airliner King," *Newsweek* (January 13, 1969), 73.
31. *Ibid.*
32. Malnic, 35.
33. Lacy interview.
34. Kvassay interview.
35. The author noticed the sign while attending an auction at the California Airmotive warehouse.
36. Malnic, 35.
37. Lacy interview.
38. Hovdey, 48.
39. Jay Miller, "Pony Power," *Air & Space* magazine (February/March 2005).
40. Richard Sweeney, "TT-1 Demonstrates Acrobatic Capability," *Aviation Week* (September 21, 1959), 128.
41. Miller.
42. "Pilot's Arrival Exciting One," *Reading* (PA) *Eagle* (June 8, 1976), 2.

Chapter 7

1. Jeffrey Lenorovitz, "Electra Cargo Conversion Finds Market," *Aviation Week & Space Technology* (February 6, 1978), 42.
2. McCaw interview.
3. Hugh Field, "Launch pad for Hustler," *FLIGHT International* (October 16, 1976), 118.
4. Peter Viemeister, *Start All Over* (Bedford, Virginia: Hamilton's, 1995), 397.
5. Clark interview.
6. McCaw interview.
7. Donald E. Fink, "Turboprop to Utilize Turbojet Backup," *Aviation Week & Space Technology* (November 24, 1975), 65.
8. Lacy interview.
9. Allen E. Paulson, "Aircraft with Combination Power Plant," United States Patent 4,089,493, filed September 29, 1976; issued May 16, 1978.
10. Fink.
11. Allen E. Paulson, "Loner Groaners," *Flying* (August 1976), 84.
12. William H. Gregory, "Innovation and Competition," *Aviation Week & Space Technology* (September 2, 1985), 13.
13. Hugh Field and Warren Goodman, "Reading Show," *FLIGHT International* (July 3, 1976), 31.
14. Field, "Launch pad..."
15. "Reading show report," *FLIGHT International* (June 24, 1978), 1953.
16. Gordon Baxter, "People Who Fly: Tom Peterson," *Flying* (May 1977), 130.
17. McCaw interview.
18. O'Sako interview.
19. McCaw interview.
20. Clark interview.
21. Gregory Ford Henderson, *The Henderson Family and the California Perfume Company* (June 2013), accessed online May 2014.
22. *Ibid.*
23. F. Andrew Taylor, "Underground home was built as Cold War-era hideaway," *Las Vegas Review Journal* (June 17, 2013).
24. "Founder Jerry Henderson," Alexander Dawson School website, accessed online June 2014.
25. John F. Berry, "Aircraft Refitter's Fi-

nancial Angel," *Washington Post* (July 30, 1978), G1.

26. "Hustling Off the Runway," *Flying* (April 1978), 22.

27. "American Jet Hustler flies," *FLIGHT International* (January 21, 1978), 159.

28. "Allen Paulson: Pursuing…," 40.

29. "General aviation," *FLIGHT International* (September 9, 1978), 975.

30. Jeffrey M. Lenorovitz, "Hustler Utility Aircraft Redesigned," *Aviation Week & Space Technology* (March 27, 1978), 20.

31. Lacy interview.

33. Viemeister, 353.

34. Donald E. Fink, "Grumman American Sale Approved," *Aviation Week & Space Technology* (July 24, 1978), 19.

35. O'Sako interview.

36. Christensen interview.

37. Glenn interview.

38. Murray Smith, author interview, July 27, 2016.

39. Skurla, 138.

40. *Ibid.*, 133.

41. Lacy interview.

42. Skurla, 138.

Chapter 8

1. George M. Skurla and William H. Gregory, *Inside the Iron Works* (Annapolis, Maryland: Naval Institute Press, 2004), 133.

2. Sutton, Michael, "Behind the Brochure," *FLIGHT International* (March 19, 1964), 425.

3. Skurla, 135.

4. *Ibid.*, 134.

5. *Ibid.*, 135.

6. *Ibid.*, 137.

7. Edwin J. Bulban, "Gulfstream I Turbofan Version Studied," *Aviation Week & Space Technology* (September 9, 1974), 53.

8. Skurla, 135.

9. Rodengen, 75.

10. Berry.

11. Skurla, 143.

12. Viemeister, 334.

13. *Ibid.*, 335.

14. Skurla, 138.

15. Viemeister, 344.

16. Albert "Goldie" Glenn, author interview, May 14, 2015.

17. Lacy interview.

18. Rodengen, 75.

19. Hovdey, 46.

20. Viemeister, 344.

21. *Ibid.*, 345.

22. Lacy interview.

23. *Ibid.*

24. Viemeister, 345.

25. Glenn interview.

26. Viemeister, 346.

27. *Ibid.*

28. Lacy interview.

29. Glenn interview.

30. McCaw interview.

31. Viemeister, 350.

32. McCaw interview.

Chapter 9

1. Rodengen, 83.

2. Glenn interview.

3. Paulson transcript.

4. Glenn interview.

5. *Ibid.*

6. Skurla, 143.

7. Glenn interview.

8. *Ibid.*

9. "AJI and Allen Who," *Aviation International News* (August 11, 1978), 76.

10. Paulson transcript.

11. Glenn interview.

12. "Tesoro Petroleum: The Irony of Becoming a Takeover Target," *Business Week* (October 6, 1980), 61.

13. Paulson transcript.

14. *Ibid.*

15. "Allen Paulson: Pursuing…," 41.

16. Glenn interview.

17. David M. North, "Gulfstream to Expand, Sell Piston Line," *Aviation Week & Space Technology* (May 21, 1979), 20.

18. Glenn interview.

19. *Ibid.*

20. McCaw interview.

21. Glenn interview.

22. *Ibid.*

23. McCaw interview.

24. "Allen Paulson: Pursuing…," 40.

25. O'Sako interview.

26. Clay Lacy, "A salute to Allen Paulson," *Professional Pilot* (September 2000), 188.

27. "Gulfstream American Seeks VFW-614 Rights," *Aviation Week & Space Technology* (March 19, 1979), 28.

28. North, "Gulfstream to Expand…," 20.

29. "Gulfstream American Ends VFW-614 Talks," *Aviation Week & Space Technology* (July 16, 1979), 20/

30. "Allen Paulson: Pursuing...," 40.
31. Email, Scott Morris to author (October 20, 2015).
32. "Allen Paulson: Pursuing...," 40.
33. *Ibid.*, 41.
34. "Gulfstream goes military," *FLIGHT International* (June 20, 1981), 1919.
35. Accident report, *Gulfstream Peregrine N600GA, El Reno, Oklahoma, November 23, 1983* (Washington, D.C.: National Transportation Safety Board).
36. "Allen Paulson: Pursuing...," 39.
37. Smith interview.
38. Lacy interview.
39. "First Flight of Peregrine Trainer Scheduled," *Aviation Week & Space Technology* (May 4, 1981), 56.
40. "Peregrine—Gulfstream's ultimate single?" *FLIGHT International* (March 3, 1984), 563.
41. "Gulfstream Plans Peregrine Production," *Aviation Week & Space Technology* (February 27, 1984), 73.
42. Smith interview.
43. Mary Lou Paulson interview.
44. O'Sako interview.
45. Dorsey.

Chapter 10

1. "Allen Paulson: Pursuing...," 41.
2. O'Sako interview.
3. Christensen interview.
4. "President's Message," Gulfstream Aerospace *Southern Exposure* newsletter (November 23, 1982), 1.
5. Skurla, 139.
6. Paulson transcript.
7. *Ibid.*
8. Agis Salpukas, "Cockpit Entrepreneur: Allen E. Paulson," *New York Times* (May 1, 1983).
9. *Ibid.*
10. "Gulfstream Workers Get Nearly $1,000 in Stock," *Savannah Morning News* (April 21, 1983), D1.
11. Glenn interview.
12. "Paulson made presence felt in background of sports world," *Savannah (GA) Morning News* (July 21, 2000).
13. Glenn interview.
14. "Intended Victim Kills Kidnapper," *Lewiston* (MN) *Journal* (December 12, 1983), 8.
15. "Kidnapping Attempt Backfires," *The Dispatch*, Lexington, NC (December 12, 1983), 2.
16. Mary Lou Paulson interview.
17. David M. North, "Gulfstream Terminates Production of Turboprop Commander Line," *Aviation Week & Space Technology* (January 28, 1985), 24.
18. North, "Gulfstream to Expand..."
19. O'Sako interview.
20. Paulson CNN interview.
21. David M. North, "Rolls-Royce Alters Speys To Meet Pollution Rules," *Aviation Week & Space Technology* (July 2, 1984), 34.
22. *Ibid.*
23. Clay Lacy, "A salute...," 188.
24. Glenn interview.
25. "Gulfstream IV is launched with Tay," *FLIGHT International* (March 12, 1983), 645.
26. Lee Iacocca, with William Novak, *Iacocca* (New York: Bantam Books, 1984), xv.
27. McCaw interview.
28. Rodengen, 122.
29. Paulson transcript.
30. "Chrysler Deal for Gulfstream," *New York Times* (June 20, 1985).
31. "Paulson flies the GIV in," *FLIGHT International* (October 12, 1985), 25.
32. Paul William Kroll, "One Woman's Love Affair With The Martial Arts," *Black Belt Magazine* (November 1976), 42.
33. Christensen interview.

Chapter 11

1. "Gulfstream founder gave generously..."
2. Paulson CNN interview.
3. Mary Lou Paulson interview.
4. Sikorsky S-76 helicopter advertisement with Paulson endorsement.
5. "Paulson flies..."
6. Paulson transcript.
7. Allen Paulson, news conference at Gulfstream Aerospace (March 20, 1990).
8. "Gulfstream 4B Targets First-Class Airline Service," *Aviation Week & Space Technology* (March 25, 1985), 36.
9. Lacy interview.
10. "Gulfstream claims global record," *FLIGHT International* (June 28, 1987), 3.
11. Paul Dean, "Aboard Friendship One: A 6-Mile High House Party," *Los Angeles Times* (February 1, 1988).
12. *Ibid.*

13. J. Mac McClellan, "Record Breaker," *Flying* (June 1988), 70.

14. *Ibid.*

15. Lacy interview.

16. Kvassay, *Alex in Wonderland*, 230.

17. Lacy interview.

18. Clark interview.

19. McClellan, 72.

20. Kvassay, *Alex in Wonderland*, 233.

21. Mark David, "South Mapleton Drive Houses a Bevy of the Rich and Famous," *Variety* (August 28, 2014).

22. O'Sako interview.

23. Glenn interview.

24. Jay Hovdey, *Cigar: America's Horse* (Lexington, Kentucky: Blood-Horse Publications, 2003), 30.

25. Associated Press, "Insurers Agree Cigar Is Infertile," *Southeast Missourian* (March 25, 1997), 7.

Chapter 12

1. James Risen, "Chrysler Sells Unit After Loss of $664 Million," *Los Angeles Times* (February 14, 1990).

2. Paulson transcript.

3. Paulson news conference.

4. *Ibid.*

5. Daniel J. Kadlec, *Masters of the Universe* (New York: Harper-Business, 1999), 173.

6. Paulson transcript.

7. *Ibid.*

8. Benjamin Hebebrand, "Paulson Purchases Gulfstream Again," *Savannah Morning News* (February 14, 1990), 1.

9. *Ibid.*

10. Agis Salpukas, "Ex-Owner of Gulfstream Buys It Back," *New York Times* (February 14, 1990).

11. Benjamin Hebebrand, "Gulfstream, Learjet Both Appear Delighted by Planned Purchase," *Savannah Morning News* (February 14, 1990), 5A.

12. *Ibid.*

13. *Ibid.*

14. *Ibid.*

15. *Ibid.*

16. Paulson news conference.

17. Benjamin Hebebrand, "Gulfstream's Marriage With Learjet Junked," *Savannah News-Press* (February 25, 1990), 8F.

18. "Remarks at Colorado Springs to the Graduating Class of the U.S. Air Force Academy, June 5, 1963," *The American Presidency Project*, accessed online September 2016.

19. The speed of sound (Mach 1) varies with temperature and altitude, and at sea level is about 760 miles per hour. The Mach number is the ratio of airspeed to the speed of sound.

20. "Remarks Announcing Decision To Continue Development of the Supersonic Transport, September 23, 1969," *The American Presidency Project*, accessed online September 2016.

21. Paulson news conference.

22. "Gulfstream ponders SST," *Flying* (December 1988), 9.

23. Postlethwaite.

24. "Sukhoi meets Gulfstream on SST," *FLIGHT International* (July 8, 1989), 5.

25. *Ibid.*

26. Postlethwaite.

27. Paulson news conference.

28. "Sukhoi meets..."

29. Eric Weiner, "U.S.–Soviet Makers Plan Supersonic Business Jet," *New York Times* (November 28, 1989).

30. *Ibid.*

31. Glenn interview.

32. Edward H. Phillips, "Gulfstream, Rolls-Royce Developing Hushkits to Extend Business Jet Life," *Aviation Week & Space Technology* (June 17, 1991), 209.

33. Clark interview.

Chapter 13

1. Glenn interview.

2. Paulson news conference.

3. O'Sako interview.

4. Glenn interview.

5. Kadlec, 177.

6. Glenn interview.

7. In addition to Rumsfeld, the board included George Schultz, former secretary of state; Robert Strauss, former U.S. ambassador to Russia; Colin Powell, former chairman of the joints chief of staff; and Henry Kissinger, former secretary of state. Other members were heads of major corporations or friends of Forstmann.

8. Glenn interview.

9. O'Sako interview.

10. Kadlec, 178.

11. *Ibid.*

12. Anthony Blanco and William C.

Symonds, "Gulfstream's Pilot," *Business Week* (April 14, 1997), 4.
13. Smith interview.
14. Glenn interview.
15. O'Sako interview.
16. *Ibid.*
17. Kadlec, 178.
18. Blanco, 2.
19. Kadlec, 182.

Chapter 14

1. O'Sako interview.
2. *Ibid.*
3. Mary Lou Paulson interview.
4. "Paulson Remembered as 'Champion in Life,'" *The Blood-Horse* magazine (July 26, 2000).
5. Clay Lacy, "A salute…," 189.
6. O'Sako interview.
7. "GSU receives first installment of $7.5 million gift," *Savannah Morning News* (December 5, 2003).
8. Blanco, 4.
9. When Lockheed hired engineers in 1943 to design the XP-80 jet, there wasn't enough factory space. They moved into a circus tent having a strong odor; the "Skunk Works" description stuck and was trademarked.
10. Julian Moxon, "Supersonic Business," *FLIGHT International* (December 23, 1998), 34.
11. Smith interview.

Bibliography

Accident report, *Cessna A150K, registration N8321M; Eagle, Idaho, October 10, 1970.* Washington, D.C.: National Transportation Safety Board, NTSB Identification: SEA71AS022.

Accident report, *Gulfstream Peregrine N600GA, El Reno, Oklahoma, November 23, 1983.* Washington, D.C.: National Transportation Safety Board.

Air Safety Board Report, *Accident Involving Aircraft NC-16066 of United Air Lines, Off Port Reyes, California, on November 29, 1938,* Civil Aeronautics Authority.

"AJI and Allen Who." *Aviation International News,* August 11, 1978.

"Allen Paulson: Pursuing Aviation Fame and Fortune." *Flying,* July 1981.

"American Jet Hustler Flies." *FLIGHT International,* January 21, 1978.

Aviation/Space Writers Association 1938–1988. Columbus, Ohio: Aviation/Space Writers Association, 1988.

Baxter, Gordon. "People Who Fly: Tom Peterson." *Flying,* May 1977.

Berry, John F. "Aircraft Refitter's Financial Angel." *Washington Post,* July 30, 1978.

Blanco, Anthony, and William C. Symonds. "Gulfstream's Pilot." *Business Week,* April 14, 1997.

Bowen, Edward L. *Legacies of the Turf.* Lexington, Kentucky: Blood-Horse Publications, 2004, 242.

Bulban, Edwin J. "Gulfstream I Turbofan Version Studied." *Aviation Week & Space Technology,* September 9, 1974.

"California Airmotive Acquires Firm." *New York Times,* July 17, 1962.

Cerra, Frances. "Plane Racing: Its Revival Is Still Up in the Air." *New York Times,* March 18, 1978.

Christensen, Crystal. Author interview, June 1, 2015.

Christine, Bill. "Longtime Owner Paulson Loses Battle with Cancer." *Los Angeles Times,* July 21, 2000.

"Chrysler Deal for Gulfstream." *New York Times,* June 20, 1985.

Clark, Evert. "Czechoslovakian Refugee Seeks U.S. Air Crown." *New York Times,* September 11, 1964.

Clark, Joe. Author interview, June 15, 2016.

David, Mark. "South Mapleton Drive Houses a Bevy of the Rich and Famous." *Variety,* August 28, 2014.

Davies, R.E.G., *Airlines of the United States since 1914.* Washington, D.C.: Smithsonian Institution Press, 1972.

Dean, Paul. "Aboard Friendship One: A 6-Mile High House Party." *Los Angeles Times,* February 1, 1988.

Dorsey, Jasper. "Allen Paulson an Incredible Man." *Rockmart* (GA) *Journal,* March 28, 1990.

Doty, L.L. "Airlines, Curtiss-Wright Tackle Problems of Turbo-Compound." *Aviation Week,* April 21, 1958.

"The E.F. MacDonald Company." Harvard Business School Baker Library: Lehman Brothers Collection—Twentieth-Century Business Archives.

Field, Hugh. "Launch Pad for Hustler." *FLIGHT International*, October 16, 1976.

_____, and Warren Goodman. "Reading Show." *FLIGHT International*, July 3, 1976.

Fink, Donald E. "Grumman American Sale Approved." *Aviation Week & Space Technology*, July 24, 1978.

_____. "Turboprop to Utilize Turbojet Backup." *Aviation Week & Space Technology*, November 24, 1975.

"First Flight of Peregrine Trainer Scheduled." *Aviation Week & Space Technology*, May 4, 1981.

"Five Dead in Freak S.F. Plane Disaster." *The Stanford Daily*, Stanford (CA) University, November 30, 1938.

"Founder Jerry Henderson." Alexander Dawson School website.

Garrison, Glenn. "Used Plane Market Soft, but Not Glutted." *Aviation Week*, March 21, 1960.

Geere, Stacy T. *Lucky Me: The Life and Flights of Veteran Aviator Clay Lacy*. Virginia Beach, Virginia: The Donning Company Publishers, 2010.

"General Aviation." *FLIGHT International*, September 9, 1978.

Glenn, Albert "Goldie." Author interview, May 14, 2015.

Gregory, William H. "Innovation and Competition." *Aviation Week & Space Technology*, September 2, 1985.

"GSU Receives First Installment of $7.5 Million Gift." *Savannah (GA) Morning News*, December 5, 2003.

"Gulfstream American Ends VFW-614 Talks." *Aviation Week & Space Technology*, July 16, 1979).

"Gulfstream American Seeks VFW-614 Rights." *Aviation Week & Space Technology*, March 19, 1979.

"Gulfstream Claims Global Record." *FLIGHT International*, June 28, 1987.

"Gulfstream 4B Targets First-Class Airline Service." *Aviation Week & Space Technology*, March 25, 1985.

"Gulfstream Goes Military." *FLIGHT International*, June 20, 1981.

"Gulfstream IV Is Launched with Tay." *FLIGHT International*, March 12, 1983.

"Gulfstream Plans Peregrine Production." *Aviation Week & Space Technology*, February 27, 1984.

"Gulfstream Ponders SST." *Flying*, December 1988.

"Gulfstream Workers Get Nearly $1,000 in Stock." *Savannah Morning News*, April 21, 1983.

Gunther, Max. *The Very, Very Rich and How They Got That Way.* London: Harriman House Ltd., 1972.

Hebebrand, Benjamin. "Gulfstream, Learjet Both Appear Delighted by Planned Purchase." *Savannah Morning News*, February 14, 1990

_____. "Gulfstream's Marriage with Learjet Junked." *Savannah News-Press*, February 25, 1990.

_____. "Paulson Purchases Gulfstream Again." *Savannah Morning News*, February 14, 1990.

Henderson, Gregory Ford. *The Henderson Family and the California Perfume Company,* June 2013.

Hoffman, David H. "Hearings Threaten Supplementals' Status." *Aviation Week & Space Technology,* January 15, 1962.

Hogan, Jan. "Casino Executive Paulson, 78, Dies." *Las Vegas Review-Journal,* July 21, 2000.

Hovdey, Jay. *Cigar: America's Horse.* Lexington, Kentucky: Blood-Horse Publications, 2003.

"Hustling Off the Runway." *Flying,* April 1978.

Iacocca, Lee, with William Novak. *Iacocca.* New York: Bantam Books, 1984.

"If I Can Learn to Fly, You Can Learn to Fly." *Popular Science,* January 1967.

"Insurers Agree Cigar Is Infertile." Associated Press. *Southeast Missourian,* March 25, 1997, 7.

Jehl, Douglas. "Horse Racing; Cigar Hangs On in Desert Sand to Win 14th in Row." *New York Times,* March 28, 1996.

Kadlec, Daniel J. *Masters of the Universe.* New York: Harper-Business, 1999.

"Kaye an Official For Lear Jet." *Lawrence* (KS) *Journal-World,* March 1, 1966.

Keefe, Howie. *Galloping on Wings with the P-51 Mustang "Miss America."* Newcastle, Washington: Aviation Supplies & Academics, Inc., 2013.

Kroll, Paul William. "One Woman's Love Affair with the Martial Arts." *Black Belt Magazine,* November 1976.

Kvassay, Sandor "Alex." Author interview, January 12, 2017.

Kvassay, Sandor (Alex). *Alex in Wonderland,* Tucson, Arizona: Westernlore Press. 1995.

Lacy, Clay. "A Salute to Allen Paulson." *Professional Pilot,* September 2000.

_____. Author interview, January 6, 2015.

Lear, Moya Olson. *An Unforgettable Flight,* Reno, Nevada: Jack Bacon and Company, 1996.

Lear, William P., Jr. *Fly Fast ... Sin Boldly,* Lenexa, Kansas: Addax Publishing Group, Inc., 2000.

Lenorovitz, Jeffrey. "Electra Cargo Conversion Finds Market." *Aviation Week & Space Technology,* February 6, 1978.

_____. "Hustler Utility Aircraft Redesigned." *Aviation Week & Space Technology,* March 27, 1978.

Malnic, Eric. "Aging Planes Bring Profit." *Spokesman-Review,* Spokane, WA, December 14, 1968.

McCaw, Bruce. Author interview, July 10, 2015.

McClellan, J. Mac. "Record Breaker." *Flying,* June 1988.

McLellan, Dennis. "Bill Murphy, 92; Southland Car Dealer, Top California Sports Car Racer in '50s." *Los Angeles Times,* July 21, 2005.

McNall, Bruce, *Fun While It Lasted.* New York: Hyperion, 2003.

Miller, Jay. "Pony Power." *Air & Space* magazine, February/March 2005.

Moxon, Julian. "Supersonic Business." *FLIGHT International,* December 23, 1998.

Neal, Ronald D. "Development of the Lear Jet Model 23." *American Aviation Historical Society Journal,* Fall 1989.

North, David M. "Gulfstream Terminates Production of Turboprop Commander Line." *Aviation Week & Space Technology,* January 28, 1985.

_____. "Gulfstream to Expand, Sell Piston Line." *Aviation Week & Space Technology,* May 21, 1979.

_____. "Rolls-Royce Alters Speys to Meet Pollution Rules." *Aviation Week & Space Technology,* July 2, 1984.

O'Sako, Kathy. Author interview, May 15, 2015.

Paulson, Allen. "Loner Groaners." *Flying,* August 1976.

_____. *Pinnacle* television interview on *Cable News Network,* January 26, 1985.

_____. News conference at Gulfstream Aerospace, March 20, 1990

_____. Speech accepting the Horatio Alger Award, New York, 1985

_____. Transcript of dictated personal history, July 23, 1995.

Paulson, Allen E. "Aircraft with Combination Power Plant." United States Patent 4,089,493, filed September 29, 1976; issued May 16, 1978.

Paulson, Mary Lou. Author interview, August 2, 2015.

"The Paulson Estate Battle." *Forbes,* May 12, 2003.

"Paulson Flies the GIV In." *FLIGHT International,* October 12, 1985.

"Paulson Made Presence Felt in Background of Sports World." *Savannah Morning News,* July 21, 2000.

"Paulson Remembered as 'Champion in Life.'" *The Blood-Horse* magazine, July 26, 2000.

Peddicord, Ross. "Pilot/Inventor Paulson Knows Meaning of Speed." *Baltimore Sun,* April 28, 1992.

"Peregrine—Gulfstream's Ultimate Single?" *FLIGHT International,* March 3, 1984.

Phillips, Edward H. "Gulfstream, Rolls-Royce Developing Hushkits to Extend Business Jet Life." *Aviation Week & Space Technology,* June 17, 1991.

"Pilot's Arrival Exciting One." *Reading* (PA) *Eagle,* June 8, 1976.

"Plane Crash Brings Death to Bill Stead." *Spokesman-Review,* Spokane, WA, April 28, 1966.

"Plane Drifts to Rocky Shore at Foot of Light." *San Rafael* (CA) *Independent,* November 30, 1938.

"President's Message." Gulfstream Aerospace *Southern Exposure* newsletter, November 23, 1982.

"Radio Log Tells Tragic Story of Plane Disaster." *Chicago Daily Tribune,* November 30, 1938.

Rashke, Richard. *Stormy Genius: The Life of Aviation's Maverick Bill Lear.* Boston: Houghton Mifflin Co., 1985.

"Reading Show Report." *FLIGHT International,* June 24, 1978.

"Remarks Announcing Decision to Continue Development of the Supersonic Transport, September 23, 1969." *The American Presidency Project.*

"Remarks at Colorado Springs to the Graduating Class of the U.S. Air Force Academy, June 5, 1963." *The American Presidency Project.*

Rempel, William C. *The Gambler.* New York: HarperCollins, 2018.

Risen, James. "Chrysler Sells Unit After Loss of $664 Million." *Los Angeles Times,* February 14, 1990.

Rodengen, Jeffrey L. *The Legend of Gulfstream.* Fort Lauderdale: Write Stuff Enterprises, 2000.

Rummel, Robert W. *Howard Hughes and TWA.* Washington, D.C.: Smithsonian Institution Press, 1991.

Salpukas, Agis. "Cockpit Entrepreneur: Allen E. Paulson." *New York Times,* May 1, 1983.

_____. "Ex-Owner of Gulfstream Buys It Back." *New York Times,* February 14, 1990.

Serling, Robert. *Howard Hughes' Airline.* New York: St. Martins/Marek, 1985.

"Sinatra Has Now Become Aircraft Tycoon." *Sarasota Herald-Tribune,* August 29, 1965.

Skurla, George M., and William H. Gregory. *Inside the Iron Works.* Annapolis, Maryland: Naval Institute Press, 2004.

Smith, Murray. Author interview, July 27, 2016.

"Sukhoi Meets Gulfstream on SST." *FLIGHT International,* July 8, 1989.

Sutton, Michael. "Behind the Brochure." *FLIGHT International,* March 19, 1964.

Sweeney, Richard. "TT-1 Demonstrates Acrobatic Capability." *Aviation Week,* September 21, 1959.

Taylor, F. Andrew. "Underground Home was Built as Cold War-era Hideaway." *Las Vegas Review Journal,* June 17, 2013.

"Tesoro Petroleum: The Irony of Becoming a Takeover Target." *Business Week,* October 6, 1980.

Thompson, Gary. "Paulson: Big Plans in Gaming." *Las Vegas Sun,* September 11, 1997.

"The Used Airliner King." *Newsweek,* January 13, 1969.

Viemeister, Peter. *Start All Over.* Bedford, Virginia: Hamilton's, 1995.

Weiner, Eric. "U.S.–Soviet Makers Plan Supersonic Business Jet." *New York Times,* November 28, 1989.

Werner, Jeffrey R. "What Can a Passenger Do If the Flight is Booked Solid? The Human Fly Has One Solution." *PEOPLE* magazine, July 19, 1976.

Wilen, John. "Suit Details Failure of Riviera Sale." *Las Vegas Sun News,* June 2, 1998.

Winchester, Jim. *Lockheed Constellation.* St. Paul, Minn.: MBI Publishing Co., 2001.

"Winners Get $200, Atlantic Passes." TWA *Starliner* newsletter, April 12, 1951.

Index

accidents, aircraft: Cessna 150 with
Robert Paulson (1970) 81, 89–91;
Goodyear Racer with Bill Stead (1966)
57; Grumman F-14 with Bob Smyth
(1970) 122; Gulfstream Peregrine 600
with Bill Lawton (1983) 151; LANSA L-
749 Constellation (1966) 132; Lockheed
L-1049H Constellation with Fish
Salmon (1980) 65; Lockheed 10 Electra
with Amelia Earhart (1937) 23; National
Airlines Douglas DC-8 (1978) 104–105;
Navy AD-1 Skyraider with Clint Eastwood (1951) 15; North American P-51C
with Bill Odom (1949) 54; Pitts Special
with Sherman Cooper (1972) 66; Standard Airways L-1049G Constellation
(1963) 49; Stinson with Marvin Hornbeck (1965) 82; Tupolev Tu-144 SST
(1973) 197; United Air Lines DC-3A
(1938) 7,11–13, 15
Aero Commander, Inc. 88–89, 128, 163
Aero Union Corp. 106, 151
Aeroconversion U.S.S.R. 202
Aeronca, Inc. 99–100
Aerospatiale 196
Air Force, U.S. 39–40, 57, 95–97, 99–100,
115, 117, 144–145, 149, 151, 194
Air Progress 98
Air Race Management 66
air races: California 1000 Mile Air Race
59, 178; California Air Classic 66; California National Air Races 67; Cleveland
National Air Races 54; National Cham-
pionship Air Races 53, 57, 97; Pacific In-
ternational Air Races 23; Reno Air
Races 53–57, 59–61, 66; United States
Cup 64–65
air shows: Farnborough Air Show 198,
216; Hannover International Air Show
143; National Business Aircraft Association (NBAA) 89, 139, 146, 154, 176; Paris
Air Show 100, 113, 149, 151, 157, 179–181,
197, 199; Reading Air Show (National
Maintenance and Operations Meeting)
10, 110–112, 124; Transpo 72 100
Airbus Industrie 107
Aircraft Engines and Metals Corp. 50
Aird, Neil vi
Airline Deregulation Act of 1978 147
airlines: Air France 197; Air North 147;
Air US 147; Alaska Airlines v, 73; American Airlines, Inc. 60; American Flyers
Airline Corp. 58; Associated Air Transport 49; British Airways 197; California-
Hawaiian Airlines 58; Eastern Air Lines
58; Filipinas Orient Airways, Inc. 104;
Flying Tiger Line 102; Garuda Indonesia
105; Great Northern Airlines 103;
Hawaiian Airlines 103; Horizon Air x,
73; Imperial Airlines 49; Japan Air Lines
67; Lineas Aereas Nacionales (LANSA)
132; Modern Air Transport, Inc. 58; Na-
tional Airlines 104–105; Orchid Line 55;
Pacific Southwest Airlines (PSA) 105;
Pan American World Airways, Inc. 172,
180; Philippines Airlines 104; President
Airlines 49; Qantas Airways 64, 92;
Slick Airways 50; Southwest Airlines
Co. 77; Standard Airways, Inc. 48–49;
Swift Aire 104; Trans World Airlines,
Inc. (TWA) 4, 27–39, 43–46, 48, 59, 92,
94, 160; Transcontinental & Western
Air, Inc. 27; United Air Lines, Inc. 7, 12,
40, 57, 64, 180; United States Overseas
Airlines (USOA) 77; Varig 64; Western
Airlines 45; Zantop Air Transport 58–
59; Zantop International Airlines 103
Airport (movie) 28
Airport Journal vi
airports: Boise Airport 82; Burbank 1, 44–

233